LITERARY SCHOLARSHIP

Literary Scholarship

Its Aims and Methods

by

NORMAN FOERSTER

JOHN C. McGALLIARD

RENÉ WELLEK

AUSTIN WARREN

WILBUR L. SCHRAMM

Chapel Hill

THE UNIVERSITY OF NORTH CAROLINA PRESS

1941

TYPOGRAPHY, PRINTING, AND BINDING IN THE U. S. A. BY
KINGSPORT PRESS, INC., KINGSPORT, TENNESSEE

Preface

WITHIN AND without our graduate schools, there is a widespread feeling that the present state of American literary scholarship is by no means satisfactory. For more than a decade the opinion has been gaining that our theory of scholarship, while not unsound, has been too limited in its scope and too vague in its ultimate aims. Dissatisfaction with the kinds of production characteristic of the learned journals has been increasingly expressed, and a conviction has been growing that considerable changes will have to be made in the training of the scholars of the future. Sporadic experiments toward new types of training have already been undertaken at Chicago, Harvard, and other institutions.

Before changes are introduced generally, the teaching profession will doubtless wish to reconsider thoroughly the proper ends and means of literary scholarship. In America as in England, most scholars have been disinclined to rational examination of the basic nature of their division of learning. Perhaps they have been wise in preferring practice to theory; perhaps they have not been wise, however, in leaving virtually uninspected the theory upon which their practice rests, or in proceeding as if that theory were an absolute good for all

v

time. A few interesting studies have been published in this country on restricted problems of methodology, but as yet scarcely any attempt has been made to consider broadly the rationale of literary scholarship.

To make such an attempt is the object of the authors of the present study. They have worked out, in close collaboration, a statement of the total scope of literary scholarship and an analysis of the special functions of its several provinces. In their conception of the responsibilities of the scholar they have tried to take into account, not merely the production typical of the past half-century, but the entire history of literary scholarship. They have sought a clear-minded view of the relation of their division of learning to other divisions, especially history, philosophy, and the fine arts, with which it has deep-seated relations. They have endeavored to suggest some of the services which literary scholarship is not offering but is capable of offering to society. And they have presented for consideration a plan for the higher study of letters which in their opinion is sounder than the plan now generally followed.

Members of the teaching profession have found many different causes of our present discontents. Among those most frequently mentioned are: (1) the heavy burden of teaching, especially of routine elementary teaching; (2) the common dependence of academic preferment upon the sheer quantity of research published, which encourages an aimless continuance of stereotyped kinds of scholarship; (3) the less and less liberal education offered by the secondary school and college, which fails to provide a sound basis for the higher study of letters;

and (4) the low morale of our graduate students of letters today, who too rarely possess a genuine "calling" to scholarship and teaching and are too often motivated by laziness and fear, the desire to find the lines of least resistance. The pressure of these and other conditions will unquestionably handicap efforts to improve our scholarship. But the fundamental cause of our discontents appears to lie elsewhere. The shortcomings we deplore can be ascribed only secondarily to the social milieu in America, since they manifested themselves likewise in various European countries where the milieu was very different. American has followed European scholarship in responding, for better and worse, to the intellectual climate of an age of science. The effort to apply to letters the spirit and method of science produced the qualities for which our scholarship is notable, and produced also the defects of our qualities. Enthusiasm for science led us to expect of science more than it can accomplish in the field of the humanities. For this we are responsible; for this the remedy lies within our reach. It consists, in a word, in determining what science can and what it cannot do for us—what we must do for ourselves.

No claim is made that the proposal offered in this book has any final validity, or that any program can be devised which will not need, in practice, protection against new shortcomings. Nor is it conceived that mature and productive scholars who find themselves largely in agreement with the argument should be expected to attempt tasks to which they are not inclined. The book is primarily designed, indeed, not for those who are masters now, but for the apprentices who will be masters tomorrow. The future of literary scholarship belongs to the young men and women, in our graduate schools, who are widening and deepening their literary culture, learning about "Bibliography and Methods," pursuing special studies under direction, and otherwise preparing to carry on the torch. If we are to keep faith with them, we shall have to do more than make them like ourselves, we shall have to suggest ways by which they may one day become better than we are. We shall need to display a better leadership in the field of scholarship than the statesmen of our time have shown in the field of politics, if the place of the humanities in education and life is to be effectively asserted. More and more the responsibility for the creation of such a leadership seems to devolve upon England and America.

Whatever merits this book may possess are due in no small measure to the critical reading of portions of it by a number of scholars, whose objections, reservations, and positive suggestions have been carefully considered and in many cases have resulted in important revisions, but who are nowise responsible for the defects of the book as it stands. Acknowledgments are gratefully made to the heads and various staff members of the School of Letters at the University of Iowa, and also to Albert W. Aron, Leonard Bloomfield, Kenneth Burke, Harry Caplan, Gilbert Chinard, George R. Coffman, Ronald S. Crane, Norman W. DeWitt, Miles Hanley, G. A. Harrer, Percy W. Long, Robert K. Root, Horatio Smith, Edgar H. Sturtevant, J. S. P. Tatlock, John A. Walz, Robert Penn Warren, Karl Young, Morton Zabel.

The Authors

Contents

Preface   v

1. THE STUDY OF LETTERS.
                    Norman Foerster   1

2. LANGUAGE.
                    John C. McGalliard   33

3. LITERARY HISTORY.
                    René Wellek   89

4. LITERARY CRITICISM.
                    Austin Warren   131

5. IMAGINATIVE WRITING.
                    Wilbur L. Schramm   175

Notes   215

A Bibliography   239

Index   257

LITERARY SCHOLARSHIP

THE STUDY OF LETTERS

Norman Foerster

§ I

LITERARY SCHOLARSHIP has reflected the scientific spirit of our age. Like literature itself, it has been realistic, appropriating the aims and methods of the natural sciences and more recently the social sciences. It has aimed at truth, especially factual truth; it has sought exactness and thoroughness; it has cultivated detachment and impersonality; it has risked tediousness and triviality. It has employed as its dominant concept the idea of change, growth, development, in harmony with the scientific hypothesis of evolution. Finding the subject of language—one of its two main branches—eminently suited to such an approach, it has founded a new anthropological science, linguistic philology, which has occupied till very recently an extensive place in the training of all scholars in letters.

Its other main branch, literary philology, proved to be far more recalcitrant to the aims and methods of science, but at least an effort could be made, and has been made, to study it as scientifically as its nature permits. Among the various fields of literary philology the one that has most generally invited this effort is literary history. Many scholars have thought of literary history as concerned primarily with the literary relationships of writers, the sources to which they were indebted and to which they added something, the influences which they passed on to subsequent writers. Many other scholars, conceiving that the causes that produce literary results are infinitely complex, have been concerned with the relation of literary works to the milieu, the particular time and place, the cultural situation out of which they emerged. In order to widen the domain of literary history such scholars have tended to merge it in general history, the history of civilization, the manifestations of which are political, social, economic, intellectual, psychological, religious, and artistic. Reacting against the tendency to study the history of literature *in vacuo,* some of our scholars have gone so far as to produce studies in fields lying mainly or wholly outside their professed subject.[1]

It would be superfluous to celebrate the achievements of this scientifically inspired scholarship—its solid triumphs in linguistics, in many kinds of historical studies, in the making of trustworthy texts, variorum editions, bibliographies, and concordances, above all in firmly establishing a respect for fact. Everyone is aware of these triumphs. Everyone is agreed as to the values of the important books that are the fine fruit of this scholarship, works like Prokosch's *Comparative Germanic Grammar,* Klaeber's *Beowulf,* Manly-Rickert's *Text of the Canterbury Tales,* Young's *Drama of the Mediaeval Church,* Bredvold's *Intellectual Milieu of John Dryden,* Lowes' *Road to Xanadu,* Lancaster's *French Dramatic Literature of the Seventeenth Century,* and Flickinger's *Greek Theater and Its Drama*—an exemplary list to which could be added many works of equal distinction. Such works have given American scholarship a high place. They have made valuable contributions both to the sum of human knowledge and to the understanding of our lingual and literary heritage.

§ II

Yet it is undeniable that the literary scholarship of our scientific age—an age permeated with scientific thought and scarcely any other—has been limited in its kind of excellence. The fact has been conceded by the scholars themselves, who commonly refer to their labors and the results of their labors as *research*. The connotation of the word is ordinarily scientific. The use of it suggests a limitation of scholarship to those activities which it can reasonably share with science. On the other hand the connotation of the traditional term, *scholarship*, is ordinarily humanistic. For example, a writer like Dr. Flexner habitually pairs as contrasting terms *sciences* and *humanities* and, correspondingly, the terms *science* and *scholarship*, *scientist* and *scholar*.[2] Among the humanities is literature, and scholarship concerned with literature has always implied not merely research but various literary activities, research included.

In the light of the history of literary scholarship, what is a scholar? He is "a man of intelligence who is well versed in literature"[3] and who is continually growing in understanding of the intellectual and artistic aspects of his subject. Such a man was Aristotle, perhaps the greatest of all scholars, to whose literary treatises, the *Poetics* and the *Rhetoric*, little of central importance has been added since, unless by the author of the treatise *On the Sublime*. In penetration to essentials, in fertility of suggestion, these works have never been surpassed, and they are still the scholar's best textbooks. The ancient pattern of our recent scholarship is not to be found, however, in the perceptive and speculative energy of Aristotle, but rather in the learned researches of the

Alexandrians in grammar, prosody, antiquities, mythology, et cetera, which put Greek literature in a form that assisted the understanding of it by later times, though even the Alexandrians, it may be noted, presented much of their learning in the form of "creative writing": epical and elegiac poetry accomplished in versification if not in the animating spirit of letters.

The history of modern scholarship begins with the humanists of the Renaissance, who were concerned with discovery, arrangement, translation, criticism, and creation, taking all of literary scholarship as their province. If the generality of humanists deployed at random in this province, the greatest of them, such as Petrarch, Poliziano, or Erasmus, were not aimless researchers but scholars, willing to perform preliminary labors but intent upon humane ends, critical and creative. It would seem that the diverse yet unified literary activities of a *Poetphilolog* like Erasmus afforded a better model for emulation today than that Renaissance herald of modern science, the author of the *Advancement of Learning*.[4] During the succeeding age of neo-classicism the alliance of learning, criticism, and creation was continued in such dominating men of letters as Malherbe, Boileau, Voltaire, Dr. Johnson, and Lessing. In the remarkable cosmopolitan culture which Europe owed mainly to France, a scholar was essentially a man of intelligence well versed in the Classics, finding in them the authoritative voice of reason or nature, basing upon them standards of universal validity, studying them in the belief that literary values are timeless and unchanging. In the battle of the books which disturbed the literary peace of the Enlightenment, admirable moderns were commonly justified—as Shakespeare was justified, e.g., by Lessing—on the ground that they were really in harmony with the ancients.

A way of escape from the authority of the timeless ancients was gradually worked out by the advancing romantic movement, especially in Germany.[5] Among the ideas of great significance for scholarship which were brought to clarity by romanticism, perhaps the central one is that of organic growth, associated with the idea of natural goodness. It was applied to an individual's "genius," to works of art, to the culture of a given time or nation. The relativity implicit in this conception undermined the belief in absolute standards. The proper approach to antiquity was held to be historical, since it too, like all cultures, went through stages of birth, growth, and decay according to organic forces expressing themselves in time and space. Among the results of this conception was an immense widening of sympathies, a zeal for the translation and appreciation of the neglected early national literatures of Europe (Italian, Spanish, Portuguese, English, French, German, Scandinavian, Celtic) and even of Asia, which opened the way to comparative literature. At the same time the study of language and languages considered as organic developments opened the way to linguistic philology. While a fresh cosmopolitan spirit came into scholarship, recognizing the contributions of various nations to the sum of human culture, even stronger was a renewed nationalistic spirit, a patriotic enthusiasm for the tradition and the destiny of an intimately felt native culture. An organic culture must have its roots in the soul of the people and therefore in the past of that people, not in an alien classical antiquity but in the old "romantic" period, i.e. the Middle Ages and the Renaissance, the natural basis for a fresh romantic period in which the yoke of pseudo-classicism should be discarded and each nation assert its inborn genius. A new creative expression should find its inspiration in such productions as the plays of Shakespeare, the old ballads, and the *Nibelungenlied*.[5]

Of this second "Revival of Learning" the prophet was Herder, whose *Ideen zur Philosophie der Geschichte der Menschheit* now seems commonplace only because it has been thoroughly absorbed. Herder's most illustrious successors were A. W. Schlegel and Friedrich Schlegel, who, with the zeal of Renaissance humanists, turned in every direction for new light. German thought, literary art, and scholarship were brought to France by Mme. de Staël, to England by Taylor, Coleridge, and Carlyle, to America by Ticknor, Hedge, Longfellow, and Lowell. In the first half of the nineteenth century, American scholarship was giving relatively less attention to the Classics, expanding its field to include the modern literatures of the Old World, dividing its labors on the lines of national cultures, pursuing the historical method in language and literature, substituting "appreciation" for judicial criticism, and countenancing scholars with interests in translation and creative writing.

The romantic spirit of the age could never alone have brought about such a reorientation of scholarship: it needed, and received, the support of the scientific spirit. The distinguishing virtue of the romantic spirit is breadth of sympathy, not strict truth; its favorite method, a dreaming or divination, not a discipline. Frequently, however, romantic poets or critics who came to dream remained to learn, and, more and more, scholars imbued with the advancing scientific spirit sought to transform the romantic dream of the past into a world of substantial reality. Subjectivity and objectivity together made possible the recreation of the "Gothic" past which Europe had so long neglected and the Hellenic world which it had never really comprehended. For example, the new attraction to fairy tales, which caused them to be one of the most characteristic forms of creation in the German romantic school, was soon reflected in the carefully collected *Kinder- und Hausmärchen* of the Grimm brothers. Later, Jacob Grimm, uniting the cultural patriotism and the scientific passion of his times, produced such works as *Deutsche Mythologie, Geschichte der deutschen Sprache,* and *Deutsche Grammatik.* In his hands linguistic philology at last became a science. Never the narrow specialist, he pursued in many directions his love of historical investigation of the Germanic heritage. Meanwhile F. A. Wolf assured the development of a new Hellenism. If Bentley had founded historical philology, it was the author of the *Prolegomena* to Homer who now established the scientific type of scholarship represented by the term *Altertumswissenschaft,* thanks to which the nineteenth century became "a second Renaissance of Greek studies, destined perhaps to be as important as the first." [7]

The great age of science had now arrived, an age of exploration of the natural and human past by geology and paleontology, an age dominated by the idea of change through evolution, an age of realistic and naturalistic philosophy and literature, of methodical and meticulous objectivity in the historical study of literature and its backgrounds. In the 1860's came the brilliant effort of Taine to apply naturalistic concepts and scientific methods to a national literature. His *Histoire de la littérature anglaise* opens with the words, "History has been transformed, within a hundred years in Germany, within sixty years in France, and that by the study of their literatures" as transcripts of past states of feeling and thought. Literary works were to be regarded as documents, by means of which the scholar could reconstruct the mental structure of an author and establish the causal relationships that explain literary phenomena, literary phenomena being essentially like natural phenomena. Making similarly dangerous assumptions, Brunetière, in *L'Évolution des genres dans l'histoire de la littérature,* attempted to apply to the phenomena of literature a formal classification based on the Darwinian theory. Whatever their shortcomings, it is worthy of note that men like Taine and Brunetière were cast in a larger mould than most of the cautious and tireless specialists who followed them. Although French scholarship became on the whole the most accomplished in Europe—the most fully aware of the balance and integration of qualities requisite for humane scholarship— it also proved, when it wished, its capacity to equal the Germans in massive pedantry.

In America, during the latter half of the nineteenth century, the scientific type of literary scholarship and the German method of training literary scholars were pursued with striking success. Symbolical of a new era was the opening of the Johns Hopkins University in 1876, sanctioned by an address by Thomas Henry Huxley. This was the first American institution to follow the pattern which the liberal and scientific German universities, beginning with Halle and Göttingen in the eighteenth century, had established for the life of the scholar as master and as apprentice. In the years that followed, it no longer seemed necessary for young Americans to migrate to German centers of learning. One after an-

other our universities made provision for library facili-
ties, seminars, theses, and the degree Ph.D., and incul-
cated a scientific discipline in linguistic and literary
philology. The tendency to a one-sided scientific vision
of life and of scholarship was offset by the still vital humanistic and Christian traditions; hence the type known
as the "scholar and gentleman," scholarship not having
yet lost its associations with taste and a finely tempered
nature. One must regret that the new dispensation broke
down, in time, this happy fusion. Fortunately, however,
it also purged scholarship of the most obvious defects of
romanticism, its irresponsibility and its aversion to hard
and systematic work. There was need of the exacting
discipline which Germany had formulated and exemplified, and which at length attained its American culmination in the early twentieth century under the inspiring
leadership of such men as Gildersleeve, and Grandgent,
and Hohlfeld, and Manly, and Kittredge.

By the second quarter of the new century the triumph of scientific literary scholarship in America was
impressive.[8] But with triumph came a flagging of excitement, a loss of vision, a tendency to mechanical expert-
ness, a sense of diminishing rewards, even though these
symptoms of inadequacy were disguised by the opening
up to scholarly exploration of the most recent periods
of literary history. No serious efforts were made to alter
or enlarge the pattern of what was more and more called
research. While European scholarship was seeking to
renew its vitality by fresh purposes and methods, American scholarship persistently confined itself to the accumulation of *Materialien* for the description of historical phenomena.[9] In this atomistic view of learning it
was apparently assumed that the facts, once in, would
of themselves mean something. Synthesis, interpreta-

tion, and application were postponed to a steadily re-
ceding future. In all fields specialists were setting a huge
and crowded stage for a drama that might some day be
produced. If an enormous apparatus of learning was
prerequisite to the understanding of an author and his
age, specialists seeking to command this apparatus were
in grave danger of losing the aesthetic, intellectual, and
spiritual qualities upon which the understanding of a
great writer primarily depends. There were, of course,
exceptions, scholars superior to these tendencies, but
the tendencies were marked enough to threaten an im-
pending decadence.

At the same time the neutrality of the scientific point
of view led American scholars to banish from their professional domain activity in imaginative and critical
writing, and to minimize interest in values of any sort.
As a man, a scholar might indulge in the hobby of writing verses or stories, and even publish them, but such
trifling had nothing to do with his scholarship. As for
criticism, there were said to be only two kinds, the dog-
matic and the impressionistic, and though the latter was
the more excusable, both were bad. In general, a scholar
as such could not afford to concern himself with ideas,
except historically, or with the problems of his own time
in either letters or life itself. Thus came about a ruinous
divorce between writers and critics, on the one hand,
and researchers and historians on the other. The higher
interests of literary scholarship were to be entrusted to
the ignorant and undisciplined, while the ancillary labors were to be multiplied *ad infin.* by expert scholars
for their mutual enlightenment. Scholars were now to
show their dedication by retreating from the life and
letters of the day into a tower of ivory where they could
pursue their mysteries undisturbed.

§ III

But recent years have brought signs of change. We have become aware of an increasing aimlessness and bewilderment, especially among young scholars whose careers are ahead of them. We have become aware that the premises upon which our conception of scholarship are based may be open to suspicion. We are inclining to the conclusion that literary scholarship must reclaim some of its historic purposes and interests, without losing what is really valuable in the method borrowed from science.

Though most of these signs of change are recent, they may be said to have begun, in America, with James Russell Lowell, poet-critic-scholar and an early president of the Modern Language Association. In two addresses, one before this organization and one at the Harvard Anniversary, he deplored certain results of scientific training in letters. Though himself deeply indebted to the method of the Germans, he conceived that they were misleading us into pedantry, and declared that it was wrong "to train young men in the languages as if they were all to be editors, and not lovers of polite literature." Linguistic study was getting, it seemed to him, "more than its fitting share," for our deeper concern is with "philosophy, as Milton understood the word," or with "Literature." To the claims of the scientific specialist he answered that, "after all, the noblest definition of Science is that breadth and impartiality of view which liberates the mind from specialties." Himself a scholar in the modern humanities in the period of their triumph, he yet asserted that the classical languages speak to us today "with a clearer voice than that of any living tongue."

Eight years after Lowell's M.L.A. address another teacher at Harvard, Irving Babbitt, began to say much the same thing in a series of articles gathered, in 1908, into a book on *Literature and the American College*. He freely acknowledged "the services that nineteenth-century scholars, especially those of Germany," had rendered to learning, but declared that their type of scholarship, having fulfilled itself, was on the way to becoming an anachronism. He admitted that "the historical method is invaluable, but only when it is reinforced by a sense of absolute values." He welcomed the fact that knowledge is advancing in increasing volume, but insisted that it must be assimilated by an equivalent effort of thought in order to be vital knowledge; as he repeated from Buddha, "Without knowledge there is no reflection, without reflection there is no knowledge." He made it plain that he would destroy nothing, except excess, since the spirit of the humanities was, above all, the sense of proportion or "humane balance." He found in the tradition of humanism a way of escape from the excesses into which the modern world, and modern scholarship with it, had been led by the romantic and the scientific movements. So vigorously did Babbitt urge the case for proportion in life, in letters, in scholarship, through a series of learned and brilliant critical works, that in some respects his own books were disproportionate, as was pointed out especially by the scholars whose excesses he was attacking—those in whom scholarship had passed into pedantry and those in whom it had passed into sentimentalism and dilettantism.

A similar position was taken by Albert Feuillerat of Yale University in a suggestive article entitled "Scholarship and Literary Criticism." He welcomed the scientific method of the nineteenth century as a corrective of mere subjectivism, but deplored the degeneration of it into a pedantry that converted the means into an end, that accumulated facts without regard for any purpose beyond them. In divorcing itself from literary criticism, scholarship had betrayed the cause of literature in the American college, had abandoned the ambition of "playing a part in the education of the nation at large," and thus had divorced itself from the public as well. "Let us frankly acknowledge," he proposed, "that we have made a mistake. When the twentieth century began, two ways were open to us. One of them prolonged in a straight line the beaten trail; the other diverged. By some error on our part we took the oblique way, and now it has proved to be a blind alley. . . . Let us therefore retrace our steps to the cross-roads where scholarship and criticism began to separate."

By the close of the nineteen-twenties discussions of the function of literary scholarship were taking on the semblance of a debate. A few years later came the address of the president of the Modern Language Association on the occasion of its fiftieth anniversary. John Livingston Lowes used this occasion for a reconsideration of the purpose of such a society of scholars. He pointed out that the original constitution had stated the purpose to be "the advancement of *the study* of the Modern Languages and their literatures," and that in 1927 it had been altered to read "the advancement of *research* in the Modern Languages and their literatures." [10] He found the change to the narrower term unhappily significant. Research seeks knowledge, exhaustive and exact, but such knowledge is properly only the prerequisite to the higher study of letters. "Some day somebody may use our accumulations to constructive ends—but why in Heaven's name not more often *we?*" We appear to have forgotten that humane scholarship "moves and must move within two worlds at once —the world of scientific method and the world, in whatever degree, of creative art. The postulates of the two are radically different. And our exquisitely difficult task is to conform at once to the stipulations of each without infringing on those of the other." It is time for us to remember that "the ultimate end of our research is *criticism,* in the fullest sense of an often misused word."

Though not strictly reasoned, this address by a distinguished leader in research was widely interpreted as a sign of the times. Other signs, within the same association, were the deliberations of a committee on Trends of Scholarship, the organization of discussion groups on Contemporary Literature and on General Topics,[11] and the establishment of an English Institute for the leisurely consideration of aims and methods in literary studies. Meanwhile, Ronald S. Crane was putting into effect a revolutionary change in graduate study at the University of Chicago, based upon a group of four "disciplines" and assigning a novel prominence to literary criticism. The rationale of the new plan was explained, in part, in an article on "History *versus* Criticism in the University Study of Literature." According to Professor Crane, "Literary History has occupied, especially during recent years, altogether too privileged a place." We forget that, while literary history conceived as a genetic construction has its special task and justification, its service as a discipline prior to criticism is apparently humble and largely negative. Understanding *why* an author said what he said does not enable us to understand *what* it is that he said. There is, however, a kind of literary history concerned with the recovery of texts and meanings, with *what* the author said, and this kind of literary history offers an important service to criticism. The final understanding of the work itself, as a work of art, lies in the field of criticism, which is "a discipline concerned with the analysis and evaluation of particular literary works in the light of general principles of aesthetics." In contrast with literary history, which studies the relations of authors in time, literary criticism studies imaginative works in regard to "those qualities which can truly be said to be timeless . . . in the light of general aesthetic principles quite apart from any knowledge of their origin or historical filiation." [12] To shift the emphasis in our scholarship to criticism, Professor Crane concludes, will demand nothing less than a complete reversal of the policy of our academic departments of literature during the past generation, a reform which can hardly be brought about by the few excellent critical scholars in the country: we shall in the end have to rely on "the younger generation of students and instructors, many of whom show much promise for the kind of literary study I have in mind and a genuine enthusiasm for its advancement."

Unlike Professor Lowes, Professor Crane definitely recognizes that criticism must have reasoned, conscious, coherent principles, and he thus clears the way to the reunion of scholarship with criticism, that is, with a type of aesthetic evaluation which is not sentimental and impressionistic. This would bring the literary scholar, once more, close to literature. At the same time it would bring him close to philosophy. For a disciplined consideration of literary works as works of art, Professor Crane insists, must rest upon a theory of literary art, and this in turn, if the theory is to be subjected to rational examination, requires a philosophy of art, and this, again, requires an "adequate metaphysics." [13] Nothing is said, however, of the need of an ethical philosophy, apparently on the ground that the ethical effects of literature, equally with their historical causes, lie outside the scope of specifically literary criticism.

To cite one more scholar, the ethical aspect of literature has been placed in the foreground by Douglas Bush, professor of English at Harvard, in a suggestive passage at the close of his book on *The Renaissance and English Humanism.* In words that grate on modern ears he reminds us that "The chief Renaissance humanists, in common with most of the ancients, held a didactic and religious view of literature." [14] This view endured as long as humanism endured, but when "the study of literature and rhetoric was divorced from the study of virtue" and humanism suffered itself to succumb to decay within and to rivals without, men turned to science and the solid realities it promised to discover. In this, he continues, lies "a moral perhaps for us official custodians of the humanities. The modern world, apart from proletarian authors, has long abandoned the didactic and religious view of literature, and the result has been irresponsible journalism on the one hand and irresponsible scholarship on the other. When literature ceases to be studied as a guide to life, the zest for discovery begins. We might say that the appearance of Bentley marked the death of Renaissance humanism in England. In recent times we have witnessed the virtual extinction of the classics, and at present even the modern humanities are yielding ground daily to the social sciences. With much help from external enemies we English scholars are toiling mightily to bring about the death of English."

From the time of J. R. Lowell to the present day, and especially since about 1930, dissatisfaction with the main drift of our literary scholarship has increased. We are now so far from the inspiriting sense of purpose and value which characterized the romantic and scientific revivals, that scholars have actually proposed a moratorium on scholarship, often more or less facetiously or, as in the case of Professor Bush, "timidly." We are now well aware that we have lost our bearings and that only a new orientation can bring us closer, once more, to literature and to life.

§ IV

If literary scholarship in the coming years is to regain its lost prestige, it will have to reclaim its lost provinces. And if it is to reclaim its lost provinces, it will need the support of a new plan of education of scholars. This will involve the entire period of formal education from the earliest years to the end of graduate study. While the pivotal change must be the restoration of liberal education in the so-called liberal college,[15] there must also be important changes in the apprenticeship leading to the degree doctor of philosophy in the several departments of letters.

The aims of advanced discipline in letters to which we have given serious attention in the established system are so familiar that they may be stated in few words. We have sought:

1. To inculcate the scientific habits of accuracy and thoroughness and the sense of time or historical sense.

2. To assure a general acquaintance with a language and a literature viewed in their historical development and environment.

3. To develop a capacity of research in a limited field of language or literary history.

These aims are simple, definite, and attainable, and have produced results, as has been said, which have given American scholarship high distinction within narrow limits. Reflecting what was felt to be, in the nineteenth century, a new need in the history of scholarship, the established system has succeeded in making its contribution. Few would deny that whatever is essential in this contribution should be and will be preserved hereafter; perhaps few would deny, also, that today a new need in the history of scholarship has again arisen, the need of a scholarship more closely affiliated with the creative and critical interests of letters, and more concerned with the values which the humanities have to offer a world threatened with a barbarism expertly scientific in war and peace.

In accordance with this new need, the aims of advanced discipline in letters may perhaps be stated as follows:

1. To encourage a common intellectual life among students of letters, in which the discipline of letters will be integrated with the other humanistic disciplines—history, the fine arts, philosophy, and religion.

2. To restore the full meaning of literary scholarship so that it shall imply not only accuracy, thoroughness, and the sense of time, but also aesthetic sensitiveness, the ability to write firmly, a concern for general ideas, and an insight into the permanent human values embodied in literature.

3. To offer a rigorous discipline in the specialized types of literary activity—the study of language, the study of literary history, the theory and practice of literary criticism, and the art of imaginative writing.

4. To restore a vital relationship between scholarship and letters by preparing scholars for careers as teachers (collegiate as well as graduate), as critics, or as writers.

In comparison with the aims of the old system, these aims are complex, indefinite, and elusive of "objective" attainment. In other words, while the old system followed the ways of science, the new ventures to go farther, to follow also the ways of the humanities. Herbert Spencer was of course correct in saying that every subject can be studied scientifically, but he paid scant attention to the relative advantages of so studying different subjects. Formulas, for example, are possible and fruitful in a science like chemistry and even in a science like linguistic philology, but the attempt to erect them in the study of literature must always lead to inconclusive and dismal results. In the field of literary historiography, as soon as we get beyond the preliminary stages of assembling and arranging materials and aspire to be really historical, the method of science must be supplemented by quite different techniques. Surely it is time for scholars in the humanities to make clear to themselves the fact that science is not the only respectable kind of inquiry. Any kind of inquiry is respectable if it uses the means appropriate to its subject-matter. In literature, a subject lying in the realm of values, the most appropriate means of learned inquiry is critical argument, fortified by aesthetic perceptiveness and historical awareness. Sooner or later this will have to be generally recognized and acted upon in our graduate schools, regardless of the difficulties involved. There will always be room for the scholar with a natural gift for scientific investigation and a desire to employ it exclusively, so far as that is possible, but it would seem manifestly inappropriate to continue to train the oncoming generation of scholars as if they were all to be limited to the task of being scientific. The literary approach to literature, not the scientific, first attracts the young to the study of the subject, and the literary approach should normally dominate throughout the period of study and the professional life of the scholar. To insist that all scholars must be primarily scientists, to be scandalized by a plan of higher study of which the aims are admittedly complex, indefinite, and elusive of "objective" attainment, is to shirk obligations imposed by the nature of the subject, to close one's eyes to the fact that the field of the humanities is humane, the field of literature literary.

An obvious means of bringing home to the student that literature is a department of the humanities is to expect of him a sufficient acquaintance with the other humanities. He should have—wherever and whenever he secured it—a decent notion of human history, ancient, mediaeval, and modern, of which the history of literature is only one line of development. He should have some competence in at least one of the fine arts— its theory, history, and if possible practice as well—especially since the belles-lettres are themselves one of the fine arts. He should have at least a modest discipline in philosophic types of thinking and a first-hand knowledge of the works of some of the great thinkers since Socrates, if only because of the rôle played by ideas in literature. He should have some understanding of religion, since the Christian tradition enters largely into the literature he studies and literature itself is in a sense a profession of faith, involving as it does visions of reality and ethical affirmations. If he is a student of the Classics, his understanding of the ancient world and ancient literature will be wanting in vitality unless he also knows much of the modern world and modern literature. If he is a student of one of the modern literatures, he will need not only some command of other modern literatures but also a direct knowledge of the ancient literatures, because of their profound effect on European culture and, in the case of Greek literature, because of its surpassing achievement. Systematic work in these subjects should dominate liberal education before the graduate years begin,[16] and should continue so far as possible in the years leading to the doctor's degree. Prior education being what it is, the attainment in the humanities that can safely be required in the graduate school is uncertain and subject to experiment.[17]

Having a fairly rich background in the other humanities, the student will be in a position to deal fruitfully with his chosen subject, imaginative literature. There appear to be four ways of dealing with it: the disciplines of language, literary history, literary criticism, and imaginative writing. The current system of training has virtually been limited to the first two. Plainly, discipline in language (in understanding of the nature of language in general, and of the nature and history of the language in which a given national literature was written) is an essential part of a reasonably complete literary culture. Plainly, again, discipline in literary history (in understanding of the continuity of the phenomena of letters, with special reference to the development of a given national literature) is an essential part of a reasonably complete literary culture. Both language and literary history may be regarded as ends in themselves, as branches of learning worthy of dedicated study. They may also be regarded as "tool" subjects, as means to the understanding of literature, enabling us to see literary works more nearly "as they really are." If the light they yield is far less than we commonly assume, it should nevertheless be prized and sought after.

Thus, in relation to literature, both language and literary history are background subjects, ancillary to the main enterprise, which is the interpretation and evaluation of imaginative literature, of the poem, the play, the novel.[18] Finally arrived at literature itself, how are we to deal with it? How are we to come to understand it, in the fullest sense?

The answer, in simplest terms, would seem to be obvious: by learning, on the highest plane, how to read. As the scientist is a man like other men, observing and reasoning as others do, only more expertly, so the scholar is a man who reads literary works but reads them with superior understanding and judgment. He must not only use what aid his linguistic and historical study affords, he must also and especially read them closely, thoroughly, seeking to grasp *all* of their meaning as works of art and to place them in the order of values. This the graduate student can accomplish only by developing, day in and day out, his aesthetic discrimination, his command of general ideas, his insight into enduring human values. Here his most valuable instrument is natural sense, if he is blessed with it, for no amount of factual knowledge will avail in its stead.[19] And certainly whatever sense or tact he is endowed with needs constant exercise and training, such as are afforded by the admirable method of critical reading known as the *explication de textes*.[20] While this method has dominated literary education in France from the lower schools through the university, it is all but ignored in the United States and no general effort has been made to achieve the same end by other means. Certainly some means must be found immediately if we are to avoid sending forth countless doctors of philosophy, as we do at present, who are rich in lore but cannot read.[21] Along with practice in close analysis of concrete literary works or passages, there is need also of an abstract approach—the study of literary theory, or the philosophy of literature. By acquainting himself thoroughly with selected treatises from Aristotle to Eliot and Richards, the young scholar will gradually escape from the ideological prejudices and limitations of his own time, arrive at a clearer understanding of the rationale of the classic, romantic, and realistic theories, and enter upon the search for a point of view competent to give shape and meaning to all his scholarly activities.

At least until the romantic movement, there was a fairly consistent scale of values in the tradition of humane letters, stretching all the way from Homer to Goethe, perhaps the only scale of values really appropriate for the scholar who would deal seriously and sympathetically with the artistic thought of the past. Nevertheless the young scholar should of course be permitted to occupy a point of view hostile to this tradition, such as that of modern naturalism, provided that he works his way to it honestly, for in criticism as in philosophy the scholar has a right to freedom and integrity. From *some* point of view he must learn to deal with the three questions framed by Goethe: "What did the author propose to himself? Is what he proposes reasonable and sensible? And how far has he succeeded in carrying it out?" To answer the first question, he must know how to read; to answer the last, he must have a literary aesthetic; to answer the second, the most difficult question, he must possess at least a tentative "working philosophy," a conception of life developed by experience and reason. Since reasoned literary principles and skill in using them come only to a man well versed in both life and letters, these capacities cannot reach their full development in the years of graduate study. But rapid progress is possible in these years, if the higher as well as the lower responsibilities of the scholar are constantly kept before the student by means of instruction and requirements for the degree.

The scholar, being primarily a reader, must learn to read well. He must also learn to write well, within the limits of his talent. One of the best ways of understanding imaginative literature is to write it, since the act of writing—the selection of materials, the shaping of them, the recasting and revising—enables the student to repeat what the makers of literature have done, to see the processes and the problems of authorship from the inside.[22] The time he spends in writing poems, stories, or plays, if he has any talent whatever, will not be lost; pen, paper, and waste basket are the apparatus of a laboratory second only in importance to the central laboratory of the literary scholar—the library. If he accomplishes nothing more, he will acquire the habit of writing about literature in a language tolerably fresh, alert, and apt. Naturally a capacity to write readable English is especially appropriate to the student of English; but it cannot be amiss for the student of a foreign language who will express himself in English in the learned journals. Doubtless it is also desirable that the student of a foreign language, ancient or modern, should attain some skill in writing in that language, even though the age of the Ciceronians is far in the past. If literary scholarship is to become literary once more and not merely scientific, the restoration of imaginative writing to its domain would seem to be imperative. Several decades ago Albert S. Cook remarked, truly, that "the philologist,

as such, is not necessarily a creative literary artist. . . .
Yet he may be." [23] It seems clear now that he should not
only be permitted but encouraged to be, in view of the
vitalizing interrelation between creation and scholarship.

What has been said thus far concerns the general literary culture of the student. There must also be a special literary culture, determined by the special aptitude
of each candidate. Having passed a searching general
examination, he should be permitted to concentrate, in
the last year of his candidacy, upon one of the four disciplines. If his ability lies in the field of linguistics, he
will acquire a scientific knowledge of language phenomena and a thorough acquaintance with the history
of his chosen language and of the principal languages
from which it developed. If his ability lies in literary
history, he will immerse himself in the literary phenomena of his chosen period, in their relations to the milieu,
and in the most relevant portions of earlier periods. If
it lies in literary criticism, he will focus, upon a particular problem in theory or practice, all his accumulating
competence in the understanding of art and philosophy
and their relation to literature. Finally, if it lies in imaginative writing, he will seek both to discipline his
vision and to master his medium. The fruit of this process of specialization will be a linguistic monograph, a
historical monograph, a theoretical or practical critical
study, or a work of imaginative literature, the standard
in the last case being equivalence to the quality of the
books issued by the best American publishers.

It must be granted that such a program of general and
special studies is difficult and exacting. But so was the
German program when it was introduced and developed at Johns Hopkins, Harvard, and elsewhere. The

colleges from which graduate schools derived their students in the days when the degree Ph.D. was adopted were still essentially secondary schools. Today they are on a far higher plane, though they expend much time and effort upon illiberal subjects of study. Further, the number of students seeking the highest degree has grown so rapidly that, if the requirements for admission to candidacy and for the degree itself were slowly advanced, graduate schools would still train an adequate supply of students, not merely because of higher standards but also because of the nature of the training offered, which would bring into the departments of literature many who are richly gifted but who are today repelled by what they see there. In any case, whatever the effect, a better type of literary scholarship can be brought about only by some such gradual modification of our established system.

The product of the new system would be, first, teachers well prepared for college instruction. At present we tend to prepare teachers narrowly for graduate instruction and then send them out to the colleges, a type of maladjustment which would not be tolerated in such professions as law and medicine. Under the proposed plan doctors of philosophy would be equipped for their teaching because the primary object of their training would be the widening and deepening of their literary culture. A proportioned training in the four disciplines —language, literary history, literary criticism, and imaginative writing—is precisely what should be attempted if we were thinking only of preparation for the instruction of undergraduates. Secondly, the product would be teachers well trained for the supervision of graduate studies. Prepared to contribute to scholarship in one of the four disciplines, they would also be prepared to guide graduate students in that discipline. Within both college and university, writers and critics would represent points of view capable of assuring scholarship of a constantly renewed vitality and purposefulness.[24] Finally, the product would be writers and occasionally critics (for good critics are always rare) who would establish themselves outside the universities and enrich the literary life of the nation.

§ V

Some such system of training scholars might be expected gradually to reunite the hostile elements in our national literary scene. Today the academic and non-academic servants of letters are in derisive conflict, the public itself, with substantial common sense, siding with the authors and critics against the professors. We have a sharp divorce between the journalist critics, who despise learning yet need it, and the men of learning, who despise criticism yet need it. We have a divorce between the creative authors, unhappily indifferent to the letters of the past, and the scholars, unhappily indifferent to the letters of the present. Patently, the result of these artificial divisions has been nothing less than the impoverishment of our national literature and culture. The urgent need of the time is a centripetal effort, a pulling together toward a common center as the condition of clear purpose and fruitful diversity of achievement hereafter. While the search for new facts, methods, and problems should not be suffered to lapse, the central task of scholarship in the middle twentieth century is to use—to sort, order, weigh, apply—what the scholarship of the nineteenth century and the early twentieth so devotedly accumulated. In the era of the second world war, we must still repeat what Edwin Greenlaw said in the crisis of 1917: "Our greatest need is for the reinterpretation of literature in the light of our immense accumulation of facts. To prevent a new scholasticism, to make full use of the deeper and richer interpretation which will come to us if we seek it, to complete the union between scholarship and life which was one high aim of the early humanists, is the greatest duty confronting graduate departments of literature." [25]

This can only mean that academic scholarship must reconcile its scientific passion with that absorption in values which is characteristic of imaginative writers, literary critics, philosophers, and others in the realm of the humanities. It is quite true, as Dr. Flexner has said, that the humanistic disciplines have gone under a cloud, and that "when they assert themselves, they are prone to do so apologetically, on the ground that they too are, or can be, scientific." Now science as such is neutral, unconcerned with use and effect, while the humanities, the value subjects, have as their high social responsibility the determination of use and effect. "In the modern university, therefore, the more vigorously science is prosecuted, the more acute the need that society be held accountable for the purposes to which larger knowledge and experience are turned. Philosophers and critics, therefore, gain in importance as science makes life more complex." [26] Science did not cause, nor can it cure the grave ills of the age of science; cause and cure alike are the responsibility of the several humanities. Indeed, ours is an age of science only in the sense that science is the greatest achievement of our time; it is not true in the sense that science has guided our civilization. The ends for which science has been a means have been determined by the humanities—exceedingly inadequate ends, judging by the results. Our decisive ends appear to have been satisfaction of an unbounded appetite for material power, combined with the self-deception of flimsy ideologies from eighteenth-century sentimentalism to twentieth-century totalitarianism.

However that may be, the remedy for the confusion and bewilderment that are rendering purposeful action so difficult today lies in the province of the humanities, which includes literary scholarship. If our academic curators of literature are inclined to limit their activities to investigations that have no relation to the present conflict of values, this indicates not that the humanities but that they themselves are aloof. Even in relation to politics, the values expressed by men and women in the humanities may be regarded as highly pertinent, as European dictators have shown by segregating or exiling numberless men of letters, scholars, artists, historians, philosophers, churchmen, and the like. A better compliment could not be paid, a better recognition that the forces which guide action, feed the imagination, provide resolution, are the immeasurable forces of human preferences and beliefs. More and more the importance of these forces is being brought home to us by world events. Even the scientifically trained mind is becoming convinced, as President Conant's report in 1941 testifies, that the preservation of "the dignity of the individual man" may finally depend on scholar-teachers in the humanities. For if the university in a free society has as its central function "the guardianship of eternal values," if it must keep values accessible to the individual and help him to develop "a constructive, critical faculty" competent to choose wisely among them, it follows that education must be primarily "concerned with 'value judgments' in art, in literature or in philosophy."

Signs are multiplying that a grave responsibility may be placed, gradually or suddenly, upon American professors of literature and the other humanities. Are they prepared to receive it?

2

LANGUAGE

John C. McGalliard

THE IMPORTANCE of language in human life has been rediscovered in our time. Interest in the signification and use of words has never been more general or more diversified. The revolutionary character of contemporary politics, philosophy, and literature has motivated many inquiries into the relationship between words and things. Intensive propagandists, who often fool the public by bending words to their ends, have drawn attention to the power of language. Words are heavy explosives; sometimes they are used by airplanes to bomb populations.

Despite this renewal of interest in language, despite also the profound interest of our age in science, linguistic science has generally suffered neglect. It has neither sought nor attracted publicity; it seems to have a "bad press"—or none at all. Few of those who have recently tried to illuminate political, economic, or aesthetic problems have built their analyses upon the basic data of linguistic science. Some are apparently unaware that there is such a thing as a science of language, though it is older by three decades than Darwinian biology and presents a solid and steadily growing body of facts and principles. A closer relationship between linguists and thinkers in other fields who deal critically with important words would profit both. How relevant linguistics is, or should be, for those who venture into applied linguistics may be suggested by glancing at some recent well known books.

Assistant Attorney General Thurman W. Arnold's two books,[1] *The Symbols of Government* and *The Folklore of Capitalism*, might well have been entitled "Language and Government" and "Language and Capitalism." For Mr. Arnold's symbols are words used uncritically, irrationally, and unrealistically; and his folklore consists chiefly in the use of words as fetishes. One chapter, in fact, is entitled "The Use of the Language of Private Property to Describe an Industrial Army," and another deals with "The Traps which Lie in Definitions and Polar Words." Much of the author's effort can be summed up in an emphatic exclamation or two: "Don't you see that you can't change a thing, really, by adopting a legal fiction and calling it something which it isn't? Can't you get rid of your prejudices about words and look at the things they designate?" Sound philosophy has heeded these warnings for upwards of twenty-five centuries. But linguistics—specifically, etymology and semantics—has offered conclusive scientific data on the subject since the middle of the nineteenth century. These tangible data, readily available in historical dictionaries, comparative grammars, etc., demonstrate the wholly arbitrary relationship between words and things, as well as the perpetual possibility—and frequent occurrence—of drastic change in the denotation and connotation of words. No one who has assimilated the elements of linguistic science can be excused if he falls into the word-traps against which Mr. Arnold cries his loud and useful warning.

Much the same holds good in other fields of contemporary thought. Professor Bridgman's *The Logic of*

Modern Physics offers an example.[2] The author makes a strenuous effort to give his reader an insight into some of the concepts of the new physics. In order to do this he examines our familiar associations with such words as *time* and *space*, analyzing these associations critically in the light of the scientist's "operational" approach to phenomena. He shows a keen realization of the obstacles to any substitution in the concepts habitually linked with words. Bridgman's reader, like Arnold's, will have an easier task if he has learned to regard words as arbitrary, conventional symbols, subject to change of meaning in the course of human experience.

Probably the most widely known book of our time in the borderland between philosophy and psychology is *The Meaning of Meaning* of Ogden and Richards.[3] Here, too, the approach is made via words, beginning with an attempt to analyze language. This brilliant and provocative book sharply demands a more critical attitude toward language on the part of the educated public. By its famous Symbol-Thought-Referent triangle, it focuses attention upon a basic inductive conclusion of linguistic science firmly established in the nineteenth century. This, once more, is simply the "imputed" or conventional nature of the relationship between words and things, although the spectacular presentation and the insistent emphasis of Ogden and Richards are salutary and desirable in our chaotic century.

Another recent book has brought the term *semantics* out of its compartment in linguistics, extended its application, and given it an immense popularization. This is Korzybski's vast and, in many ways, fantastic volume, *Science and Sanity*.[4] Semantics in the past usually designated the study of the meanings and changes of meaning in words. Korzybski uses it to include any sign-or-

symbol system of statement or communication; for instance, mathematical symbols and equations constitute
a scheme of semantics. This thinker believes that our
ordinary use of language habitually adheres to an illu-
sory static norm. We say things are such and such, without qualification, when we should say that a particular
thing acts in such and such a way at a definite time.
Language should be adjusted to the emergent and
eventive behavior of the universe. Practically all statements should be empirical, tentative, positivist. In this
way generalization upon inadequate evidence and verbal abstraction would be avoided. It is far beyond my
scope or power to evaluate as a whole Korzybski's far-
flung proposal for the reform of our intellectual life and
civilization in general. Since, however, he proposes a
reform of language as the chief instrument for the re-
habilitation of the world, it may be remarked that he
has apparently given little consideration to the phenomena of language in human history. He seems unaware
of the strength of tradition in the forms and usages of
language; at the same time, he neglects the fact of profound and far-reaching change within a single language
or family of languages.

Moreover, it is necessary to avoid mistaking shortcuts
of language for lapses of logic. The Victorian label "a
bad woman" is no proof that its users were unable to
perceive the good traits of the person in question. They
were quite aware that she might be kind to her mother,
friendly with children, scrupulously honest in financial
matters, etc. The term is simply evidence of the central
and predominant importance of a particular moral code
in the life of that period. At that time, "bad woman"
was a label almost as specific and limited as "spy" or
"traitor." The history of word-meanings is everywhere

rich in such examples; they are known as specializations of meaning and are described in all standard works on vocabulary.

The work of Ogden and Richards and of Korzybski has received a rather remarkable popularization and adaptation. The most widely known book of this nature is Stuart Chase's *The Tyranny of Words*.[5] It is a simplified yet extravagant version of the originals. Chase ignores linguistic science entirely. To him semantics is virgin soil, and he does not hesitate to violate it. But he shares Ogden and Richards' distaste for "abstractions" and philosophy to the full, and makes a ruthless and undiscriminating application of their distinction between cognitive and emotive meaning.

I began the chapter with "applied linguistics" for two reasons. First, it is this field which has attracted the greatest interest recently. Probably more writers and readers have turned their attention to the relationship between language and thought, conduct, and art in the last fifteen years than ever before. Secondly, the comparative neglect of linguistics as a system of scientific data and principles on the part of these writers, at the same time that they base much of their work on the inductions of linguistic science, seemed to demand a primary emphasis. It is surprising, indeed, to find long established principles laboriously established logically, *ad hoc;* to find commonplaces of traditional semantics sensationally proclaimed, as by explorers; to find such intensive examination of contemporary language, with little or no recognition of a long and continuous past, as though language were a static institution. To say nothing of the work of European linguists such as Jespersen, Paul, Meillet, de Saussure, Bréal, Vendryes, it is astonishing that the fundamental texts by contemporary

Americans like Bloomfield, Sturtevant, and others are seldom even mentioned.[6] For the application of linguistics is still an activity that should be guided by linguistic criteria.[7]

§ II

What, then, is linguistics? What does it do? What has it accomplished? What does it offer? In view of the situation of contemporary thought in relation to language, it may be worth while to attempt a rapid survey of the field.

The aim of linguistics is to describe scientifically all phases of language activity accessible to objective study. Like other sciences, it examines data and proceeds to inductive conclusions and generalizations. Language is a human invention and a social activity. The individual man acquires his language and transmits it as he acquires and transmits other traditions and institutions. In this respect, language is like government, for example. But since language is not instinctive, like walking or crying, but has to be learned, it must be classified also as a practical art, like cooking or shaving. The only difference here from the other practical arts is that every normal human being acquires the art of language if he lives a few years beyond birth. The corresponding phase of linguistic science—historical or descriptive grammar—is analogous to a scientifically descriptive manual of any other art as practised at a particular time and place. Historical grammar is thus comparable to scientific archaeology: each studies data inductively in order to give an account of the practice of an art in the past. But, although the symbols of language are voluntarily produced, the symbols themselves are not in all respects voluntary. For example, the sounds employed in the production of a particular word often change within a given period of time. So far as the speakers of the language are concerned, these changes are usually both involuntary and unconscious. What is more, they occur not in isolated words here and there, but in every situation in which certain ascertainable articulatory situations are present. Only, for a particular language at a particular time and place these changes may be formulated with a remarkable uniformity. Linguistic science thus includes the study of a human activity which is at once a social institution, a practical art that shows a wide variety of tools and technique, and a set of involuntary habits of behavior. In addition to and apart from all this, the unique function and purpose of language is to act as a system of communication by means of arbitrary signs or symbols. Linguistic science is, accordingly, centrally concerned to give an account of the workings of this symbolic system of communication.

Like biology, anthropology, and the other sciences developed in the nineteenth century it asks what? how? when? by what process? Like other sciences, its methods are descriptive, historical, comparative. It came as an innovation, a century and a quarter ago, in the long tradition of the study of language. From the time of the Greeks to the beginning of the last century the guiding direction of language study was normative and prescriptive. The Greeks, the Romans, the mediaeval peoples, and the men of the eighteenth century sought to describe language in direct conformity with the "laws of thought," of which formal logic was the instrument. Aside from, or sometimes in conjunction with this attitude, the usual purpose of a work on language—grammar, dictionary, or rhetoric—was to determine the "correct" linguistic form or practice and enforce it. Such was the intention, for instance, with which Doctor Johnson began work on his *Dictionary,* although his empirical good sense led him in time to see the impossibility of anything like complete success. The linguist as such has no interest in imposing logic or enforcing correctness. He tries simply to record accurately, to understand, to analyze, to trace. In proportion to the amount of data available, he is ready to devote as much time and energy to "non-literary" Greek dialects, known only through inscriptions, as to Plato; he is as much interested in illiterate and "backwoods" English as in Milton. For he is seeking to determine not what people "ought" to say but what, in fact, they do or did say.

It does not follow from this distinction, however, that there can be no legitimate connection between descriptive and prescriptive grammar. As, free from bias in favor of any particular form, the scientific grammarian examines the record of actual usage, he may discover that a form forbidden in the textbooks is frequently employed by a large number of writers whose language usage is recognized as "standard" and "correct." This happened in regard to the use of a preposition at the end of a sentence and the use of the split infinitive in English. Long ostracized in school grammars, these are abundantly justified by the citation of usage in such Modern English grammars as Curme's and Jespersen's. This does not mean that all infinitives should be split or that all sentences should end with a preposition when possible. It indicates, instead, that the issue must be determined in every instance, not by specific rule, but by the character of the whole phrase or sentence in which the infinitive or preposition occurs.

Thus, what was once regarded as a point of grammatical correctness is shown to be a question of effectiveness of expression. More than this, it is the historical and comparative grammarian who has enlightened us as to the real nature and criteria of correctness. For instance, the multiple negative has long been avoided in standard English. Logical grammar forbade it on the ground that "two negatives make an affirmative." (One wonders whether an imaginative schoolboy ever undertook to square things by using three or five!) Then historical and comparative grammar disclosed that the multiple negative—double, triple or quadruple—flourished in English from the beginning until some time in the seventeenth century, as well as in many other languages. It is absurd to say that King Alfred, Chaucer, and Shakespeare did not customarily use correct language. In their centuries the multiple negative must clearly have been correct. Equally clearly, it is not correct in Modern English. Evidently it is not a matter of logic but of usage. To be sure, logical considerations may have influenced the change in usage, but logic cannot be applied directly with consistent results as a criterion of language practice. For example, it is illogical to have separate pronouns for the singular and plural in the first person (*I* and *we*) and only one for both numbers in the second (*you*); or to have *he* and *she* but only *they*. In other words, linguistic science demonstrates that no language form is intrinsically correct or incorrect; everything depends on usage. Language is a social institution and is governed by social criteria.

The language data that a linguist examines are sounds, forms, relational groups of these, and meaning. The study of sounds is subdivided into *phonetics* and *phonology*. Phonetics includes the examination of the vocal apparatus used in language. It describes and defines the total range of speech sounds which can be produced by the activities of the vocal cords, tongue, lips, etc. To it we owe the scientific classification and descriptions of vowels, diphthongs, voiced and unvoiced consonants. Recently phoneticians have given us accurate instrumental measurements of such elements of speech as duration (of sounds), pitch, quality, and stress. Phonetics, in short, tells us in full detail how the physiological apparatus of human speech functions in all its operable parts. It is a kind of X-ray that reveals the actual phenomena of spoken language, which are often disguised by conventional spelling and terminology. Thus, we say that the "vowel" in the Modern English word *bite* is "long *i*" and that in *bit* "short *i*." The phonetician observes the facts of pronunciation and tells us that the sound referred to in *bite* is actually a diphthong made up of the vowel written by phoneticians usually α plus the vowel i; our customary paired contrast with the vowel in *bit* is out of accord with the facts of the two cases. He will show us, also, that the traditional terms "long" and "short" may not correspond actually to the comparative duration of the sounds to which they are applied in any given language at a particular time. It is phonetics that shows us—if that be any comfort!—just why it is so difficult to learn to speak a foreign language accurately in adult life. Thus, most Americans pronounce imperfectly the *ch* sound of German *acht* simply because that is a variety of guttural consonant which does not occur in Modern English, Americans have never had occasion to pronounce it in their own language and their vocal apparatus has not learned how to produce that particular sound, that is, has not formed the requisite articulatory habit.

And this illustrates the usual situation. According to the report of phonetics, any particular language employs only a part of the total range of speech sounds, generally only a few dozen. Every language has its own set of sounds recognized and distinguished by the speakers of that language. Many, or most, of these sounds may not coincide exactly with the sounds used in any other language. The sounds represented by *u* in French *but* and the nasal vowel of French *an* are not found in English. Neither French nor German, on the other hand, employs the sound represented by *th* in English *thin*. But the uniquely distinguishing features of the sounds of a language include also intonation, pitch, stress, position of accent, and other things. Teachers of French often remark that practically no French sound is exactly the same as any English sound. Phonetics explains why, therefore, it is necessary to acquire a whole set of new speech habits in order to speak a foreign language correctly. In modern terminology, the complete set of particular sounds employed in any given language (speech community) at a definite period are called the *phonemes* of that language. According to Bloomfield, a phoneme may be defined as "a minimum unit of distinctive sound-feature." [8] Thus, the English word *thin* contains three phonemes, represented in our conventional present spelling by *th, i,* and *n.* (Letters and phonemes do not necessarily coincide. Two letters are here used for one phoneme. And the same two letters "spell" a different phoneme in the word *then.*)

Phonology is concerned with a particular set or sets of phonemes. That is, it deals with those sounds, among the total range reported by the phonetician, which are employed by a specific language at one or more periods of its history: or with those sounds which occur in languages which are to be examined in conjunction, or compared. The phonologist, thus, may undertake to give an account of the phonemes of standard Modern English as spoken by the educated classes of contemporary England. Such an account would be a phonology of standard Modern English, that is, British English. Phonology forms a section of all comprehensive scientific grammars of any language. If the English phonologist takes Australia or America as his field he must observe such differences in sounds as actually occur in English as spoken in those countries. That is, he must record and describe Australian or American English; he cannot "assume" the phonemes found in standard London English. Indeed, American English alone offers a considerable variety in its phonemes. In some regions the first vowel in "Mary" and "merry" is the same, in others not. Or take the differing pronunciations of the *r* in *hard* and the *a* in *class*. Such differences as these, hitherto roughly classified along broad regional lines—Southern, New England, Middle Western—are now being carefully investigated. An American atlas is being prepared to record and demarcate accurately our actual speech usages in the sounds of our language. This great enterprise involves a vast amount of field work by trained observers, who go patiently all over the land, carefully recording the pronunciation of carefully selected residents of every district. The section covering New England, already in print—or in maps—reveals a complexity unsuspected by the ordinary well educated and well traveled American.[9]

The historical phase of phonology is the one which has produced the most remarkable and spectacular achievements. It is primarily by the aid of this instrument that we are able to detect clearly and trace re-

liably the development of a (spoken) language over
periods of many centuries and to understand the true
character of the connections among related languages.
To take a very simple—in fact, a simplified—example.
Suppose that you are curious about the derivation of the
word *home*. Looking in the dictionary, you discover
that the earliest form in English was *hām*. "The word
has changed a bit," you conclude. Now the phonologist,
surveying the sounds found in English words, comes
upon the same fact. But instead of closing the dictionary
with a mild wonder he continues his catalogue. He finds
that the earliest form of *bone* was *bān*; of *stone*, *stān*;
etc. When he finishes his compilation he is prepared to
say, "The sound (or phoneme) *a* ("long *a*" in conventional language) of the earliest period (Old English)
has become *o* ("long *o*") in Modern English." The uniformity of the evidence leads to this generalization and
we obtain a statement, not about isolated words, but
about the sounds of whole classes of words. This regularity of sound change is one of the most impressive
discoveries of linguistic science. The formulae which
express such changes are often called *phonetic* or *sound
laws*. But they are in fact simply statements of changes
occurring in a particular speech community over a particular period of time. The discovery of this phenomenon of uniformity of speech behavior, however, introduced a principle of language unknown before the
nineteenth century. It was soon found that, as every
language has its own set of phonemes, so every language
known for any extended period of history shows its distinctive and independent sound changes. These phonemic changes are always uniform in tendency or direction within a single language. In other words, the
phonemes of a language, taken together with the vari-

ous definite articulatory situations in which they are found—that is, other phonemes, position of accent, initial, medial, or final position in the word, etc., constitute an involuntary pattern or set of speech habits. A change of phoneme is uniform for all occurrences of the same sound in the same phonemic context—hence, in all words in which these are found—because all these occurrences are comprised in a single articulatory habit. A change in such a habit consequently involves sound change in all words produced by the activity of this uniform habit. Historical phonology consists in large part in the accurate statement of the many and complex changes of habit found in the development of each language throughout the various periods of its recorded existence. These results constitute the sections devoted to "phonology" in the scientific and historical grammars of English, German, French, Latin, Greek, Russian, Finnish, Arabic, etc., etc.

But this is not all. The principle of regularity of sound change enables us to go beyond single languages and discover and define relationships among several languages of the same ultimate derivation. In fact, the scientific methods of phonology were first applied in the study of such relationships. Let us take another very simple example. The word for "father" is *pater* in Latin, *patēr* in Greek; *pitá* in Sanskrit, an ancient language of India. In English the word is *father,* in German *Vater,* in Old Norse, a mediaeval form of the Scandinavian languages, it is *faþir.* The word for "foot" is *pedem* in Latin, *poda* in Greek, *pádam* in Sanskrit (accusative singular); in English, *foot,* in German, *Fuss:* in Old Norse *fōt.* Not to prolong the list, we may abridge the story by saying that a complete catalogue of the vocabularies of these and other relevant languages led to the generalization: "The sound represented by *p* in Latin, Greek, and Sanskrit corresponds to the sound represented by *f* in English, German, and the Scandinavian languages." Similar correspondences, showing either regular change or regular identity, could not be due to chance. We are thus led to the inference that all these languages, along with many others that I have not mentioned, are independent developments of a common ancient language. This parent language, not actually recorded anywhere, is called Indo-European.

The present direction of linguistic research is leading toward a more precise and refined understanding of the processes involved in sound change. Phonetics, to be sure, has long served as a general guide along the path of phonologic history. But the students, if not the instructors, in courses in linguistics have sometimes concentrated rather too exclusively on the results of phonetic change. It is easy to learn and remember that "Old English long *a* becomes long *o* in Modern English." If we look carefully at the language in the intervening period—Middle English—we discover that this change did not take place at one fell swoop. Chaucer, for instance, pronounced words of this group differently than words with "long *o*" in Old English. Both are spelled *o* or *oo* in Middle English: *hoom, stoon,* like *good* (from Old English *god*); *flood* (from Old English *flod*); but words of the two groups do not rhyme with each other. Those with "long *o*" in Old English, moreover, have developed differently in Modern English—into some variety of *u* sound, as in *good, flood.* The two long *o*'s of Middle English, then, were different sounds. The data of phonetics make it clear that the Old English long *a* changed first into the sound called "open *o*" in Middle English times and then went on to the "closed *o*" sound of Mod-

ern English. That is, the point of articulation moved
forward and upward in two stages. Historical phonology records the fact of change; phonetic analysis
clarifies the process.

The physiological and psychological character of the
phoneme is receiving intensive examination at the present moment. The effort is aimed at a more accurate
description of its nature and behavior—and hence at a
more precise definition of it as an element in the speech
process. In Prokosch's *Comparative Germanic Grammar,* 1939, each of the steps and stages of the great Germanic consonant shift receives careful discussion. A previous era of linguistic science firmly established the
results of the shift; the linguist of our day seeks a closer
knowledge of the manner, the order, and the method
of change.[10]

This intensive study of the relations within the phonetic system of particular languages delimits and focuses
attention upon a new range inside the total area of phonetics and phonology. Twaddell's formidable monograph, *On Defining the Phoneme,* surveys the wide variety in the conception of the term among linguists.[11]
Most of them, however, regard the phoneme as a reality,
psychic or merely phonetic or both.

The recently very active Linguistic Circle of Prague
has concentrated especially upon phonemes and systems
of phonemes. It is centrally represented by Trubetzkoy's
Grundzüge der Phonologie, 1939. The identification of
the phonemes of a language; their systematic grouping;
the relevant phenomena of intonation, quantity, accent,
pitch in word-phonemes—these are basic concerns of
the investigator in phonemics. But he examines also the
rules of structure that determine the forms of syllables
and words; the functional load of the various phonemic

oppositions; and the relationship between phonemic and non-phonemic phenomena of speech. Besides these features of a language synchronically considered, he seeks to discover what forces determine the diachronic (historical) development of a phonemic system and its constituent parts and how these forces operate.

The new conception of language sounds, not as isolated phenomena amenable to merely physical analysis, but as uniquely related units with a fixed relationship within a phonological system, has become the focus of the new departure in linguistics which we may call phonemics. Illustrative of its point of view is Trager's requirement that the phonemic table of a language should be based not on the type of sound, but on the function and structure of its phonemes.[12]

It will be interesting to see what light the intensive phonemic investigation of the future will throw on the operation of the "sound laws." But the controversy over their "invariability," if it has not yet ended in a complete reconciliation of adversaries, has been refined and redefined with increasing precision in the last generation. First, it was recognized that speech sounds are not automatic or autonomous phenomena; they do not behave like inanimate objects under the direct impact of "natural laws" or like biological organisms directed by evolutionary laws. They are, instead, highly contingent elements of human behavior. The modern "orthodox" linguist, accordingly, prefers to speak of "regular phonetic correspondences" rather than "exceptionless sound laws." In formulating his correspondences he is careful to specify the chronological period, the area, and the linguistic community or communities to which they apply. He excludes from his formula those sound phenomena which are due to the borrowing of words by one

language from another; the operation of other corre-
spondence-systems which may not be clearly formulated; and the effects of analogy, dialect mixture, ono-
matopoeia, or rhyme-words. The data of linguistic geography—scientific study of dialects and dialect relations
—do not infringe the principle of regularity. But they
enable the linguist to delimit the formulae of change
with greater precision as to time, place, and speech-
community, and to determine more accurately the effects
of "borrowing" as opposed to independent tradition in
particular words.

Close scrutiny of the linguistic context of sound
change has led to a more precise conception of the phenomenon of change. De Saussure thus declares that it
is not the phonological species ("espèce phonologique")
that is transformed, but the phoneme as it occurs in certain conditions of context, accent, etc.[13] It was not the
consonant s as a species of sound that became r in Latin
between ca. 450 and ca. 350 B.C. It was s between vowels
and in a few other positions; elsewhere s remained unchanged. The modern statement of the old principle of
"sound laws" is accordingly, "phonemes change."[14] Jespersen, who has consistently opposed the rigidly mechanical view of exceptionless sound laws, declared in
1933 that when a sound "really as such" ("wirklich als
solcher") changes, the change is regular and uniform.[15]
He quotes as essentially his own doctrine Bally's statement that words undergoing the operation of a phonetic
law do not all undergo it in the same way, but in different ways, according to the rôle they play in speech
("discours"). It will be the task of future students to
define these distinctions in precise detail.[16] Now that
phonemes and phonological systems are receiving at
once minute analysis and structural classification, it is

not inconceivable that the gap may some day be closed between the adherents and opponents of uniformity in sound change. Phonemics, the latest development in the study of language sounds, by discovering new distinctions and new identities may be able to formulate the facts on the basis of principles as yet unknown. The hostile camps may be reconciled on a terrain hitherto unmapped.

The causes of sound change continue to elude detection, although numerous hypotheses have been proposed. Older explanations on the basis of climatic conditions, anatomical changes, and racial differences have been discounted in the light of the wider data available in our time. For the Germanic and German consonant shifts, Prokosch tentatively suggests a change in habits of articulation accompanying the stress and strain of population movements.[17] Others point to the possible effect upon a language of its rapid acquisition by peoples who previously spoke a different language—the sub-stratum theory. Inaccurate transmission—through the mistakes perpetuated by children—from one generation to another has been mentioned as a possibility. But, on the whole, the tendency to-day is to start from the well attested fact of individual variation in the utterance of phonemes and to see a sound change as a spread or generalization of such a variation through imitation. This view is in harmony with the fact that language is social behavior. Sound changes are thus considered analogous to fashions in dress or deportment. Sturtevant has recently re-defined the basic problem. It is not: "Why do phonetic innovations affect all the applicable material of the speech in the district in which they arise?" but, rather: "Why do phonetic innovations spread over the whole phonetic material of a region instead of infecting

isolated words?" [18] As noted above, the phenomena of
sound change are included in the subject matter of contemporary phonemics, and further light may eventually
be expected from that new science.

The sounds of language are employed to produce patterns of speech, or morphemes. Such patterns are recognized in the cases of the various noun, pronoun, and adjective declensions, for example, and in the conjugation
of verbs in a system of numbers, persons, moods, voices,
and tenses—in short, in the whole prefixing and suffix-
ing inflectional machinery. The descriptive and historical study of these is called *morphology*. The pupil in the
first year of study of any foreign language learns, if
things turn out well, quite a bit of morphology. But the
pupil's interest in forms is static; he is interested in mas-
tering fixed patterns. This is also a part of the work of
the linguist. He seeks to determine and record accurately the forms of every language at every period of its
history—classical Latin, seventeenth century French,
English in the time of *Beowulf*. But he also wishes to
trace the development, the emergence, decline, or
change in the forms of the language. Historical morphology thus corresponds to historical phonology. Indeed, the two often converge in their account of change.
For example, the noun in Modern English has only two
case morphemes. One of these we call the possessive or
genitive: *day's*. The other form, *day*, we designate as
nominative or accusative or dative according to its function in the sentence. But there is no difference of pattern among these. From this latter point of view, we
should really speak only of a genitive (or possessive)
form and an all-other-purpose form. In the earliest period of English (Old English), however, there were, in
the "declension" to which the older form of *day* be-

longed, three separate case forms in the singular and
three in the plural. Thus: Singular: nominative and accusative *dæg*, genitive *dæges*, dative and instrumental
dæge; Plural: nominative and accusative *dagas*, genitive
daga, dative and instrumental *dagum*. (The alternation
between *ae* and *a* is a matter of phonetics; it was not
used to distinguish singular and plural.) Historical phonology tells us that the slighter force with which unaccented syllables were pronounced reduced *dæges* and
dagas alike to the uniform sound which we now spell,
according to function, *day's, days, days'*. Thus, whereas
the Old English had distinctive forms for the genitive
singular and the nominative accusative plural, the modern spoken language has one form for all three functions. The case endings of the dative instrumental singular and of the genitive and dative instrumental plural
disappeared in the same way—by gradual phonetic
weakening. A morphological fact, the smaller number
of case forms in Modern English, is thus explained by a
phonological fact. The same thing could be shown for
the verb forms, notably in the subjunctive. Similar developments, it should be said, can naturally be found
in other languages. The Latin nouns had four or five
case forms in both singular and plural. As the pupil fresh
from his Latin finds to his joy, the Romance languages,
developed from the Latin, have, in the modern period,
no case forms. Broadly speaking, this happened much
as it did in English: through phonetic weakening and
loss of the final, unaccented syllable, which carried the
distinctive case endings.

Most people are at least a bit puzzled by the few ir-
regular plural forms of nouns in Modern English: *deer,
oxen, men*, etc. From the historical point of view, the
remarkable fact is that there are not many more forms

of this kind in English. For these words are merely the survivors of whole classes of nouns that formed their plural in other ways than by adding -s (formerly -as, as we saw in *dagas*). That is, there were many types of noun declension and hence many different nominative-accusative plural forms. Gradually, in Middle English times, nearly all of the words belonging to these declensions "came over" into the *dæg-dagas* declension. Or, in other words, they adopted the -s plural. This event, it is evident, was not a sound-change. It is called analogical change: other nouns were given -s plurals on the analogy of the type which already had this form. The term analogy, apparently accurate from an external, logical point of view, may be misleading. No deliberate, conscious decision was made; people simply began to form the plural of more and more nouns with -s until almost all plurals had this form. Similar changes by analogy account for the relative uniformity of the plurals in any one of the Romance languages as contrasted with the parent Latin variety.

These examples must suffice as an illustration of the methods of historical morphology. Looking over the field more summarily, it may be said that sound change and analogy are the two greatest forces that have brought about the transformation of the highly inflectional patterns of the Indo-European into the relatively simpler morphological system of the derived languages. The linguist studies the development of this change. He discovers a great variety among the various tongues. Sanskrit retains the eight cases of the original language, ancient Greek five, Latin six, modern Russian six. Two things are evident: that the general tendency is toward a smaller number of forms, and that different languages move at greatly differing speeds in carrying out this general tendency. Most types of declensional forms and case endings can be traced to an Indo-European pattern, as might be expected in view of the common origin of the extant languages. On the other hand, the inflection of the verb was apparently less elaborately developed than it came to be in ancient Greek, with its extensive system of tenses and voices and its fairly full conjugation in four moods, indicative, optative, subjunctive, and imperative. Here the comparative linguist has something surprising to tell us. Our emphasis on time, represented in language by tense, was not such a predominant concern in the Indo-European parent language. The interest there was centered in the character or aspect of the action denoted by a verb. The aspects primarily distinguished were the *durative* (corresponding approximately to the English "he is working"); the *aorist*, or punctual, denoting the mere occurrence of an event, as such; and the perfective, denoting a completed state of the action. Since they were not oriented primarily according to time, none of these exactly coincides in function with our tenses. In the course of the development of the various languages, the indication of time was combined with and, so to speak, imposed upon these distinctions of aspect. This happened notably in Latin and Greek. But not all languages went nearly so far. The Germanic languages in the earliest period known had only a present (the old durative) and a past, made up partly of old aorist forms, partly of forms from the old perfect. That is why English and German today have no inflectional future tense and hence employ "auxiliary" words like *shall, will,* and *werden.* Thus the chain of events which started the lively controversy in the eighteenth century over the uses of *shall* and *will* can be traced to the absence of the modern time-orientation in the Indo-European language perhaps four thousand years ago!

The development of means of expressing future time throws some light on the operation of the trend away from inflectional endings and toward the use of auxiliary words. A language rich in inflections is called a "synthetic" language, whereas one that makes use of auxiliary terms is said to be "analytic." No extant Indo-European language is a pure type of either; prepositions for example, are found even in Sanskrit, with its eight cases. But, in the matter of forms for the future, it is interesting to note that Greek and Latin independently evolved (quite different) inflectional tenses. As we saw, the Germanic languages use auxiliaries. It was not until late in the Middle Ages, however, that these came to be felt as constituting a tense form. Old English, employing the old durative, relied on context to indicate the time as present or future. The Latin future was not continued in the Romance languages; nor was the future perfect. But new futures and "conditionals" were formed in these languages by the addition of forms of the word for *have* to the infinitive of the verb. These coalesced with the verb to produce new inflectional forms. Hence, although the general tendency of the Indo-European languages is undoubtedly toward the analytic type of structure, they seem likely to present a mixture of synthetic and analytic elements for a long time to come.

The study of the use or function of the forms of language is called *syntax*. The emergence and transformation of patterns of phrase and sentence structure; coordination and subordination, indirect discourse, the functions of the various moods and the circumstances governing their occurrence; conditional sentences, the sequence of tenses—these are some of the phenomena of language described and traced by the linguist. The results of his work are to be found in the comprehensive historical and descriptive grammars of the several languages. Comparative syntax indicates to us the typical character of discourse in the oldest period of our common language, the Indo-European. Since inflectional forms fully indicated the grammatical relations of words, their order could be determined according to other functions. Some notion of this linguistic era may be gained from the structure of discourse in the Homeric epics. Then, for example, in Attic Greek prose or classical Latin, we find subordination (dependent clauses and "phrases") highly developed, with elaborate and complex conventions in the use of the various moods. In the modern languages, when a great many inflections had disappeared, word order, formerly a rhetorical instrument, became a grammatical form. As has so often been pointed out, only the fixed position of subject and object enables us to distinguish accurately the active and the passive participant in the action reported by the sentence, "The dog bites the man."

The historical development of syntax in the modern languages is one of the most illuminating parts of the whole story of language. In the twentieth century, especially, the results of earlier study of the oldest periods have been utilized to trace and describe accurately the present state of these languages. The English grammars of Jespersen, Poutsma, and Kruisinga are notable examples. Perhaps the most remarkable and interesting of all is Professor Curme's 575-page *Syntax* of English in the modern period. The forty pages devoted to the subjunctive make fascinating reading for anyone interested in the ways and usages of his own present-day language.

He may be surprised by the discovery that, although most of the traditional inflectional forms and some of the older uses of the subjunctive have gone out of the language, a rich variety of new forms has arisen to express the range of thought and feeling for which the obsolete forms were once employed.

Concise illustration is difficult in the realm of syntax. Professor Curme has summed up the intellectual rewards of its study so vividly and enthusiastically that I shall venture to quote a few sentences from the Preface to his *Syntax:*

On the grammatical categories: These categories are the means by which we present our thought in orderly fashion and with precision, and are intimately associated with the expression of our inner feeling. The story of the development of these categories constitutes the oldest and most reliable chapters in the history of the inner life of the English people. Serious efforts have been made everywhere throughout this book to penetrate into the original concrete meaning of these categories, in order to throw light upon the interesting early struggles of our people for a fuller expression of their inner life and to gain suggestions for their present struggles in this direction.

On development in English from the early Modern English period: Everywhere attention has been called to the loose structure of the English sentence at that time and to the subsequent development of our simple, terse, differentiated forms of expression—an eloquent testimony to the growing intellectual life of the English-speaking people.

On standards and correctness: . . . The author

defends in this book the recommendations of conservative grammarians wherever they contend
against the tendencies of the masses to disregard
fine distinctions in the literary language already
hallowed by long usage. On the other hand, the author often takes a stand against these conservative
grammarians wherever they cling to the old simply because it is old and thus fail to recognize that
English grammar is the stirring story of the English
people's long and constant struggle to create a fuller
and more accurate expression of their inner life.[19]

Syntax is something very much alive for all speakers
of all languages, though not all of them would call it by
this name. Everyone is more or less keenly aware of the
differences that separate standard dialects from local or
illiterate speech. Several investigators have recently
tried to discover exactly what is predominant usage
among various kinds of persons. S. A. Leonard's *Current
English Usage,* 1932, and a continuation by Marckwardt
and Walcott, *Facts about Current English Usage,* 1938,
canvass the views of a wide variety of educated people
on some 230 usages.[20] Their results seem to indicate that
as a whole linguists are the most tolerant and school
teachers of English the least. Another investigation under the direction of Professor C. C. Fries surveys the
inflections and syntax of some thousands of letters in
the files of the federal government.[21] He divides the
writers into three classes, corresponding roughly to un-
skilled labor, with formal education less than eighth
grade; skilled labor, with education varying from ninth
grade to one year in college; and the professions. The
data are interesting as they stand; when the study is
complete we shall have a useful check on the language

practices of a large number of representative citizens. Already there is enough evidence to prove that the school grammar and handbook tradition is at many points inaccurate in its account of good usage. Human nature being what it is, especially pedagogical nature, it will take about a generation to bring this tradition into line with the habits of the best speakers and the judgments of the best students of the language. The syntax of contemporary English is an inviting field for research.

Phonemes, morphemes, and phrase or sentence patterns are the vehicles of meaning. They are like the root, trunk, and leaves of a tree; words are its fruit. Words furnish a tempting topic, and many popular books have been written on their wonderful ways. Nor have they been ignored by the linguist. Most standard histories of the several languages accord generous space to the vocabulary. A host of special studies in the various languages has gradually accumulated the data that make such general accounts reliable. This research has been concerned with the word stock of a given language at the earliest period of which we have knowledge; with the loss of words and the creation of new ones in every succeeding period; with words used in a given period within a particular sphere of activity or culture, such as plants, animals, war, government, philosophy, literary criticism, etc., with words adopted or "borrowed" from other languages: etc., etc. As a result, we have a pretty good knowledge of the external history of the vocabulary in most of the major languages.

Scientific etymology is the instrument of precision which assures the validity of these and all other studies of vocabulary. No phase of language demonstrates more impressively the achievement of linguistic science. Be-

fore the nineteenth century—as to this day for the linguistically innocent!—the origin of words was a happy
hunting ground of weird theory and irresponsible imagination. Establishment of the basic lines of development within and among languages put an end to all that
—for the linguist. These lines, we remember, were set
up primarily by historical and comparative phonology.
Phonological data are the indispensable framework, the
guide and the check, of etymology. Without them it is
sheer guesswork, for they alone tell us what a given
word was like in the past, what sounds it had—in short
what it was. For example, *light* and the last syllable of
delight are identical in sound and spelling in Modern
English. They seem to invite spontaneous etymologizing. But as we look back, say, to English in the time of
Chaucer, we find that *light* had a "short *i*" (like the
sound of Modern English *bit*), and that the *gh* represented a guttural consonant, now "silent," but then pronounced. If we go back to Old English, we find that the
earliest form of the word was *leoht*. Turning to *delight*,
we find that in Middle English, when it first appears in
the language, it had the form *delit(e)* and the accented
vowel was pronounced like that in Modern English *beat*.
Chaucer would never have been able to make it rhyme
with *light*. Investigation of the French language of the
mediaeval period shows that *delit* is borrowed from that
language and that its ultimate base is the same as that
of Latin *delectare*, a verb meaning "entice." The English words happen to coincide in appearance in Modern
English as a result of two sound changes and an analogical influence on the spelling of one. When the *gh* ceased
to be pronounced and the vowel was lengthened in
light, its sound became identical with that of the last
syllable of *delit*. Then it became customary to spell *delit*

according to the pattern of *light, bright, knight,* etc.

Thus the linguist tests the constituents and sources of words with an accuracy at least approaching that of a chemist testing an unlabeled liquid for identification. A few of the specimens of language remain "unknowns," however, when the data are too scanty. The results of research in the origins of words are to be found in the great etymological dictionaries of the various languages and groups of languages. Notable among these is the vast *New English Dictionary,* in ten huge volumes, with a supplement. Within the last few years has appeared Walde's comprehensive comparative etymological dictionary of Indo-European roots or bases, in three volumes.[22] This kind of collection is indispensable if the history of a word is to be carried into the past beyond the earliest period of English—or French or German, for example—or, in the case of borrowed words, beyond the immediate source in another language, such as Latin. Study of the Indo-European bases opens astonishing vistas to the "layman" as well as the linguist. For example, one learns that Latin, *video,* "see," Greek (*w*)*oida,* "know," Sanskrit *véda,* "know," and English *wit* developed from the same base; and that the base of our verb *be,* than which no word seems to have a "simpler" or more "fundamental" meaning, signified "exist." What seems to us the fundamental meaning is a weakening of the earlier signification! The making of dictionaries is a notable feature of recent years. *A Dictionary of American English* is in process of publication in Chicago. Dictionaries of Middle English and early Modern English are in preparation at the University of Michigan. These will shed enormous light on periods of the language hitherto, according to our present high standards, but sketchily known.

The history of a vocabulary is the history of a civilization and a culture. Thanks to linguistic science, which has fixed the authentic data in a reliable and coherent framework, we can now read that kind of history. Even the world of ancient Indo-European, where everything has to be inferred from reconstructions, has been partially brought to life by Hirt and other scholars.[23] Much in this sphere naturally remains speculative, but with the data—that is, the words—of an actually recorded language we are on much surer ground. Meillet's delightful *Esquisse d'une histoire de la langue latine* skilfully unfolds the Latin dress of Roman civilization, thought, institutions, and mores.[24] To drop the figure, he shows how Latin and Rome developed in parallel lines. Vossler has carefully described Old French as the "mirror" of mediaeval social institutions and cultural history.[25]

In his *History of the English Language*, 1935, Baugh has traced the growth and change of our word stock in close relation to political, social, and cultural change, demonstrating fully the clear reflection of the facts of civilization in the data of vocabulary. The Germanic settlers of England had relatively little contact with the native Celts; the few words borrowed in Old English represent the slight relationship. Yet the adoption of words like *crag* and the original of *-combe* in modern place names illustrates the occasion of word borrowing. The immigrants came upon features of the landscape unknown in their continental home and for which they doubtless had no words. Hence, it was natural to learn about the thing and acquire the name of it simultaneously. The adoption of American Indian words for animals and plants of the New World offers a parallel. The impact of Latin upon Old English was in direct proportion to the impact of Roman civilization in its various elements—articles of commerce, military artifacts, the Christian religion, etc. *Wall, wine, Chester,* (*-caster, -cester*), *mint, pepper, bishop,* and *priest* are examples. But this is only one side of the story. The English did not always borrow the Latin word; sometimes they borrowed merely its meaning and added this to a native term, as in *Ghost,* the term, still in use, chosen to designate the third person of the trinity. *Trinity,* incidentally, is a later borrowing from French; the Old English word was a translation of *trinitas—þryness* ("threeness"). Sometimes, apparently, a new word was created by suffixes to render the Latin: *divinitas* is represented by *godcundness.* Borrowing of this kind should always be taken into account in the study of a vocabulary. It may occur at any time in any language. Modern German *Fernsprecher* is none the less a borrowing from *telephone* for the fact that it has substituted German words for the originals. The Scandinavian settlers in mediaeval England brought no notably higher or influentially different culture. Accordingly, the words which they contributed to English usually denoted the concrete objects and activities of everyday life. It is difficult to determine whether some Middle and Modern English words are Scandinavian or native English; others are distinguished only by phonological tests.

The political, social and literary relations between England and France after the Norman Conquest brought about an enormous incorporation of French words into English. This is one of the amplest illustrations to be found anywhere of the coincidence of linguistic and cultural influences. Indeed, it is so overwhelming that it has sometimes led to wrong conclusions. Since in Modern English a large proportion of words connected with the "higher" aspects of life and civilization were borrowed from the French, it has been inferred that the English people and their language before the Conquest were crude or, shall we say, unintellectual. A glance at a dictionary of Old English—which suffered a loss of about eighty-five per cent of its vocabulary—will dispel this illusion. What happened was that the people who took control of the cultivated aspects of life in England spoke French for two centuries or so after the Conquest. Naturally, the "cultural" English words disappeared: there was nobody to use them! Then, as English gradually became the native tongue of the upper classes, this "unnatural" deficiency was supplied from the vocabulary of French, always readily accessible through contacts with the court, with French literature, and with France itself.

In all the later borrowings of English from other languages this same principle will generally hold: that words are accepted as the vehicles of new things, new ideas, new attitudes, or new points of view. This applies, for example, to such spheres as music (Italian), ships and nautical matters (Dutch), "abstract" ideas and conceptions (Latin). This situation is not essentially changed when we coin a word from Greek to supply a technical purpose or designate a mechanical invention: we adopt a new name for a new thing.

Change of meaning in words is one of the most frequent and far-reaching phenomena of language. Recognized more or less casually before the nineteenth century, it was never adequately studied before the advent of scientific etymology. After that, evidence of it was so ubiquitous that the linguists, so to speak, took it for granted, along with some of the principles that certain recent books, referred to earlier, have created quite a stir about. It is, obviously, an induction of comparative linguistics that words and things are not identical, that words are arbitrary symbols. It was clear, also, that their meanings depend on their users. Since the users are successive participants in a changing, developing world, it follows that change may be expected in the meanings with which they employ words. But the linguists of the mid-nineteenth century, and some of them even later, did not emphasize these facts so clearly as we might expect. Some of them were so impressed by the regularity of phonetic change, which was seemingly proved more "absolute" with each succeeding decade, that they thought of linguistic phenomena as virtually independent and automatic. This was the age that invented the term "sound law." Some of them regarded languages as evolving like an organism, after the analogy of biology according to the contemporary theory of evolution.

The first studies of meaning, or, rather, change of meaning, were undertaken in this atmosphere of evolutionary hypothesis. *La vie des mots*, 1886, by A. Darmesteter, traces the birth, growth, proliferation, decline, and death of words. He finds specialization and extension of function as normal phenomena.

Bréal's *Essai de Sémantique*, 1892, corrected both the automatic, mechanical and the evolutionary orientations. He pointed out that meaning and changes in meaning are the result of the activity of the human mind and spirit, as language in general is a form of human behavior and is created, conditioned, and changed on that basis. It is intelligent behavior directed to social purpose by a conscious will. He showed that words have no innate or intrinsic "tendencies," such as the pejorative or meliorative. A word like *mistress* does not decline in the moral scale of its own nature: its change of meaning is due to human politeness, finding expression in euphemism of language. Restriction of meaning Bréal regarded as the result of a particular adjustment between a traditional word and a specific thing—e.g., the development of specific words like Latin *tectum;* French *toit,* "roof," from the Latin root *teg-* with the more general meaning of "cover." *Adultery* and *wit* are examples of similar specialization, each in a particular social and environmental context. Change described as expansion of meaning he also attributes to the events of (social) history, for example, Latin *pecunia* (from *pecus,* "herd"; *pecunia* means "money") or the parallel case of English *fee.* The post-Bréal terms "horse-cavalry" and "mechanized cavalry" would be similarly explained—as due to the adoption of a new means of transport and combat.

Bréal's book is still in many respects sound and basic. His successors in France and Switzerland were to stress even more fully the influence of special social groups— occupational groups and others—in both the adoption and development of special meanings in words. Meillet, particularly, belongs here, and Bally. The lead which they followed is undoubtedly right; it derives from the primary fact that language is a social institution.

Semantics, as, since Bréal, the study of meaning and change of meaning has been designated, has not hitherto discovered a framework of regularity or fixed patterns, like morphology. Carnoy's *La science du mot,* 1927, offered at least an elaborate scheme of subdivision and a formidable nomenclature. In 1932 Gustaf Stern in *Meaning and Change of Meaning* sought to bring semantics into line with a general theory of language and to classify semantic change according to seven types of internal, linguistic process—as distinguished from merely assigning a name to the results of social and environmental influences. He finds that language in actual use (1) symbolizes things (ideas, emotions, etc.); (2) expresses a view (idea, attitude, emotion, etc.); (3) communicates this to hearers or readers; and thus (4) "performs its effective function"—that is, does a particular job, fulfils a specific purpose.[26]

These are his seven types of change of meaning—I summarize them briefly because Stern's book is both important and at present out of print.

1. *Substitution:* Contrast the meaning of *ship* in the twentieth and in the seventeenth centuries. This type of change due to "non-linguistic" causes—changes occurring entirely outside the psychic sphere of language.

2. *Analogy:* Development of meaning "quick" in adjective *fast,* which previously meant "firm," "immovable." A borrowing from the adverb *fast* (formerly *faste*) which developed the meaning "quickly" by regular stages.

3. *Shortening: Private soldier* is "shortened" to *private,* which acquires the total meaning of the previously used phrase.

4. *Nomination:* Calling a thing something else— metaphor, as *cowslip* (from *cow's lip*).

5. (Regular) *Transfer* of name for one thing to another, without the more or less conscious intention of metaphor found in Nomination. *Leaf* of a book, from *leaf* of a tree.

6. *Permutation:* Example: development of meaning "balls of a rosary" from previous meaning "prayers" in the word *beads.*

7. *Adequation: Horn* first an animal's horn used to make music; then a musical instrument made of something else.

How permanently illuminating or useful Stern's classification will prove remains yet to be seen. His book is, I think, the most comprehensive and symmetrical in recent years on the field of semantics as a whole—linguistic, psychological, social aspects are combined in this analysis of meaning and change of meaning. A vast amount of semantics study remains to be done. The etymologists have long agreed that the history of each word must be studied and traced independently as well as in connection, of course, with other words. This is as true of the meaning as of the sounds and forms which it exhibits.

Linguistic science has introduced order and the possibility of rational comprehension into a sphere where anarchy and untested speculation would otherwise prevail—as they did until the nineteenth century. It has discovered the true center of language—and hence the true center of its study—in human speech. It studies sounds, not letters. It has shown us what a particular language was like in the past, tracing its history and development from its first emergence in written records down to the present, or to the disappearance of the language or its transformation into another. Thus it enables us to see the whole course of development of a language and to orient ourselves accurately in any period of its history. It has given us an adequate and accurate conception of any stage of a language—Modern English, Old French, classical Latin—as a particular stage in a continuous tradition of language behavior. It has discovered and carefully described the various kinds of relationship between languages, grouping them according to genetic sources and showing the manner and effects of contact between languages. It has demonstrated that language is a human invention and a social institution governed by social forces and esteemed according to social criteria. In this way it has freed us from the illusion of intrinsic meaning and from the misconceived effort to apply the instrument of external logic directly as a criterion of language correctness. It has demonstrated that community (as also difference) of language is independent of community of race or nationality. On the other hand, it has established the linguistic community—and hence the ultimate identity of linguistic origin—of all the branches of the great Indo-European family, which includes parts of Asia, most of Europe, and, in modern times, North America, South America, and Australia. In consequence of this, we are able to trace the emergence of an intricate social, physiologic, and mental pattern—the developments of the Indo-European language—over a fairly continuous period of about four thousand years. This is an achievement without parallel in social and intellectual history. Similar, if less spectacular, are the identification, delimitation, and description of other language families—the Semitic, the Finno-Ugric, the Algonkian, and others. Finally, linguistic science has given us a true, a profound, and a comprehensive insight into the greatest invention of man, language.

§ III

The vitality of linguistic studies in our time is manifested by the abundance and variety of their development. In the traditional historical and comparative field, Indo-European horizons have been widened in the last decade by Sturtevant's work in Hittite.[27] He has apparently demonstrated that Hittite is a sister-language of the

Indo-European family rather than a branch of the latter. Since Hittite is related to a whole group of languages of the second millennium B.C. not previously clearly connected with Indo-European, Sturtevant's achievement at once traces new genetic relationships, broadens their geographical and sociological range, and pushes our chronological perspective many centuries farther into the past. Our *ultima Thule* is no longer Indo-European, but Indo-Hittite.

The recording and analysis of the languages of primitive peoples, often previously carried on with inadequate methodology, is proceeding apace. The learned journals and other avenues of publication are rich in studies, for example, of American Indian, South Pacific, and African languages. Most of these exemplify the latest techniques of transcription as well as of phonemic and morphemic analysis. They are usually free from the irrelevant terminology and grammatical classifications of the Indo-European linguistic tradition.

Notable in our generation is the increased attention devoted to the modern period of the European languages. The nineteenth century concentrated on the classical languages and the pre-Renaissance phases of Germanic and Romance. Without neglecting these, the twentieth century has turned seriously to Modern English, French, German, etc.—witness the histories and grammars of Jespersen, Curme, Brunot, et al. The extension of scientific interest beyond the sociologically thin stream of the "standard" or "correct" language practices is attested by studies like those of Leonard and Fries (cited above, p. 61), Frei's *Grammaire des fautes*, and the numerous recent studies of slang and colloquial language.[28] Material which may eventually lead to a history of English pronunciation since the Renaissance is being collected in the laboratory of Professor Miles Hanley at the University of Wisconsin. His file of rhymes already fills about three-quarters of a million slips.

Linguistic theories and linguistic techniques have naturally developed in close relationship. One of the principal methods developed in the present century has been linguistic geography, together with the consequent transformation of dialect study. This technique is based on a sociological view of language: language as a social institution or set of practices subject to change by social influences. The data of linguistic geography, in turn, sustain and define the sociological view. They bring language into closer relation with the rest of human life. Words studied geographically and dialectically in their migrations and transformations are revealed as close concomitants of the changing facts of civilization. Their emergence, borrowing, and disappearance are intimately and minutely related to the history of things. When phonetic change produces inconvenient homonyms, neologisms are introduced from other dialects or from the literary language. These processes Gilliéron called linguistic pathology and therapy; he describes them in a famous study of the words for "bee" in the French dialects.[29] The close scrutiny of speech communities made possible by investigation on the spot and mapping in atlases reveals differences of language (phonemes, morphemes, lexical units) according to sex, age, occupation, family antecedents—that is, according to social milieu. Linguistic geography, moreover, studies not merely dialects in isolation but the relationships among them. It charts the "journeys of words" across the map of a large region, like Northern France. Linguistic community is shown to be dependent on a common civilization and a common life. Innovations radiate from urban centers. They are at a minimum in isolated places and chronological periods; at a maximum in areas and ages in close contact with great centers or cultural capitals.

Linguistic geography not only sets forth the facts about modern dialects; it supplements general linguistic principles at various points. It is a forceful reminder that etymology must take careful account of the possibility of dialect borrowing; it cannot rely merely on sound laws and analogy. The true character of literary or standard languages becomes clear: they are the linguistic practices of particular (not necessarily geographically adjacent) social groups. The study of the vocabulary of standard languages as sociological phenomena has gained impetus since the advent of linguistic geography. In general, linguistic geography tightens the links between the history of language and other phases of social history. The American atlas, referred to earlier, will present the data of American speech in close relationship to the antecedents, regions, ages, education, etc., etc. of the individuals interviewed and the group represented. The phenomena of language will thus be placed accurately in the context of civilization. A modern linguistic atlas is, among other things, one kind of sociological survey just as language is for modern linguistics, among other things, a pattern of social action.

The twentieth century, primarily, has added the synchronic and the structural orientation to linguistic study. Nineteenth century linguists, we have seen, traced the history of "dead" languages and set up correspondences between them. The regular practice, by no means entirely superseded even now, was to explain later stages of a language in the light of earlier: French on the basis of Latin, Modern English as derived from Old English.

But independent analysis of contemporary languages revealed the inaccuracy of purely historical analysis. The historical method, moreover, could not be applied, usually, to the languages of primitive peoples, for the data are often exclusively contemporary. The synchronic view leads to scientific description of languages as working systems at a particular time and place: Classical Greek in Athens in the age of Pericles, Old High German in the ninth century, American English in the twentieth, etc. It asks for scientific analysis of the linguistic forms and functions once summarily recorded as descriptive or static grammar. It asserts that the full meaning of a linguistic form is found in a complete description of its use; historical derivation is irrelevant to analysis of the working of a language at any given moment. What is needed is a full account of all the contemporaneous elements of the system.

The synchronic linguist therefore applies the structural method of description and classification. As one of its strong advocates recently said, "The structural method is basically the placing together of any formal features of a language which in respect to any criterion are similar." [30] A language is "a system of units and their relations." Thus phonemes are arranged according to their relations in the language studied, morphemes according to the position of each in respect of others, the types of combination into which it can enter, the other morphemes with which it combines. Descriptive statements and classifications of any language can be organized in terms of the particular units and the relations existing among them.

The synchronic and structural approaches, earlier recognized by de Saussure and Jespersen, for example, and applied by the latter to English grammar, are becoming increasingly influential in general linguistic methodology. Their impact is especially felt in questions of grammatical classification and terminology. The structuralists have shown us, for example, that case is not an objective reality, much less a universal reality, but a relationship among some morphemes in some languages. Prepositions are not "substitutes" for case morphemes; from the synchronic point of view they are simply elements in the structure of particular languages at particular times. Structural analysis shows that definitions of the "word" or "sentence" based on the Indo-European languages may not be applicable to languages outside that family, and hence cannot be used as general or universal linguistic criteria.

Structural investigation leads to practical as well as theoretical and scientific applications, and to controversy. Since the traditional terms employed in grammars of the modern languages derive from Latin grammar and are often structurally inaccurate for synchronic study—which is or should be the orientation of language study in elementary and high school classes—what terminology should be used in the description and classification of contemporary English, French, German, etc.? Should the "convenience" of traditional terms, relevant to Latin, Greek, and to some extent to German, lead us to continue them, at the cost of inaccuracy and misrepresentation of structure, in English? Far from being settled, such questions are just now receiving enlightened discussion. Apart from pedagogical texts, moreover, the practices of eminent grammarians still differ widely. Curme's description of Modern English retains much of the case and mood classifications morphemically distinguished in Old English but not in the contemporary language. Jespersen, a more thorough-going structuralist, recognizes only distinctions represented by different morphemes and introduces a new terminology.[31] But if questions of terminology and classification are not yet determined, we are at least now in position to discuss them in their proper light; we understand the issues involved. I believe the future belongs to consistent structuralism, but the practical problem of a feasible, especially a pedagogically feasible, terminology remains to be solved.

Linguistic methodology in our time depends, further, on the view of language which the investigator adopts as basic. Less than a generation ago nearly all linguists would have accepted Sapir's definition of language as "a purely human and non-instinctive method of communicating ideas, emotions, and desires by means of a system of voluntarily produced symbols." [32] A majority, doubtless, would still accept it. But a very active group, represented in America by Bloomfield and his followers, would object to the inclusion of what they regard as undefined, mentalistic terms in this formulation—"ideas," "emotions," "desires," and perhaps "voluntarily." To them linguistics is an exact science, or should be. Since the activities of the mind are inaccessible to objective observation, they prefer to exclude it from statements. Thus Twaddell declares, "The scientific method is quite simply the convention that mind does not exist: science adopts the nominalistic attitude toward the problem of universals, in matters of procedure." [33] Carefully distinguishing between an attitude toward the universe—a philosophy of life?—and scientific procedure, Bloomfield would limit scientific statements to those which can be made in terms of strict behaviorism, mechanism, operationalism, and physicalism.[34] In *Linguistic Aspects of Science,* 1940, he gives this description of language:

Language creates and exemplifies a twofold value of some human actions. In its *biophysical* aspect language consists of sound-producing movements and of the resultant sound waves and of the vibration of the hearer's eardrums. The *biosocial* aspect of language consists in the fact that the persons in a community have been trained to produce these sounds in certain situations and to respond to them by appropriate actions. The biosocial function of language arises from a uniform, traditional, and arbitrary training of the persons in a certain group. They have been trained to utter conventional sounds as a secondary response to situations and to respond to these slight sounds, in a kind of trigger effect, with all sorts of actions.[35]

The mechanist school of linguists, accordingly, excludes psychological formulations or explanations of language phenomena of any kind. Such statements cannot be checked or verified by scientific means; let the linguist limit his formulations to such features as another scientific linguist can distinguish and measure objectively. Linguistic meaning must not be described in psychological terms. Instead, "the meaning of a form class is the contrast between its positions and combinations and those of the other form classes; the meaning of individual morphemes is approximated by contrasting the situations in which they occur in an utterance with the situations in which the same utterance occurs without them, and so on." [36] Since a language is a system of units and their relations, "correlations between the occurrence of one form and that of other forms yield the whole of linguistic structure." [37] Terms once scientifically defined, "the work of linguistics is reducible, in the last analysis, to establishing correlations." [38] " 'Parole' [utterances] is merely the physical events which we count as language, while 'langue' [a given language] is the scientist's analysis and arrangement of them." [39] The use of semantic or mentalistic terms in statements about linguistic structure muddies the water; it introduces unknowns into formulations which should be restricted exclusively to knowns. The mechanist has no objection to psychological or sociological interpretations of language, provided they do not conflict with linguistic data. But he considers any and all such interpretations irrelevant to linguistics itself; their desirability must be determined by other sciences. [40]

If the mechanists derive their conceptions and methodology in linguistics from the example of the exact sciences, the followers of Vossler base theirs on the philosophy of Croce. For Vossler language is an expression of the human spirit; language is an individual phenomenon; there are as many styles—or distinctive ways of expression in language—as there are individuals. It is thus "parole," or individual utterances, that Vossler primarily identifies as language. But, according to him, every speaker is influenced by two impulses, one leading him to go his own independent way in speech, another leading him to use language as his fellows use it. All innovation, all that is particular and distinctive in language is due to individual creative activity. All that is general in language—in a community of speakers—is due to social intercourse. Changes in a language are due to the distinctive genius of the language—that is, the combined genius of the several speakers in their predominant directions of expression. Sound changes thus follow certain lines according to the genius of the language at particular periods. Likewise syntactical change:

the word order of Modern French was developed from
tendencies in the speakers of French, the loss of case
endings was incidental. Change in the meaning of
words, or semantic change, is always through metaphor.
For language equals expression equals intuition. It is an
individual and an aesthetic fact. Because of social intercourse, communication, and social influences, it is also
a cultural fact.

Vossler sought to apply his views in a study of French
culture in the light of the development of the French
language—*Frankreichs Kultur im Spiegel seiner Sprachentwicklung*. Here he attempted "eine Betrachtung
des gesamten französischen Geisteslebens, soweit es sich
am Sprachgebrauch der Franzosen erkennen lässt." [41]
An example of his method is the interpretation of the
partitive construction with the definite article (j'ai des
pommes), which became common in the Middle French
period, as an expression of the "praktische, messende,
teilende, rechnerische Auffassung der Dinge" in that
age. [42] As mentioned earlier in this chapter, Vossler
traces the *Geistesleben* of the French people through
the development of the vocabulary of French and the
changes in the meanings of words.

Vossler himself is primarily interested in the literary
languages; indeed, his studies of Italian, French, and
Spanish poetry belong to literary history rather than to
linguistics. This dual interest in language and literature is characteristic of his followers as well. Professor
Leo Spitzer, now of Johns Hopkins University, for example, advocates—and practices—a study of literary
history in close relation to language. Occupied chiefly
with style, he analyzes an author's language as a key to
the mental state of the author. [43]

Bally and his followers combine some elements of

both the French sociological and the German idealistic schools. Bally has devoted himself primarily to the linguistic expression of emotional attitudes. For him neither life nor language is primarily a purely intellectual or logical activity or experience. Life is a struggle in which men alternate between, or combine, submission and domination. Language is fashioned in such a way as to represent these attitudes. It is fundamentally social; the variations of emotional attitude are shown in the choice of language, which is always shaped by a particular purpose. In this process the intelligence operates, not coldly and abstractly or always premeditatedly, but often unconsciously. Bally uses the term *Stylistique* (stylistics) to denote the study of the "expressive" types employed by language to render emotional attitudes.

Since language is arbitrary in both signifier (*signifiant*) and signified (*signifié*), it can express emotion only through the play of implicit associations. These associations are attached either to the *signifier*, in such a way as to evoke a sensory impression (through the sound of the word), or to the *signified*, so as to transform the concept into imaginative representation. These associations are loaded with (emotional) expressivity to the extent that the imaginative representation agrees with the emotive content of the language utterance. The study of the linguistic mechanism of these processes is stylistics. One of the methods of discovering and defining the expressive characteristics of a language is to compare its means of expression with those of another language (Bally regularly compares French and German). Another method is to compare the principal expressive types in a single language, taking account of the social milieus to which they belong, the circumstances of their use, the intonations they involve, and, finally, the effects they produce on the sensibility of speakers and hearers.

Stylistics takes as its field the whole domain of language phenomena, sounds, syntax, and vocabulary. Bally holds that little is yet known of the expressive value of sounds; nor has vocabulary been much studied from this point of view. Syntax is in somewhat better case. Stylistics studies not one part of language, but all of language from a particular angle. Ordinary language is full of expressive elements, though rarely of consciously produced aesthetic effects. Street urchins often "create style without knowing it." Bally finds a parallel between such spontaneous creations of ordinary speakers and the artistic creations of a great writer which constitute his style. Literary expression, he points out, rests entirely upon the facts of sensibility and the impressions produced by language. Every word in literary art aims at some kind of emotional effect—"une action sur le sentiment." The same penetration of language and sensibility is found in all spontaneous language. It is the task of stylistics to lay bare these "germs" of style latent in the most ordinary forms of language. Here we find a parallel to the study of literary style itself. How does a literary style develop out of spontaneous language? By adopting as an end what is only a means in actual, spontaneous language—emotional expressivity.[44]

Can the several schools of linguists—mechanist, idealistic, sociological, stylistic (psychological)—live at peace with one another, or is each in irreconcilable opposition to some or all of the rest? History supports the second alternative. Yet by profession each group works in a different field from any of the others, examines different data, or common data in a different way, and formulates conclusions—or should and could formulate them—distinct in character from those to which the techniques of any other group could legitimately lead. The mechanist works exclusively within the tangible data of language phenomena, which he describes, classifies, and arranges in a system. The idealist's "spirit of the language," the sociological linguist's "influence of society," and the psychological linguist's "expressive motivation" are all simply outside the picture for the mechanist. They are either external or intangible forces; since by definition he is concerned only with the internal and the tangible, he is right in ignoring them. In this way he is enabled to deal with one aspect of language with the objectivity of a physicist or a biologist. Thus one aspect of linguistics may be called an exact science. But language is a very complex kind of human activity. There is no reason why it should not be studied, like the rest of human activities, in many other ways—aesthetically, sociologically, or psychologically. If such study is carried on without falsification or contradiction of linguistic data—including the mechanist's data—there is no reason why it should be inveighed against as "unscientific." For that term carries an odium of total disapproval which may well be impertinent, irrelevant, or unjustified in the light of the investigator's professed principles and assumptions. The linguist who is not a mechanist, on the other hand, should have no hesitation and no embarrassment in agreeing that his methodology is not that of a physical science and that his conclusions cannot claim that particular kind of validity. He can take comfort, if he feels the need of it, from the situation in another branch of the study of man's activities: "strictly scientific" history, if it exists, is by no means the only valuable kind of history.

§ IV

For the linguist, as we have seen, language is a form of human behavior to be scientifically examined. For the creator and the critic of literature, it is the medium of an art. Although the scientific grammarian and the literary critic devote their attention to the same works of prose and poetry, their purposes and methods are different. The linguist may give the closest study to *Beowulf*, Racine, or Sinclair Lewis. He does so in order to determine the facts about some feature or features of the English or French language. As a linguist, he either has no interest in these authors and their works as literary art; or his interest is to determine facts about language as it is used in literary art (just as he might be interested in the use of language in advertising). The student of literature, on the other hand, is interested in language only as the vehicle of literary creation. In order to read literature, however, he must first master the language in which it is written. If he is to read the literature of a foreign language, or of the earlier periods of his own, the attainment of this mastery is a considerable task in itself. The monuments of literature in the early periods, moreover, are among the precious and indispensable data of the historical linguist.

Real dangers lurk in this situation, dangers apparently not always avoided in the past. The effort to learn the language is initially great in any case. If the instructor is primarily a linguist, this effort may absorb the student's whole attention. He may never achieve an experience of the literary work as art at all. It may become a cadaver for scientific dissection, the aroma of which may linger long after the facts are forgotten—to discourage the student from reading the work again in after life. It is a confusion of purposes to require *Beowulf* of students on the ground that this is the greatest poem in early Germanic literature and then devote the course to unorganized notes on Germanic linguistics. A better text could be chosen, anyway, if the course and the instructor are primarily concerned with the phenomena of language. It is unfortunate that a student's most vivid memory of that noble poem, Layamon's *Brut,* should be the miniature "Grammar of an Early Southern Middle English text" that he was required to manufacture out of it. There is no question of the value of making the grammar or of acquiring some knowledge of Germanic linguistics. But somewhere provision should be made for as serious a literary and aesthetic study of Old and Middle English literature, in proportion to the quantity and quality of the texts, as is now accorded literature of the later periods. Perhaps such courses should follow those devoted to English linguistics. In courses devoted to the literature of the early periods of English, French, German, etc., the treatment of language, necessarily larger in quantity, should serve the same purpose as in a course in Shakespeare, say, or Milton. It should be a means, not primarily an end. When this state of things is reached we shall be in position to do justice to the literary art of the Middle Ages. Until that time, we may hope that the scholar who must be both linguist and literary critic in the same course will know when to be which. The two functions, of course, may be used to supplement each other; but they should not be merely mixed in confusion.

How much knowledge about a language is requisite for the critic and "higher" student of literature? In

Language and Poetry, F. W. Bateson has recently
sketched the history of English poetry as a complex variable of the development of the language. He demonstrates conclusively the parallels between the two and
their inseparable connection, whether one agrees with
him or not as to the causal influence of language. For it
is indisputably true that the language of any period is a
transient integration of sounds, forms, conventions of
word order, and symbol-associations (word meanings).
Each age has its own integration, in which the associations of a word stand in a unique relationship to the
associations of other words.

When Hamlet spoke of his "melancholy," the Elizabethan audience thought of the four humors. A footnote
in a modern text on melancholy alone does not re-create
the Elizabethan cluster of associations, for we have detached melancholy from the other three. The vocabulary
of neo-classical poetry forms a neat circle which may
remain closed on the outside to the student who does not
acquire a sense of the relations between the terms.
"Wit," "judgment," "nature," etc., not only have a different meaning than they have now as individual words;
in the poetry of the time they are skilfully balanced
against one another. The adequate reader must become
familiar with the literary language of the late seventeenth and early eighteenth centuries as a whole. The
critic of Milton is at a disadvantage if he must rely
solely on the trustworthiness of an editor's brief footnote
for the fact that "dire" is an emphatic word, representing
the Latin *dirus*, though now weak and slightly ludicrous.
He should be a bit better at home with Milton than the
reader who must be told that "argument" is not con-
troversial, and that the "subjected" plain to which Michael leads our general ancestors is merely situated be-

low the mount of vision, not under a conqueror's heel. And how is the scholar to decide the facts about the poetic language of *Paradise Lost* unless he knows the prose and poetic language of the seventeenth century?

A number of contemporary literary critics, each in his own way, emphasize and exemplify the central importance of close attention to language. I. A. Richards studies the problem of adequate reading of an author's words and phrases. R. P. Blackmur examines a poet's lexicon intensively as a whole and in single poems. T. S. Eliot and his school are basically concerned with the language of poetry. William Empson analyzes the "ambiguities" of association in the words of a poem.[45]

A good knowledge of the history of a language as a whole is necessary for the adequate interpretation of any considerable portion or period of its literature. This introductory acquaintance with the general course of development will serve as a guide and a frame of reference. Then the language as a whole *in the period concerned* should receive the special attention of the critic or historical student of the several phases of the literature. This will lend confidence to his interpretation of texts, and save him many a serious blunder. In all intensive study—for instance, in *explication de texte*—a sure knowledge of the writer's language is essential. Otherwise, the latent suggestions, the mild overtones may be missed. For they are apt to be inherent in the subtle associations of the words.

3

LITERARY HISTORY

René Wellek

THE SUBJECT of literary history has been under fire for several decades. Dissatisfaction with the haphazard accumulation of materials and facts about the literature of the past which frequently passes for "literary history" has been growing apace. Proposals to relegate literary history to a subordinate position compared with literary criticism or a general history of civilization have become frequent in recent years. Even enthusiasts for the subject do not seem to envisage a future for it. Theorizing on the principles of literary history has often been avoided, ironically enough, on almost theoretical grounds: an empirical mentality has prided itself upon its lack of clarity on questions of methodology. A great scholar like W. P. Ker—who, in his own work, was himself a highly successful practitioner of literary history in the strictest sense of the word—has even defended the point of view that "method is far less required in literary than in political history," since literary history is "more like a guide-book than a geography."[1] Routine, confusion, resignation, and scepticism seem to characterize the present attitude of most of those who should direct our studies. Thus some reflections on the fundamental problems of literary history may not be out of place at a time when the need for reorientation is widely and acutely felt.

Most discussion on questions of method are inextricably bound up with questions of the teaching of literature and university organization. I am not here concerned with such questions—how and when literary history should be taught, or whether every literary scholar should devote himself to this or that approach to literature. I propose rather to discuss the subject of literary history simply as an organized system of knowledge. I shall try to distinguish between the different methods as practised today and suggest a scheme of relationships and emphases. This is not merely a speculative question: a clarification of the place and function of each special method is highly important for the practice of scholarship. Though no individual scholar can or should limit himself to a single approach, a recognition of the boundaries of each will prevent the confusion of aims and methods which is a bane in present-day scholarship.

§ II

Literary history in a wide sense of the term can be understood to begin with the accumulation and collection of documents, their editing and placing in a chronological scheme. This preliminary work is frequently termed "research" *par excellence*, though the methods of research —a collection, arrangement and sifting of facts—must be used in any other historical or even critical investigation and should not be appropriated for one specific set of problems alone. Nobody will underrate the immense work accomplishd in these fields, especially in the last hundred years. We have mapped out the whole realm of literature and literary scholarship with systematic bibliographies; we have clean, readable texts of almost all important writings of most periods, established frequently by a laborious process called "textual criticism"; we have given answers to innumerable questions of chronology, authenticity, and authorship. A great body of scholarship has been built up, a coöperative enterprise which may be corrected and supplemented by investigators in the future.

For these preliminary studies, however well-established, are not stationary today. It is still possible to discover unknown works, even in English literature, like the book of Margery Kempe or Medwall's *Fulgens and Lucrece.*[2] Legal and historical documents which throw light on the lives of well-worked authors have been discovered in recent years, by Leslie Hotson and others.[3] Even in the editing of Shakespeare and his contemporaries great changes have taken place in recent decades. A method which calls itself rather misleadingly "bibliography," sponsored by scholars like Dover Wilson, W. W. Greg, and, more soberly by R. B. McKerrow, has put to use the results of a careful study of the methods of book production, of Elizabethan handwriting, and compositors' practices in order to arrive not only at a new text of Shakespeare, but also at audacious speculations on Shakespeare's methods of work, his revisions and adaptations, his share in plays assigned to several authors.[4] Ingenious methods have been devised to ascertain the chronology of works for which external evidence is defective, and many questions of authenticity and authorship have been solved by an increasingly subtle study of distinctions of style and a systematic search for the remotest bibliographical and documentary evidence. Organization, sheer dogged industry, but also much ingenuity and brilliant guesswork have had their rewards in results for which every scholar must be grateful. Especially in the field of mediaeval and Renaissance studies the advance has been immeasurable. It suffices to compare the task which confronted Thomas Warton when he set out to write his *History of English Poetry* (1774–81) with the modern scholar's equipment. Warton had to collect and decipher most of the manuscripts himself, he had to date them and to search them and contemporary documents for evidences of authorship: the modern student has access to a library of accurate, legible texts and to a body of well-indexed research which has put most questions of date and authorship beyond reasonable dispute.

No doubt this work will and should continue: there are still many problems unsolved and many important gaps to fill. Important authors are not available in critical and complete editions, as in the case of Layamon, Fulke Greville, Peele, Middleton, Dryden, Defoe, Johnson, Coleridge, and many others. Much is still obscure in questions of authorship and date, especially in the vexed field of Elizabethan drama. No doubt, similar questions remain unsolved in all other literatures. But there is general agreement today that the task has been accomplished in its main outlines, at least in the great Western literatures. The time has definitely arrived when all this material accumulated and sifted by several generations should be put to some further use. The task of interpretation and coördination, the task of writing literary history, cannot be put forever on the shoulders of the next generation.

The only American book which treats of the problems under discussion in a systematic fashion, André Morize's *Problems and Methods of Literary History* (1922), creates the impression that literary history is almost confined to questions of editing and authorship, sources and biography. Towards the end of the book, there is only a brief reference to literary history in connection with the history of ideas and the history of manners. Likewise, most academic teaching stresses the use of tools and the technique of preparing new ones. The usual argument in favor of such limitations upon "research" is the value of the discipline gained by training in these methods. But the results of such training seem overrated, in view of the many fantastic theories propounded by the greatest experts. W. W. Greg—to quote a single instance—made an elaborate attempt to show that the elder Hamlet was not poisoned through the ear, and that the play within the play as well as the ghost made a false accusation.[5] Erudition and expert knowledge are no guarantees of common sense. However indispensable all this preliminary work, an overemphasis on it results frequently in trivialities and useless pedantries which justly evoke the ridicule of the layman and the anger of the scholar at wasted energy. Such work has also too much attraction for minds indifferent to the values of literature, and a rigid insistence on its technicalities sometimes puts unnecessary obstacles in the way of students genuinely interested in literary art and thought.

§ III

These preliminary studies have, of course, rarely been conducted in complete isolation. Editions, discussions of date and authorship must lead to wider questions of interpretation and to the problem of literary relationships. The natural and sensible starting-point for work

in "literary history" beyond these preliminaries is the
interpretation and analysis of the works of literature
themselves. After all, only the works themselves justify
all our interest in the life of an author, in his social environment and the whole process of literature. But,
curiously enough, literary history has been so preoccupied with the setting of a work of literature that its
attempts at an analysis of the works themselves have
been slight in comparison with the enormous efforts
expanded on the study of environment. Some reasons
for this overemphasis on the conditioning circumstances
rather than on the works themselves are not far to seek.
Modern literary history arose in close connection with
the Romantic movement, which could subvert the critical system of Neo-classicism only with the relativist
argument that different times required different standards. Thus the emphasis shifted from the literature itself
to its historical background, which was used to justify
the new values ascribed to old literature. In the nineteenth century explanation by causes became the great
watchword, largely in an endeavor to emulate the methods of the natural sciences. Besides, the breakdown of
the old "poetics" which occurred with the shift of interest to the individual "taste" of the reader, strengthened
the conviction that art, being fundamentally irrational,
should be left to "appreciation." Sir Sidney Lee, in his
inaugural lecture, merely summed up the theory of most
academic literary scholarship when he said: "In literary
history we seek the external circumstances—political,
social, economic—in which literature is produced." [6] The
result of a lack of clarity on questions of poetics has been
the astonishing helplessness of most scholars when confronted with the task of actually analyzing and evaluating a work of art. Many are able only to extract its

purely intellectual content, which they proceed to discuss in isolation from its context just as if it were a statement in a philosophical dissertation or a newspaper article.

In recent years a healthy reaction has taken place which recognizes that the study of literature should, first and foremost, concentrate on the actual works of art themselves. The old methods of classical rhetoric, poetics, or metrics are found insufficient and must be replaced or at least supplemented by new methods based on a survey of the wider range of forms in modern literature. In France the method of *explication de textes*,[7] in Germany the formal analyses based on parallels with the history of fine arts, cultivated by Oscar Walzel,[8] and especially the brilliant movement of the Russian formalists and their Czech and Polish followers [9] have brought new stimuli to the study of the literary work which we are only beginning to see properly and to analyze adequately. In England some of the followers of I. A. Richards have paid close attention to the text of poetry [10] and also in this country a group of critics have made a study of the work of art the center of their interest.[11] All these recent studies have one common characteristic: they try to bridge the dangerous gulf between content and form and to overcome the isolation of individual features like meter and diction; they attempt to analyze the work of art without ignoring its unity and integrity. Among these methods, those devised by the Russian formalists seem to me most valuable, especially with the modifications of the theory propounded by the Prague Linguistic Circle. They introduce the concept of "structure" which includes both content and form as far as they are organized for aesthetic purposes. The work of art is considered as a whole dynamic system of signs serving a specific aesthetic purpose.

Investigation of a work of literary art has to proceed in close touch with linguistics, since such a work is, first of all, an organized, purposeful sequence of words. The development of linguistics in the direction of a functional conception makes this collaboration possible for the first time. By functionalizing even sounds and replacing them by the concept of "phoneme" a new analysis of euphony has for the first time become possible.[12] The functional point of view also sheds a flood of light on the problems of metrics hitherto obscured by dilettantism or preoccupation with the oscillograph. Similar methods have also been developed in the analysis of stylistic characteristics like poetic diction and the combination and arrangement of *motifs*. Because of the close association of these methods with a study of formal elements in the old technical sense of the word, they have not altogether escaped the danger of underrating the rôle of meaning in the work of art. Roman Ingarden's ingenious book *Das literarische Kunstwerk* (Halle, 1931) has shown the way out: a careful differentiation between the different strata of a work of art leads from a consideration of sound patterns and units of meaning to the objects represented and even to the metaphysical qualities implied. Thus the problem of the "idea" or the "world-view" in a work of art is reintroduced without the risk of the usual intellectualistic pitfalls. This "idea" is not to be confused with some true statement or rational system abstracted from the work of art nor of course with the pronouncement of any one personage in a book or even the commentary of the author. An interpretation of the "world-view" will be immanent in the work as well as the whole scheme of realities and relationships to which it refers. The "idea" is not without relation to the form of the work of art, since it emerges only from the units of meaning and thus ultimately from the linguistic substratum.

All these are difficult questions still in a state of flux: but that a better understanding of the coherence and integrity of the work of art and its aesthetic function is under way can be shown by the many similar attempts at a closer analysis which have been made, apparently quite independently, in different countries. Several studies of the drama [13] which stress its difference from life and combat the confusion between dramatic and empirical reality point in the same direction. Similarly many studies of the novel [14] are not content to consider it merely in terms of its relations to the social picture but try to analyze its artistic methods—its points of view, its narrative technique. All these close studies of the work of art would benefit greatly from contact with modern poetics, especially with a new theory of genres. Furthermore the close study of the "world-view" implied in a work of literature will only gain from an expert knowledge of philosophical, ethical, religious, and similar problems and attitudes.

Matters of this sort are frequently assigned to literary criticism and excluded from literary history. But literary history is impossible without the constant use of the results of such aesthetic studies and without reference to some scheme of critical standards. A critical scheme, in turn, cannot be evolved *in vacuo*, without a knowledge of the whole variegated map of literature. The usual hard-and-fast distinction between literary history and criticism is, actually, untenable. Mr. F. W. Bateson has given expression to the common view of the difference between literary history and criticism by affirming that they are based on two distinct types of judgment.[15] Literary history, that is, shows that: *A* derives from *B*, while criticism pronounces *A* to be better than *B*. The first type, in this view, deals with verifiable facts, the second with matters of opinion which imply an element of faith on the reader's part. But this distinction cannot possibly be defended. Literary history is utterly inconceivable without some value-judgments. They are implied in the very choice of materials, in the simple preliminary question of the distinction between books and literature, in the mere allocation of space to this or that specific question. They must enter into the smallest discussion of literary relationship. The literary historian "can have access to the works he proposes to deal with —his most essential facts—only if he is sufficiently a critic; only by an appropriate and discriminating response to them; a response, that is, involving the kind of activity that produces value-judgments. The judgments are not expressions of opinions on facts that can be possessed and handled neutrally."[16] Conversely, a criticism which is content to be utterly ignorant of all historical relationships would constantly go astray in its judgments: it could have no correct conception of originality in any concrete instance, and would constantly blunder from its ignorance of historical conditions in its understanding of concrete works of art. The literary critic needs such knowledge as the historian assembles, as the literary historian needs criteria supplied by some theory. The common nineteenth-century divorce between literary criticism and history has been detrimental to both. The critic has been encouraged to slipshod guesses, autobiographical "adventures among masterpieces," and a general neglect of the more remote past. The historian has shirked vital problems arising in the course of his studies as reserved for criticism or else has adopted merely conventional standards, whether romantic or neo-classic, without any examination of their presuppositions. This has frequently led him to a lack of contact with contemporary problems either in literature or in speculative thought, and thus has tended to justify the reproach that literary history has become merely academic antiquarianism.

§ IV

The analysis of the isolated work of art is, of course, to a certain extent artificial and impracticable. Along with the intensive study of its unity and integrity, there will always be the supplementary approach from its environmental context, whether we conceive of this as the literary tradition, the individual experiences of the author, or the sum-total of all the other human activities which influence and condition its production. These "extrinsic" studies have so monopolized the attention of scholars that it seems useful to draw attention rather to their limitations and drawbacks than to the undoubted light they have thrown on the process of literature. When these environmental methods are pushed to their deterministic extremes, and literature is conceived as causally determined by any one or any combination of these forces, a proper comprehension of literature has actually been hindered. All such extrinsic studies do violence to the individuality of the literary work and to the nature of literary evolution. Any causal explanation of a work of art by some external activity necessarily must ignore the actual integrity, coherence, and also intrinsic value of a work of literature. The work is reduced to an illustration or an example in a different scheme of references. This may be seen by glancing briefly at the most common traditional methods of the study of literature.

The most obvious approach to literature is through the principal cause of a work of art, its author. The biographical method has been dominant in literary studies, especially in England, from the time Leland and Bale compiled their catalogues of lives in the sixteenth century, through Johnson's *Lives* and the "lives and letters" of the Victorians down to the fictionalized biography of the present day. Biography as such is a branch of history in its own right and uses the evidence and methods of history. The life of an author is dealt with exactly like that of a general, statesman, musician, or painter. Biography is also valuable, to be sure, for the interpretation of literature, by assembling the materials for psychological and sociological study. It furnishes data on the race, the family, the social status, the individual experiences and mental characteristics of an author. Yet the value of this information for the study of literature seems frequently overrated. I am not merely thinking of the abuses of the biographical method: the usual preoccupation with trivial details of the purely private life of an author, his love affairs or his personal quarrels, which often have scarcely any literary significance. I have in mind rather a more fundamental objection. The comprehension of a work of art is, actually, seldom impaired by a lack of biographical knowledge. We know practically nothing biographical beyond the bare dates in the case of most of the older poets, nor do we know much about the intimate lives of our contemporaries, and yet we scarcely feel handicapped in understanding their writings. The biographical approach is most valid when it succeeds in demonstrating the close relationship of work and life. This will be possible with modern subjective poets like Goethe or Byron who themselves conceived of their work as a record of individual experiences. But in countless other works of art the element of personal expression is very weak, while the aesthetic value is great. The Italian *novelle,* the sonnets of the Renaissance, Elizabethan dramas, naturalistic novels, folk-poetry, classical music, and Chinese painting are obvious examples. Besides, even when there is a close relationship between the work of art and the life of its author, this must never be conceived as meaning that the work of art is a mirror or copy of life, a direct confession or piece of autobiography. Much biographical work has been marred by a mechanical conception of the relation between art and life. An ignominious hunt for models in the private life of the author has ignored the transformation every experience must undergo in the artistic process. The work of art may embody the dream of its creator, or his exact psychological opposite, or it may function almost as a mask in a subtly inverse fashion only indirectly related to the empirical personality.

In recent decades a healthy reaction against this literal-mindedness has taken place: psychological terms and criteria have refined the biographical approach. The psychological habit of an author, the processes of his creation, and even the depths and shallows of his subconscious mind have been studied. In Germany at least, the term "Erlebnis" and its skilful use by men like Dilthey and Gundolf [17] have done much to replace the idea of mere transcription, and in other countries more diffidence and subtlety in the interpretation of art through life is now almost general. And yet, whatever refine-

ments may be introduced, the art of literature can never
be fully explained by individual biography and psychology. A work of art is not simply the embodiment of
experience, but always the last number in a series of
works; it is a drama, a novel, or a poem determined, as
far as it is determined at all, mainly by literary tradition.
The biographical approach actually obscures a proper
comprehension of literature, since it breaks up the order
of literary tradition in favor of the life-cycle of an individual. Even the undeniable results of the biographical
or psychological approach seem frequently small in
scope, if we judge them strictly for their value in the
comprehension of literature. The best empirical study
of the creative process I know, Professor Lowes's learned
and brilliant *Road to Xanadu* (1926), is, in its description of the creative process itself, little more than a
string of metaphors about the "deep well," the "hooked
atoms," and the "sea-change" brought about by art.
Even Coleridge's famous distinction between fancy and
imagination seems less valuable as a distinction in psychology than as an observation of two types of imagery
which could be differentiated without the assumption
of two distinct powers of the mind.

Much psychological study of literature is concerned
with the purely private character of the man or else with
speculations on inaccessible states of mind. Thus Mr.
Tillyard in a good book on Milton complains that critics
of *Paradise Lost* ignore "what the poem is really about,
the true state of Milton's mind when he wrote it." [18] He
thus apparently assumes that poetry must be the
expression of the author's personality and that all poetry
is *about* the poet's state of mind. Even if this large assumption were true,[19] it would still be impossible to
reconstruct the mental state of an author in the moment

of creation, and it would be irrelevant, as well, since a resultant work of art is not explainable by the conscious "intentions" and "states of mind" of an author. The work of art is an objective construct whose full meaning can be exhausted only by generations of readers. This "genetic fallacy" is usually driven to grotesque lengths by the psychoanalysts, who study the poet as a case in abnormal psychology and think that his complexes and idiosyncrasies, however well documented, "explain" a concrete work of art. They make the same error which misleads historians of philosophy into disputing or disposing of an argument because they can show its origin in some experience or habit of the philosopher. In the same way much study of the psychology of the reader seems to have scarcely any relevance to the work of literature itself. Greatly as I admire the critical abilities of Mr. I. A. Richards, I cannot see any light in his chief theory, that poetry puts into order the chaos of our impulses. His theory seems completely useless in the concrete analysis or evaluation of a piece of poetry, and we are not much comforted by his constant declaration that this or that problem is still "hidden in the jungles of neurology." [20] He is driven to admit that a balanced poise can be achieved by a bad as well as a good poem, by a carpet as well as a sonata, and thus has nothing to do with the actual object of our study: literature. When literature is used as evidence or material in the field of psychology, it loses its literary character and is placed on the same level as a psychological questionnaire or experiment. It serves elsewhere and thus falls outside the scope of these reflections occupied with the study of literature. What I have been saying should not, however, be misinterpreted as implying that there is no problem of the expressive function of literature. One cannot deny that different works of art by one author may have a striking "physiognomical" similarity. There is a quality called "Miltonic," "Keatsian," etc. which can be determined on the basis of the works themselves and which is not necessarily ascertainable through any purely biographical evidence. The biographical framework will also help us in studying the most obvious of all strictly evolutionary problems in the history of literature: the growth, maturing, and possible decline of an author's art. But the mechanical determinism of the conception of art as a transcript of life should be definitely discarded.

§ V

Exactly the same fundamental criticism can be made of another common external approach: the explanation of literature by the history of humanity, whether we conceive this determination of literary evolution in the broadest terms as an assemblage of the whole range of historical factors, or, more narrowly, as any one particular activity of man, his language, his thought, the political institutions, the economic and social changes, or the biological basis in race. Literature is, of course, in constant and vital relationship with all these activities. Yet it has its own development, irreducible to any other activity of man or to a sum of all these activities. Otherwise it would cease to be literature and lose its *raison d'être*.

The most central approach to literature among these external approaches is that through the history of language, inasmuch as language is the medium of literature. This view has been stated powerfully by F. W. Bateson

in his book *English Poetry and the English Language*
(1934). But he vitiates his argument by the prejudice
that literature "is unintelligible except in reference to
something outside itself," and that it is completely dependent on the evolution of language.[21] Mr. Bateson ignores the fact that language itself is also formed by
literature and that both language and literature are
formed by other social forces. Without linguistics, it is
true, no proper study of the texture of a work of art, its
diction, meter, style, euphony, etc. is possible. But the
very fact that we can conceive of a universal history of
literature, which would also be a history of literary
forms and genres, cutting across all linguistic boundaries, shows that literature is not reducible to a simple
reflex of linguistic evolution. The overemphasis on linguistic boundaries encouraged by the growth of nationalism has led to artificial distinctions in the actual writing of literary history. The development of mediaeval
literature in the British Isles, for instance, is obscured, in
some centuries, if only documents in English are selected and literature in Latin or Anglo-Norman is ignored. Much also of the grouping of literatures along the
lines of purely linguistic families seems doubtful, as the
frequent though scarcely convincing attempts to write a
history of all Slavonic literatures show. Literature *can*, of
course, be treated purely as a linguistic document. But
then it ceases to be literature: distinctions between
good and bad poetry or between literature and a legal
document fall. Literature becomes a source for the
science of linguistics, a science which has its own criteria and aims, even though its results are highly important and useful for the understanding of literature.

In recent decades emphasis has fallen primarily upon
the study of literature as determined by the history of

philosophy, religion, ethics, or related arts, or by the general social evolution of society. No one should under-rate the substantial gains made in the comprehension of literature from the light shed by philosophers or theo-logians or economic and social historians, whether these were professionals in their subjects or literary historians who acquired the requisite knowledge themselves. But again a distinction should be drawn between the use of such studies for the interpretation of literature and the use of literature as a document for the study of the history of civilization or philosophy, religion, society, etc. Many literary historians deliberately ignore this distinction and plead for such an extension of "literary history," which would, in practice, merge it with the whole history of civilization. Edwin Greenlaw in his well-known *Province of Literary History* (1931) went so far as to say that "nothing related to the history of civilization is beyond our province," [22] and the practice of literary historians shows that he simply gave expres-sion to an actual state of affairs. Professor Kittredge wrote an imposing work on *Witchcraft in Old and New England,* and at this very moment topics like "Women as Healers in Mediaeval Life and Literature" are being accepted by the foremost American universities for the doctorate in English. Nothing can and should, of course, prevent any man from working on any subject under the sun. Universities, besides, do not recognize the his-tory of civilization as an independent subject and politi-cal historians are usually so preoccupied with diplomacy, war, and institutions, that the literary historian can feel justified in expanding into a neighboring field. But it should be recognized that this *is* an expansion: that the literary historian leaves his subject and enters another, though related, field. The objection may be made that what is here involved is, after all, merely a terminological difference. If Professor Greenlaw and his adherents are willing to call a book on witchcraft or mediaeval healing "literary history," let them have their innocent pleasure. In practice, there is, however, a very real danger that this terminological confusion of genres will be detrimental to the central aims of literary study. The study of everything connected with the history of civilization will crowd out strictly literary studies. All distinctions will fall and extraneous criteria will be introduced into literature, and literature will necessarily be judged valuable only so far as it yields results for this or that neighboring discipline.

We can clarify this situation best, perhaps, by considering first the philosophical study of literature. Again, an excessive determinism seems to me misleading. The development of literature is not a mirror of the history of philosophy. Poetic thought goes its own way and has its own development. Frequently there is a cleavage between the implied world-view of poetry and the technical philosophy of the time. Even where poetry takes over philosophical ideas, artistic form may transform every one of them almost out of recognition. The purely philosophical approach will conceive of literature as the "history of ideas in dilution," as Professor Lovejoy terms it.[23] Poetry as art will appear either insignificant or merely a troublesome and superfluous wrapper for the ideas studied. But an approach to literature which excludes or ignores the pure lyric with no philosophical or ideological content seems to me self-condemned. We may, of course, as philosophers, use literature merely as a document in a history of philosophy; but in such a study distinctions between literature and philosophical writings have to be ignored and all authors must be judged frankly as philosophers. The epistemology of a writer like Coleridge must be measured by epistemological criteria and the theological system of Milton in his *De Doctrina Christiana* must be relegated to a very modest niche in the history of seventeenth-century thought, regardless of the fact that Milton is the greatest figure in English seventeenth-century poetry. There are special dangers in such an approach. Frequently the practitioner, an English scholar, has no proper equipment for the neighboring field he has entered and is apt to overrate and isolate works which carry the names of great poets. He introduces extraneous criteria into the study of philosophy. On the other hand, philosophers are liable to impose purely philosophical criteria on *belles-lettres*. Even the most brilliant "historians of ideas" who are professional philosophers, like Lovejoy in the United States, Gilson in France, Cassirer and Dilthey in Germany, have not always escaped this danger.[24] Professor Lovejoy's own limitation of the term "history of ideas" is a case in point. It seems a highly artificial distinction to reserve the study of the great philosophers and their systems to an old-fashioned "history of philosophy," while the smaller, more popular thinkers (including poets) come under the "history of ideas." Equally artificial is the way in which Professor Lovejoy distinguishes between the history of ideas as the study of "unit-ideas" and the history of philosophy as the study of coherent systems. The history of philosophical concepts and problems belongs, in fact, simply to the history of philosophy, and was practised by historians of philosophy like Hegel or Windelband long before we had ever heard of a special "history of ideas." To study merely unit-ideas to the exclusion of coherent systems seems as one-sided as it would be to study the history of versification, diction, or imagery in preference to the study of the coherent whole of a work of art. Thus the confusion between the two disciplines, literary history and history of philosophy, either subjects literary studies to extraneous criteria or introduces foreign standards into the study of philosophy.

Exactly the same principles should be applied to the approach to literature in terms of the social, political, and economic situation. If we look at it from the point of view of literature, we have again to reject the one-sided determinism of literature by social forces. Literature is not simply determined by social evolution; it is itself a center of forces, and influences the trends of society. It stands in constant interrelations with it, of course; but frequently it may escape from it or react against it. Literature does not always mirror the actual proportions and tensions of the social and political evolution. Thus in eighteenth-century England a bourgeois literature flowered when the country was still ruled by a landed gentry, and the numerous proletariat remained almost ignored in literature. The industrial revolution, which as a social phenomenon had begun late in the eighteenth century, hardly enters literature before the forties of the nineteenth century. Thus literature may be either in advance of or behind its "times." To arrive at valid conclusions we must examine the exact relationships of literature and society in every period, and realize that literature is frequently created by a specific "intelligentsia" which is to a certain extent independent of social class-lines. We distort and pervert the actual literary evolution if we subordinate it too uniformly to the pressure of the social changes. On the other hand, it is wholly possible to use literature simply as a social document, in a history of society. Then, of course, every work of literature has to be used frankly for its information on social questions, and literature will take its place alongside a commercial treatise, a book of statistics, a government publication, or a traveller's jottings. One can argue that it is possible to derive sociological information from literature which it would be difficult to find elsewhere. For instance, E. Kohn-Bramstedt's *Aristocracy and the Middle Classes in Germany* uses the nineteenth-century German novel in order to determine social types, questions of social prestige and morality. Mr. Kohn-Bramstedt is, of course, aware that novels are used by him "not for their literary values, but only for their illustrative function" [25] and that he can and should use worthless literature as well as standard authors. In any case, literature is not easily employed as a "social document." The assumption that it presents a true picture of society is not necessarily true, as the quarrel over Restoration comedy or naturalistic novels shows. In every individual case the actual relation to social reality has to be determined by checking the literary evidence with evidence from other documents; otherwise we mistake satire or the picture of a dreamland or some very personal slice of reality for the whole of social reality, and get entangled in a vicious circle arguing for the "truth" of a picture when we know only the picture itself. The sociological method thus faces exactly the same dangers as the approach to literature from the intellectual background. It seems either to impose extraneous criteria on literature or to use literature merely as a document in other fields of studies.

Today we must also mention the relations of literature

to the "somatic" or "biological" life of man. Climate, race, the nation, the tribe, the family had been made much use of in Germany and elsewhere, long before the particular Nazi version of such questions. Again a one-sided determinism of literature by these physical conditions of life should be rejected, especially as these relations seem distant and the terms of reference vague. Usually the study of the racial characteristics of literature is not correlated with anything really physical; it is merely a study of nationalist ideologies. But even the grotesque antics of the propounders of the "Nordic" theory should not obscure the fact that there are real, though difficult and delicate, problems to solve. One can hardly deny, for instance, the distinctive contribution of different races to American literature, since a common language and tradition will make these characteristics stand out more clearly. But in the present state of affairs, it is difficult to lay one's hands on definite relationships, while the dangers of a naturalistic determinism by "blood" or "race" seem so grave that much thinking will have to be done to define these problems in a fruitful, objective way.

One external approach to literature deserves special discussion because it obviates one of the principal objections I have raised. I allude to "Geistesgeschichte" as practiced in Germany, which does not make literature dependent on any one single human activity, but rather conceives of it as an expression of the general "time-spirit." Literature is again studied as an illustration of the general mental history of mankind. A justification for the assumed parallelism of all the different activities of man in any one period belongs to a speculative philosophy of history and cannot be discussed here adequately. However, it may be remarked that an affirmative answer to the question of a parallelism of all human activities is usually given far too hastily. As to politics, one can easily show that the courses of literature and political fortune do not run parallel. It suffices to quote the example of Germany during the Napoleonic wars, when a period of political impotence coincided with the greatest flowering of German literature. Painting and music have developed very differently from literature, for the simple reason that neither had the support or dead-weight of a tradition of classical antiquity. Technical philosophy does not necessarily run parallel with the ideology embodied or implied in the poetry of the time, as witness the rule of Scotch Commonsense philosophy and of Utilitarianism during the English Romantic period. Whatever may be the possible arguments for a unified time-spirit, the actual practical examples of "Geistesgeschichte" one has seen, such as Paul Meissner's *Die geistesgeschichtlichen Grundlagen des englischen Literaturbarocks* (1934), indulge in extravagant speculations which frequently do not amount to more than the construction of an ingenious but arbitrary pattern of antithetical concepts.[26] The supposed similarities between the arts are frequently based on little more than elaborate puns or extended metaphors, and most of the work seems as far away from the actual process of literature as anything in the more pedestrian and humble studies of social or intellectual historians. The existence of a problem of a general history of mankind and its spiritual evolution is, of course, not to be denied. Literature (or rather anything printed) will always be the main source-material for speculation upon such a synthesis; but as a study it seems to me quite distinct from the history of literature.

§ VI

So far I have been concerned with literary history in the usual wide sense of the term loosely designating the study of literature in the past. I have not yet discussed the problem of literary history in the narrow sense—I am even tempted to say, in the proper sense.

The question can be raised whether it is *possible* to write literary history, that is, to write a history of literature which will be both literary and a history. It must be admitted that most histories of literature are either social histories or histories of thought as mirrored in literature, or a series of impressions and judgments on individual works of art arranged in a more or less chronological order. A glance at the history of English literary historiography will amply justify this view. Thomas Warton, the first "formal" historian of English poetry, studied ancient literature because it "faithfully records the features of the times and preserves the most picturesque and expressive representations of manners" and "transmits to posterity genuine delineations of life." [27] Henry Hallam included books on logic, political economy, astronomy, and medicine in his *Introduction to the Literature of Europe in the Fifteenth, Sixteenth and Seventeenth Centuries.* Henry Morley conceived of literature as "the national biography" or the "story of the English mind." [28] Leslie Stephen regarded literature as "a particular function of the whole social organism," "a kind of by-product" of social change.[29] W. J. Courthope, author of the only *History of English Poetry* based on a unified conception of its development, defined the "study of English poetry as in effect the study of the continuous growth of our national institutions as re-

flected in our literature." He looked for the unity of the
subject "precisely where the political historian looks for
it, namely, in the life of a nation as a whole." [30]

While these and many other historians treat literature
as mere document for the illustration of national or social
history, another group recognizes that literature is first
and foremost an art. But they seem to be unable to write
history. They present us with a discontinuous series of
essays on individual authors, linked together by "influences" without any conception of real historical evolution. Edmund Gosse, it is true, in his introduction to a
Short Story of Modern English Literature (1897), professed to show the "movement of English literature," to
give a "feeling of the evolution of English literature," [31]
but he was merely paying lip-service to an ideal then
spreading from France. In practice his books are a series
of critical remarks on authors and some of their works
chronologically arranged. Gosse later quite rightly dis-
claimed any interest in Taine and stressed his indebted-
ness to Sainte-Beuve, the master of biographical portrai-
ture.[32] The same is true, *mutatis mutandis,* of George
Saintsbury, whose conception of criticism was nearest
to Pater's theory and practice of "appreciation," [33] and
the most remarkable achievement of English literary
history in recent times, Oliver Elton's six volumes, are
Surveys of English Literature, and frankly profess to be
"really a review, a direct criticism" and not a history.[34]
This list could be extended almost indefinitely, and an
examination of French and German histories of literature would lead, with some exceptions, to almost identical conclusions. Thus Taine was obviously interested
mainly in his theories of national character and his philosophy of milieu and race, Jusserand studied the history
of manners as mirrored in English literature, and

Cazamian invented a whole theory of "the oscillation of the moral rhythm of the English national soul." [35] Thus most leading histories of literature are either histories of civilization or collections of critical essays. The one type is not a history of *art*, the other not a *history* of art.

Why has there never been an attempt to trace the evolution of literature as art, on a larger scale? One difficulty is obviously the fact that the preparatory analysis of works of art has not been carried out in a consistent and systematic manner. Literary criticism has not yet developed satisfactory methods which would enable us to describe a work of art purely as a system of signs. We either remain content with the old rhetorical criteria which are felt to be unsatisfactory in their exclusive preoccupation with apparently superficial devices, or we have recourse to an emotive language which merely describes the effects of a work of art on the mind of the reader in terms incapable of real correlation with the work of art itself. One reason for this backwardness in our faculties of analysis is that we employ erroneous conceptions of the "ontological situs" of a work of art, to use a somewhat pretentious philosophical term. [36]

The essence of a work of art is usually looked for in the individual state of mind of the writer or reader. The first alternative leads to speculations on the author's intuitions and intentions which will forever remain inaccessible to any objective study, while the second alternative must lead to complete subjectivism and ultimately to barren scepticism. A solution would be most satisfactory which would try to get away from concepts based on individual psychology and would look for the essence of a work of art in a system of signs and implicit norms existing as social facts in a collective ideology just as, for instance, the system of lan-

guage exists. Just as we can study a language apart from
the innumerable individual speech-acts, a work of art
should be accessible to objective study regardless of
the differences in the individual experience.

Another difficulty is the related prejudice which I
have already discussed that no history of literature is
possible except in terms of causal explanation by some
other human activity. A third difficulty lies in the whole
conception of the development of the art of literature.
Few would doubt the possibility of an internal history
of painting or music. It suffices to walk through any
art gallery arranged in chronological order or in accordance with "schools" to see that there is a history of
the art of painting which is quite distinct from either
the history of painters or a disjointed appreciation of
individual pictures, even in regard to some timeless
scheme of values. It suffices to listen to a concert in
which compositions are arranged in a chronological
order, to see that there is a history of music which
has scarcely anything to do with the biographies of the
composers, the social conditions under which the works
were produced, or the appreciation of individual pieces.
Such histories have been attempted in painting and
sculpture since Winckelmann wrote his *Geschichte der
Kunst im Altertum,* and most histories of music since
Burney have paid attention to the history of musical
forms.

Literary history is simply confronted with the analogous problem of tracing the history of literature as an
art in comparative isolation from its social history, the
biographies of authors, or the disjointed appreciation of
individual works. One has, of course, to admit that the
task of literary history (in this limited sense) presents its
special obstacles. Compared to a piece of painting

which can be seen at a glance, a literary work of art is accessible only through a time-sequence which makes it more difficult to realize as a coherent whole. But the analogy of musical form shows that a pattern is just as possible, even when it can be grasped only in a temporal sequence. Special problems arise, because in literature there is a gradual transition from simple statements to highly organized works of art, since the medium of literature, language, is also the medium of everyday inartistic communication and especially the medium of sciences. It is thus more difficult to isolate the artistic function of a literary work of art. An illustration in a medical or biological textbook or a military march are two examples which show that the other arts have also to deal with borderline cases of inartistic communication, and that the difficulties in distinguishing between art and non-art in linguistic utterances are only greater quantitatively.

There are, however, scholars who simply deny that literature has a history. W. P. Ker argued, for instance, that we do not need literary history, as its objects are always present, are "eternal," and thus have no proper history at all.[37] T. S. Eliot also would deny the "pastness" of a work of art. "The whole of the literature of Europe from Homer," he says, "has a simultaneous existence and composes a simultaneous order." [38] Art, one could argue with Schopenhauer, has always reached its goal. It never improves, it cannot be superseded or repeated. In art we need not find out *"wie es eigentlich gewesen"*—as Ranke put the aim of historiography—because we can experience quite directly how things are. So literary history is no proper history, being merely the knowledge of the present, the omnipresent, the eternally present. Now, one cannot deny that there is some real difference between political history and the history of art. There is a distinction between that which is historical and past and that which is historical and still somehow present. The battle of Waterloo is definitely past, though its effects may be felt even today and its course reconstructed accurately, but the *Iliad*, the Parthenon, or a mass by Palestrina are still somehow present. Yet this does not exclude the possibility that there is a real history which is more than a mirror of the social changes under which literature was produced in the past. Even an individual work of art does not remain unchanged in the course of history. The *Iliad* has gone through a long process of interpretation and criticism. The *Iliad*, as we read it today, even if we know ancient Greek well, is in many ways different from the *Iliad* read or heard by the Greeks. We cannot, for example, contrast its language with the everyday language of Homeric Greece, and thus cannot feel the deviations from colloquial speech, on which much of the effect of any poetic diction must depend. In Homer or any other poet we are unable to understand all the ambiguities which are an essential part of his meaning.[39] There is, to be sure, a substantial identity of structure which has remained the same throughout the ages. But this structure is dynamic: it changes throughout the process of history while passing through the minds of readers, critics, and fellow-artists. To speak of "eternity" is merely an expression of the fact that the process of interpretation, criticism, and appreciation has never been completely interrupted and is likely to continue indefinitely, or at least so long as there is no complete interruption of the cultural tradition. One of the tasks of the literary historian is the description of this process. Another is the tracing of the development of works of art arranged in smaller and larger groups, ac-

cording to common authorship, or genres, or stylistic
types, or linguistic tradition, and finally inside a scheme
of universal literature.

But the concept of the development of a series of
works of art seems an extraordinarily difficult one. In a
sense each work of art is, at first sight, a structure discontinuous with neighboring works of art. One can argue
that there is no development from one individuality to
another. One meets even with the objection that there
is no history of literature, but only of men writing. According to the same argument we should have to give
up writing a history of language because there are only
men uttering words, or a history of philosophy because
there are only men thinking. Such extreme "personalism" must lead to anarchy, to a complete isolation of
every individual work of art, which in practice would
mean that it would be both incommunicable and incomprehensible. We must conceive rather of literature
as a whole system of works which is, with the accretion
of new ones, constantly changing its relationships,
growing as a changing whole. But the mere fact that
the literary situation of a time has changed compared
to the situation of a decade or a century before is still
insufficient to establish a process of actual historical
evolution, since the concept of change applies to any
series of natural phenomena. It merely means ever new
reshufflings of a kaleidoscope which are meaningless
and incomprehensible. Thus the study of change, as
recommended by F. J. Teggart in his *Theory of History*
(1925) would lead merely to the abolishment of all differences between historical and natural processes and
would leave the historian helplessly thrown back on borrowings from natural science. If these changes recurred
with absolute regularity we should arrive at the concept

of law in the physicist's sense of the word. But such predictable changes called laws have never been discovered in any historical process in spite of the brilliant speculations of Spengler or Toynbee. The one ambitious attempt to arrive at such a law of English literature, M. Cazamian's "oscillation of the rhythm of the English national mind," a rhythm which is supposed to speed up its oscillations the nearer we approach the present, could easily be shown to be merely an ingenious construct which at many points does violence to the actual evolution of English literature.[40] Thus, purely psychological uniformities (as the supposed "law" of action and reaction, or convention and revolt) cannot tell us anything significant about the individual historical process.

Development means something else and something more than change and even regular, predictable change. It seems obvious that it should be used in the sense elaborated by biology. In biology, if we look closer, there are two very different concepts of evolution: first, the process exemplified by the growth of an egg to a bird, and second, the evolution exemplified by the change from the brain of a fish to that of man. Here no series of brains ever develops actually, but some conceptual abstraction, "the brain," which can be defined only by its function. The individual stages of development are conceived as different approximations to an ideal taken from the human brain. In what sense can we speak of evolution in either of these two meanings in literature? Ferdinand Brunetière and John Addington Symonds assumed that we can speak in both senses of the evolution of literature. They had the idea that one could consider literary genres on the analogy of species in nature.[41] Literary genres, according to Brunetière, as soon as they reach a certain degree of perfection, must wither, languish, and finally disappear. A genre grows, reaches perfection, declines, and dies, and also genres become transformed into higher and more differentiated genres just as do species in the Darwinian conception of evolution. I hardly need to show that the use of the term "evolution" in the first sense of the term is little more than a fanciful metaphor. According to Brunetière French tragedy, for example, was born, grew, declined, and died. But the *tertium comparationis* for the birth of tragedy is merely the fact that there were no tragedies written in French before Jodelle. Tragedy died only in the sense that according to Brunetière no important tragedies conforming to his ideal were written after Voltaire. But there is always the possibility that a great tragedy will be written in French in the future. According to Brunetière, Racine's *Phèdre* stands at the beginning of the decline of tragedy, somewhere near to its old age, but it strikes us as young and fresh compared to the learned Renaissance tragedies which according to this theory represent the "youth" of French tragedy. Even less defensible is the idea that genres become transformed into other genres. Thus, according to Brunetière, French pulpit oratory of the seventeenth and eighteenth centuries was transformed into the lyrical poetry of the Romantic movement. Actually, no real "transmutation" had, however, taken place, but merely the same or similar emotions were expressed once in oratory and later in lyrical poetry, and possibly the same or similar social purposes were served.

While we thus must reject the biological analogy between the development of literature and the closed evolutionary process from birth to death—an idea which is by no means extinct and has been revived by Spengler and Toynbee—the concept of evolution in the second sense seems much nearer to the real concept of *historical* evolution. It recognizes that a mere series of changes does not suffice but that an aim for this series must be postulated. The different parts of the series must be the necessary conditions for the achievement of the end. The concept of evolution towards a specific goal (e.g., the human brain) makes a series of changes into a real concatenation with a beginning and an end. Still there is an important distinction between this second meaning of biological evolution and historical evolution in the proper sense. In order to grasp historical evolution in distinction from evolution in biology we must somehow succeed in preserving the individuality of the historical event, while the historical process must not be left as a collection of sequent but unrelated events. The solution lies in the attempt to relate the historical process to a value or norm. Only then can the apparently meaningless series of events be split into its essential and unessential elements. Only then can we speak of historical evolution, which still leaves the individuality of the single event unimpaired. By relating an individual reality to a general value, we do not degrade the individual to a mere specimen of a general concept, but we give significance to the individual. The point of view here advocated implies that history does not simply individualize general values (nor is it, of course, a discontinuous meaningless flux), but that the historical process will produce ever new forms of value, hitherto unknown and unpredictable. The relativity of the individual work of art to a scale of values is thus nothing else than the necessary correlative of its individuality. The series of developments will be constructed in reference to a scheme of values or norms, but these values themselves emerge only from the contemplation of this process. There is, one has to admit, a logical circle in the fact that the historical process has to be judged by values, while the scale of values is itself derived from history. But this seems unavoidable, because otherwise we must either resign ourselves to the idea of a meaningless flux of change or apply extraliterary sets of standards—some Absolute which is extraneous to the process of literature.

This discussion of the problem of literary evolution has been necessarily abstract. I hope it has made clear that the evolution of literature is different from that of biology, and also that it has nothing to do with the idea of a uniform progress towards *one* eternal model. History can be written only in reference to variable schemes of values and these schemes have to be abstracted from history itself. I should like to illustrate this idea a little more concretely by pointing out some of the problems with which literary history—in this narrow sense—is confronted.

The most obvious interrelationships between works of art have been treated most frequently and certainly form a staple of traditional scholarship. But sources and influences are usually conceived in a thoroughly mechanical fashion: some single trait is isolated, the work of art is broken up into little pieces of mosaic, and nothing is established beyond the fact of relationship. The relationship between two or several works of art can be discussed profitably only when we see them in their proper place within a scheme of development, not if we list haphazard relationships which usually amount to a mere use of *motifs*, plots, or little stylistic tricks. Relationships between works of art present thus a critical problem of comparing two wholes, two systems which must be broken up into isolated components only for the sake of study. Another approach, with which it should not be confused, is the use of literature for the study of the migration of plots and *motifs;* a special field which has close relations with folklore and ethnology. In such a study the theme of *Hamlet* can be paralleled from all over the world without our saying anything relevant on Shakespeare's *Hamlet* in particular. The literary interest begins only when we are able to show how an artist handled this or that *motif* which he drew from the common stock of popular imagination. The history of such a *motif* or rather of a cluster of *motifs,* a fable or a plot, can be written with the aim of some particular version of the story in mind.

A further obvious series of works of art is the works written by one author. Here the scheme of reference must be some individual work or group of works adjudged to be his maturest, and all the other works must be analyzed and judged from the point of view of their approximation to this type. Such a task has been attempted in innumerable monographs, though rarely with a clear consciousness of the problems involved, and frequently in inextricable confusion with problems of the author's personal life. Another group of evolutionary series can be constructed by isolating a certain trait in works of art and tracing its approximation towards some ideal (even only temporarily ideal) type. We could, for instance, give an historical account of the present system of English versification. We have books like those of George Saintsbury on the history of English prosody and prose rhythm which isolate such an element and trace its history, but these ambitious books are unfortunately vitiated by the unclear and obsolete conceptions of meter and rhythm on which they are based. They demonstrate that no proper history can be written without an adequate scheme of reference, in this case some theory of rhythm, meter, rhyme, diction, or any other isolated factor of the work of art.

Histories of genres and literary types raise another group of problems. Such studies have suffered from the inadequate theory of genres now available. But we have —in spite of the attempts of Croce to discredit the whole conception—many studies, especially of oral literature and its types, which prepare the way for such a theory, and there is an increasing number of histories of genres which show a clear conception of the type whose evolution is traced. I am thinking especially of the work of Veselovskij [42] in Russia or Günther Müller's excellent *Geschichte des deutschen Liedes;* [43] there is also much of value in the books of Brunetière, if we subtract some of the extravagancies of his biological parallelism. In England, John Addington Symonds's remarkable book on *Shakspere's Predecessors* (1884) at least clearly envisages the problem: the tracing of the actual evolution of the art of drama from its beginnings to its culmination point in England—the form given to it by the genius of Shakespeare. Also a number of recent studies approach this ideal history of the genres. [44]

Exactly similar problems are raised by a history of a period or a movement. A history of Romanticism, for instance, must be written with a clear conception of the final form of Romanticism in mind, while all phenomena must be conceived as approximations towards this ideal type. A period is not merely a verbal label for any time-section, nor a metaphysical essence, as it is conceived by many German historians, but rather a time-section in which some particular system of norms is dominant. This unity of a time-section is, of course, only relative. If it were absolute, the periods would lie next to each other like blocks of stone and there would be no continuity of development. Thus a real history of a period can be written in reference to its scheme of norms which does not violate the individuality of any single work of art, as it is not an instance in a class-concept but with all other works makes up the concept of a period.[45]

The further and wider problem, a history of a national literature as a whole, is more difficult to envisage, as the term "national" is heavily fraught with purely ideological connotations. It is difficult to trace the history of a national literature as an art, when the whole framework invites to references essentially unliterary, to speculations about national ethics and national characteristics which have little to do with the art of literature. In the case of American literature, where there is no linguistic distinction from another national literature, the difficulties become manifold, as the development of the art of literature in America must be necessarily incomplete and partly dependent on an older and stronger tradition. Clearly, any national development of the art of literature presents a problem the historian cannot afford to ignore, though it has scarcely ever been investigated in any systematic fashion. Needless to say, histories of groups of literatures are even more distant ideals. The existent examples, like Jan Máchal's *Slavonic Literatures* or Leonardo Olschki's attempt to write a history of all Romance literatures during the Middle Ages are not too successful.[46] Most histories of world literature are attempts to trace the main tradition of European literature united by their common descent from Greece and Rome, but none of these have gone beyond ideological generalities or superficial compilations unless we consider the brilliant sketches by the brothers Schlegel, which hardly serve contemporary needs. Finally, a general history of the art of literature is still a far distant ideal. The existing attempts, like John Brown's *History of the Rise and Progress of Poetry* dating from 1763, are too speculative and schematic, or else, like the Chadwicks' three volumes on the *Growth of Literature,* preoccupied with questions of static types.

After all, we are only beginning to learn how to analyze a work of art in its integrity; we are still very clumsy in our methods, and their basis in theory is still constantly shifting. Thus, much is before us. Nor is there anything to regret in the fact that literary history has a future as well as a past, a future which cannot and should not consist merely in the filling of gaps in the scheme discovered by older methods. We must seek to elaborate a new ideal of literary history and new methods which would make its realization possible. If the ideal here outlined seems unduly "purist" in its emphasis on the history of literature as an art, I can only plead that no other approach has been considered invalid and that concentration seems a necessary antidote to the expansionist movement through which literary history has passed in the last decades. A clear consciousness of a scheme of relationships between methods is in itself a remedy against mental confusion, even though the individual may avowedly elect to combine several methods or even to investigate rather the wood of the partitions between the pigeon-holes than any particular pigeon-hole in the entire system of human knowledge.

What can we do in the meantime? If I should be asked to formulate my own recommendations, which, I hope, express not merely personal idiosyncrasies but rather some of the needs of the present situation in scholarship, I should stress the following points:

1. We need a clearer realization of methods and aims,

including the specific place and function of every individual literary study. One of the desiderata is a history of literary scholarship which would survey and criticize what has been achieved in the past.[47]

2. We need a synthesis and coördination of the work already accomplished, a task which cannot be left to the remote future.

3. We should perhaps restrict attempts to account for literature in terms of something else, and expect less from an excessive determinism which would reduce literature merely to a passive mirror of some other human activity.

4. We should concentrate on the study of the actual work of art in connection with and on the basis of a new critical theory of literature.

5. Finally, we should, I think, turn to the task of a history of literature as art and thus revive, in the field of literature, the lost art of history-writing.

4

LITERARY CRITICISM

Austin Warren

IN AN academic community professionally given to the study of literature, it might be supposed that criticism—or the interpretation and evaluation of literature —would be the chief as well as the final interest, that close and eager talk about contemporary poems and novels would abound, that literary theory and the discriminating judgment of literary masters and masterpieces would be the natural engagement of academic pens. Such a supposition, however, would be misleading. Members of the profession would doubtless assent to general statements concerning the importance of criticism; but in practice they have been prone to dismiss the art as too easy—or too difficult. Scorning impressionism as the facile effervescence of the dilettante, they have held real criticism to be the consequence of rare sensibility and as rare philosophical depth and scope, hence too exacting for all save the masters. In consequence of such pride and humility, criticism, save as the record of past speculation, has had no status within the university.[1]

Today, however, there are healthy and hopeful signs of a more intelligent attitude toward those ends of literary experience, its enjoyment and its judgment. This is a propitious time at which to consider, as dispassionately as may be, the whole scope and duty of criticism.

§ I

Criticism has its history, its theory, and its practice. The first, which has been the traditional province of academic scholars, is the expository chronicle or the patterned sequence of past literary judgment. It has the interest which attaches to other forms of intellectual history; and it may be pursued independently as a study in the rise, development, and decline of ideas or, in conjunction with the history of philosophy and the history of aesthetics, as a department of *Geistesgeschichte*. It profitably accompanies the analysis of specific works of literature written at the same period and under the same canons; thus a discipline in sensibility may be had by reading romantic poetry under the tutelage of romantic criticism, seeking—before evaluating it by the standards of subsequent time—to define and realize what poetry was expected to be and to do for exacting readers contemporary with it.

The history of criticism, in turn, can be properly understood only when correlated with the history of literature. The theories of earlier critics neither proceed from a vacuum nor address themselves to a void; they are generalizations (and predictions) on the basis of a specific and generally ascertainable body of literary experience: the neoclassicists, for example, generalize their experience not of mediaeval or oriental but of Greek and Roman—more specifically, of Roman—literature. In order to construe past critical language, we need to know, in the instance of each system, what concrete literary experience it subsumed.

From scrutiny of the past, we turn to present construction. Critical theory interprets, systematizes, and evaluates the literary experience of mankind, as ethics undertakes a similar survey of men's moral experience. It may profess no ampler synthesis than that of its deviser's experience: then it is the attempt of a critical reader to formulate and rationalize, by discrimination among his memories of past literary experiences, the grounds of his preferences, the hierarchy of his tastes. But, since no man's experience is totally unique, in thus rationalizing for himself, he writes at least for those who are like him. And, since all men are to some degree "like him," he may, by virtue of his sensibility, range of experience, and acumen at analysis and comparison, lead others to see and accept values hitherto imperceptible or inacceptable.

The final formulation may be purely descriptive—the definition and arrangement of the criteria upon which, as a matter of fact, men—and that not experts alone or Europeans alone but all literate persons—have judged: the result would be a psychology and a sociology of literary experience. Or it may be normative—the use of aesthetic or extra-aesthetic criteria, or of criteria both aesthetic and more than aesthetic, to define kinds or degrees in literary value. Whether descriptive or normative, it will scrutinize and arrange the criteria of past and present experts, not merely as offered in their theoretical statements but also as discovered in their practice. And like systematic philosophy, it must transcend by including its past: a new theory must differ from its predecessors not by the omission of relevant data but by more coherent and satisfactory explanation.

Normative theory, not content with an arrangement of men's actual preferences, will undertake to set forth the values which men should derive from their literary experience, or the canons by which they should judge their reading. These normative claims may be more or less metaphysical: they may be derived from a theory of transcendental beauty. Or they may rest on bases psychological, social, or moral. The "ought" of the critical theorist may mean, "You would have more pleasure from your reading if you read this or thus," or it may mean, "Aesthetic contemplation, or instruction, or incitation to the good life, is what you should derive from your reading."

Practical criticism, the third genre, takes its start from the immediate experience of literature, indeed from the experience of a particular work of literature; and it remains in much closer relation to literary experience than its theoretical allies generically represented by the "arts" and "apologies" and "defenses" of poetry.[2] Often it expresses itself in conversation; a modestly professional form is the book-review; from the time of Corneille and Dryden to the present, it has frequently appeared as the preface to a play or to a volume of lyrics, in which the author explicates the technical problems which he confronted and defends his solution of them. The critical essay, seeking to elucidate and appraise a writer, may be chiefly biographical in its method, as with Sainte-Beuve and Arnold; chiefly ideological, as with Paul Elmer More and Edmond Scherer; or chiefly technical, as with Dr. Johnson and Henry James; and often it employs a combination of these methods.[3] Its scheme of reference may be narrow or large. "Close criticism" of poetry, remembering that poetry is written in words, never moves far from the poetic text, quotes not to illustrate a generalized statement but to analyze the ingredients of the text and the nature of their mixture; and "autotelic" criticism concerns itself with a single poem, inducing, from the poem as a whole, the standard

by which its elements are judged to hamper or promote
the kind of success at which it aimed.[4] But other schemes
may seek to put the work or the writer into the widest
possible relationship, on the theoretically undeniable
principle that one can understand no thing without understanding everything.[5]

History, theory, and practice are separable but not
disjunct. History provides us with the theoretical and the
practical criticism of the past; and it is to be presumed
that we can profit, negatively and positively, by the example of past performance. As for theory and practice,
they are obviously interdependent. Every case of practice can be put in terms of its theoretical assumptions;
every theory must be validated by its ability to handle,
economically and skilfully, the cases that it subsumes.
A theory must be judged not only by its degree of internal coherence but by its external coherence with ex-
periential fact; a specific discussion can illuminate the
text only by bringing to bear upon it a mind widely and
sensitively exercised, a mind equipped with a memory
and with expectations.

§ II

The proper methods of criticism, practical and theoretical, will be implicit in the nature of literature itself.
In the broadest sense, literature is anything in print. At
its preliminary restriction, it becomes any writing which,
whatever its intent, has uncommon distinction in composition and style. If we ask why Newman is literature
and not Pusey; why T. H. Huxley is literature and not
Tyndall; why Hume is literature and not Kant, the answer is formal. Whatever the author's motive for writing,

his product—if shaped with art—becomes literature. A closer definition, however, must take account of structure and purpose. By literature we mean, centrally, not Cicero, Bossuet, F. H. Bradley but Homer, Dante, Shakespeare, Racine, Balzac, and Keats; in generic terms, the characteristic forms of literature are the epic and the tragedy, the novel and the drama and the lyric—the forms originally generalized as poetry, later as belles lettres, and now as imaginative literature.[6] In essence, literature is neither the agreeable conveyance of information nor the transcript of what is literally true: it is an art which, through myth or fable, offers an interpretation of life. The "poet" is not a transcriber but a maker, a creator, one who brings into being a world which is like life but which is not life. If style distinguishes "applied literature" from the tract, the scientific monograph, and the textbook, the difference between applied literature and imaginative literature is to be found in the presence or absence of "invention."

For most imaginative works we can conceive some approximate unimaginative equivalent by comparison with which to define the scope and intent of artistic invention. Shakespeare's *Henry IV* might have been a chronicle instead of a play; Tolstoi's *War and Peace*, a history of Russia during the Napoleonic wars; Proust's *À la Recherche du Temps Perdu*, either an autobiography or a psychological treatise; Pater's *Marius*, a monograph on Roman philosophy and religion under the Empire.[7] Imaginative literature is never creation *ex nihilo*; and the cosmos it produces suggests other possible worlds, constructed on different principles. A proper conception of literature will have to account for its linkages with informative prose and for its disjunction.

Aristotle's assignment of "poetry" to a place between

history and philosophy is one mode of defining that position. Particular literary works it is generally easy to align, some with history and some with philosophy; of novels like those of Howells and Sinclair Lewis, we say that, whatever their fate as art, they will be valuable to students of social history; the *Divine Comedy*, Mann's *Magic Mountain* and Dostoevsky's *Brothers* readily lend themselves, we see, to philosophical interpretation. History is concerned with facts, philosophy with values; history with particulars; philosophy with universals; history with the contingent; philosophy with the unconditioned. Literature mediates between these two. When it is relatively unsuccessful, it illustrates a general law by a particular instance, or follows a particular presentation with a generalizing maxim; when it is genuinely successful, its individual and its typical are so continuous that only by emphasis or tone can one tell whether the type incarnated itself or the individual implied a typicality.

But literature, and especially poetry, must also be conceived as intermediate between the fine arts (painting, music) and philosophy. Poetry uses measured and precise rhythms, like those of music, and some lyrical poetry approaches the condition of music in its reduction to euphonious sounds evocative of imprecise emotional states; poetry uses images, and some descriptive poetry approaches the condition of painting in its reduction to imagism. Other poetry makes large use of abstract ideas; most poetry makes some use of conceptual statement; the practical and ideological purposes customary to language make a poem's total reduction to sound patterns impossible. The image, visual or auditory, and the concept: these are both properties of the richest poetry; and the supreme business of poetry is to achieve and maintain a tension between the image and the concept, or to provide the identification of the two through the metaphor or the myth.

The form of literature relates it to the other arts; its matter, the interpretation of life, relates it to philosophy. The novelist portrays aristocrats or commoners, women of easy virtue or rigorous, rural and regional life or urban, introverts or extroverts; and he not only presents them but he supplies a point of view from which they are to be seen: he ennobles and dignifies one class, he gives satiric or minimizing characterization to another. In the older novels, this is ordinarily not wholly trusted to the fable: the writer acts as narrator but also as commentator, who, like Thackeray and Hawthorne and Hardy, makes certain that we comprehend aright the ethical implications of the tale. In another and more artful kind, that of Henry James, there is likely to be a character who apprehends significances for us. But even in the novel from which the novelist is most withdrawn, his moral presence is still felt as selector and colorist: he thinks this worth writing about; he makes no moral distinctions—itself a moral philosophy.

The case is not totally different with poetry. Milton certainly was concerned with poetic theory, with "that sublime art which in Aristotle's *Poetics*, in Horace, and the Italian commentaries of Castelvetro, Tasso, Mazzoni, and others teaches what the laws are of a true epic poem, what of a dramatic, what of a lyric"; but he also thought of the poet as a philosopher, saying of "our sage and serious Spenser" that he was "a better teacher than Scotus or Aquinas." [8] Point of view is present also in the short poem—whether it be Donne's "The Indifferent" or Hardy's "At Church" or Ransom's "The Equilibrists"; it is implicit in the poem and can be precipitated into prose to serve philosophical scrutiny. To be sure, point of view may be dramatically assumed, or may represent the poet's mood rather than his consistent or characteristic attitude: we must not attribute to Wordsworth, as settled conviction, the view implicit or explicit in a single poem, or in the poems of a particular period; but if we observe the proper precautions of speech we can define the conceptual or affective implications of a poem, a group of poems, or the totality of a poet's work.[9]

From this double reference of literature, to art and to life, we derive the two polar methods of criticism, which we may call aesthetic and ideological. Our attention may be focussed upon the form of literature and the motive for its differentiation from that which is not literature, or upon its matter, the experience of life and the attitude toward life to which it gives form.

The first, aesthetic or technical criticism, is an analysis of "imitation," or the devices which win and hold our attention, the principles of selection and order which turn observation and passion into art. Aristotle's *Poetics* is a document of this sort; the successive *Artes Poeticae* of Horace, Vida, Scaliger, Puttenham, Ronsard, and Boileau are chiefly devoted to technical observations on poetic diction, the structure of the epic, the tragedy, and other genres, to methodological remarks on characterization, to classification of schemes and tropes (figurative deviations from scientific prose), to tabulation of meters and stanza forms. Neoclassical criticism, whether that of Dryden, Bossu, Du Bos, or Dr. Johnson, is chiefly technical: sometimes in the large, as it concerns theory of genre; sometimes in the small, as it concerns diction, the placement of the caesura, or the status of the "conceit."

With exceptions like Poe and Henry James, nineteenth

century critics chiefly practised other methods of criticism; but, since Croce and Rémy de Gourmont, there have been many converts. The new formalism differs in certain respects from its lineage. Aristotle's concern was to induce, from an analysis of Greek tragedy, general statements concerning diction, characterization, and plot; and in this preoccupation with the general he was followed by the neoclassicists. Contemporary criticism, influenced by Croce's attack on genres and other universals,[10] has characteristically occupied itself with analysis of particular works, regarding each work as unique, a class consisting of one member; the standard of judgment is drawn from the work itself, and applied by estimating the efficacy of parts in promoting the success of the whole: the method is purely analytic.[11] A second important divergence concerns the status of "form." Following Croce in his attack upon the conception that aesthetic form is something added, by way of decoration, to a "substance" capable of statement in other terms, some contemporary critics would maintain that the "meaning" of a literary work is coterminous with its given expression, so that the whole conception of "form" as a separable aspect is false.

According to this theory of criticism, the study of literature should be formal. The "ideas" belong to philosophy; the biographical self-expression of the writer to psychology; the social milieu of writer and readers to history or sociology. But studies "in the technique of the art belong to criticism certainly. They cannot belong elsewhere . . . [They] would be technical studies of poetry, for instance . . . if they treated its metric, its inversions, solecisms, lapses from the prose norm of language, and from close prose logic; its tropes; its fictions, or inventions, by which it secures 'aesthetic distance' and removes itself from history. . . ." [12]

The aesthetic method has its parodies. In reaction against the identification of poetry with what it "says," and out of the perception that a proper poem cannot adequately be translated into prose, there may develop the notion that poetry equals its devices, and that these may be appraised in abstraction. The consequence is an industry busied with the listing of stanza forms and rhyme schemes, the classification of meters and images, or—at a more respectable level—a preoccupation with technical dogmas: assonantal terminations are censured as "bad rhymes," metaphysical conceits as "far-fetched metaphors," as though these were pronouncements which could be made without consideration of the appropriateness of each feature to the intent of its author and the character of the work within which it functions.

But formal criticism, competently practised, allows of no such atomism, nor does it limit itself to the study of surfaces. It does not postulate a "pure" poetry—imagism or echolalia: it allows, indeed cherishes, the richness of "ideas" in poetry, but it insists that they be studied only as they function in the poem. Lines like "Beauty is truth, truth beauty" or "They also serve who only stand and wait" are not to be taken as equivalents to the poems in which they occur. The meaning of a poem, not to be drawn off in a prose paraphrase, is constituted not only by its conceptual ideas but by the rhythms, the imagery, the metaphors operating in close conjunction; and these elements must properly be studied as they interact in the organism. [13]

Literature offers us, however, an imitation of life. It seems a truncation of what literature is, both to the writer and to the reader, to say that the life offered by the novelist is not to be compared with the life outside of the novel; indeed, we cannot judge of aesthetic shapings like stylization, distortion, "realism," idealization and the like without comparing the imitation with the experience to which it gives aesthetic form.[14] And if the "ideas" may be discussed only as they function within, and as a part of, the whole aesthetic structure, they receive no criticism as "ideas."

The consequence of this conception of literature is ideological criticism. This may be a moral judgment of the author's character, as intuitively assembled from his biography—on the principle that the author is the cause of his book and that a "good" book cannot proceed from a bad man, or a genetic study of his social conditioning —on the principle that his politico-economic attitudes will be determined by his class origins; but specific appeal to these causes is unnecessary and (most critics would agree) irrelevant. If the ideological judgment be of the book's intention, that intention can be discerned in terms of the book itself; if the judgment be of the book's consequence, that will be secured first by discerning its emotive effect upon the critic himself, then by his observing its effect on others and estimating its probable effect upon society at large.

Crudely handled, the ideological method consists of abstracting from their contexts and from their dramatic exponents certain sententious utterances, attributing them to their authors, and developing them with accompanying praise or censure. So one may quote Milton's

> who would lose
> Though full of pain, this intellectual being,
> Those thoughts that wander through Eternity

as though these were the poet's acknowledged senti-
ments instead of proceeding from Belial, who "could
make worse appear the better reason." Crude also is a
mechanical scrutiny of the materials: the decision that
a novel is bad because it deals with sin and sinners or because its characters are members of the leisure class.
Unsatisfactory as one must consider the eighteenth century doctrine of "poetic justice," the preoccupation of
the critic with the outcome of the plot instead of with
particular utterances of the characters or the "morality"
or "immorality" of single situations is superior to more
elementary methods. Subtle and mature ideological criticism will always be concerned with the study of moral
or political tendency in the organic work, the work taken
as a whole. It will attend to tone as well as statement;
will consider whether the author is solemnly earnest, or
lightly serious, or playful, or whimsical, or ironic. It will
abstain from using its analysis of a novelist as mere text
for a discourse inciting to virtue or rebellion. But it will
be free to estimate the accuracy or misrepresentation of
a given social class, the representative character of hero
or villain, the provinciality or inclusive largeness of the
author's philosophical attitude.

Are these two schools of criticism irreconcilable? We
recall the description of poetry as at once *dulce et utile;*
and we recognize that the Renaissance theorists differed
only on the order of precedence, on which was means,
which end: they agreed that poetry either delighted man
by its wisdom or won man to wisdom by its delight. The
Horatian formula, though imprecise and in need of interpretation, may still serve to symbolize two chief aspects of literature with which critics have been and are
concerned: the pleasure of the aesthetic experience and

the intellectual and moral enlargement which literature may provide.

So far as the issue between formal and ideological criticism is one of only method we can certainly conceive of the two as supplementary, and assert that the total critical evaluation, whether made by one man or several, will employ both aesthetic and philosophical criteria; and we can perceive that the more synoptic minds are endeavoring for adjustment and inclusiveness.

We can, with Aristotle and Maritain,[15] reconcile by distinction; that is, we can deal with literature twice— now as "poetics" and now as "politics." We can, with Matthew Arnold, use our "touchstones" as tests of poetic style but judge of hierarchic rank within literature in terms of "truth of substance" and "high seriousness." With that scrupulous critic, T. S. Eliot, we can urge that "The 'greatness' of literature cannot be determined solely by literary standards, though we must remember that whether it is literature or not can be determined only by literary standards":[16] that is, aesthetic criteria decide whether a work belongs to literature, but philosophical as well as aesthetic criteria must decide its greatness.

Another kind of mediation can be proposed: If one were to arrange all works of literature in a series beginning with forms like poetry, drama, and the novel and ending with such forms of applied literature as the sermon, the political oration, and the informative essay, one would, to approach each work most efficiently, consider where, for each, the center of gravity lay and deal with each by methods appropriate to its kind. Thus, among contemporary critics, the formal analysts, like Brooks and Blackmur, have characteristically applied themselves to poetry; ideological critics like Fox and Henderson have characteristically applied themselves to the novel, which since the eighteenth century has been the genre of widest social interest. Analogously L. C. Knights, in search of the proper genre in which to study the interaction of economics and literature "in relation to a particular place and time," chose drama in the age of Ben Jonson—drama, that is, when it occupied a position in reference to society equivalent to that occupied by the novel in the age of Dickens.[17]

The differences, however, appear not to be merely methodological but to take their rise from differing assumptions concerning both how, as a matter of fact, literature affects its readers and how, in theory, it should affect them. Formal critics, who may claim the Aristotle of the *Poetics* as their sponsor, take the aesthetic experience as being its own end. Ideological critics, whose ultimate sponsor is Plato, regard the values of art as instrumental to other values, economic, political, ethical, religious. In general, the former group interprets the proper, or aesthetic, attitude toward literature as cathartic, detached, contemplative; it makes much of the "imitation," the medium, the formal devices which disengage art from the life it "imitates." The second holds art to be incitory, an invitation to action. All art, it maintains, is more or less subtle propaganda for a way of life; and it is therefore chiefly concerned to make explicit and then to judge the doctrinal implications.[18]

In behalf of each theory there is ponderable evidence. Testimony in behalf of the former comes chiefly from art critics and philosophers, notable among them Kant, Schopenhauer, and Croce. Kant's conception of art as aesthetic purposiveness without practical purpose, Schopenhauer's conception of art as contemplation, freeing us from the blind drive of the will, Croce's denial to art of the conceptual and the utilitarian—all of which are still operative today as critical commonplaces—represent philosophic attempts at the differentiation of art from life, and of art from ethics and metaphysics. The most impressive witness to the latter comes from politicians, ecclesiastical or secular, who, like Plato, have believed that the arts should be censored. The "burning of books" and the expulsion from the authoritarian state of authors not "orthodox" are powerful testimonies to the public power of literature. If art purges instead of feeding the emotions, if it withdraws men from action instead of prompting them to rebellion, why the practical statesman's fear of "immoral" books?

One egress from this dilemma may be suggested by the practice of the Catholic Church, which, though forbidding books on the Index Expurgatorius to the uneducated or inexperienced, allows their reading to the critical and mature. To translate this distinction into terms of theory is to say that those of little reading are likely to take books too simply and directly, whereas the mature, having read many books, can distinguish art from life, opinion from opinion, and book from book. The parallels from theater and cinema demonstrate that those who attend but rarely are prone to identify art and life and to act upon the identification, whereas the experienced have adjusted themselves to that which both is and is not "life." In general, the young are probably more directly and powerfully influenced than the old; inexperienced readers take art more naïvely as a copy of life than do the experienced. Undoubtedly the majority of men make less distinction between life and art than do men of letters, who go to the arts not primarily for a vicarious life, the escape from one life to another, but for a special experience which "life" does not offer.

Another solution has already been suggested. Not only do readers vary in their responses to literature, but works of literature vary in their character: they can be ranged from photographic and phonographic works which offer an extension of the reader's life to works in which a high degree of stylization makes evident that what is offered is related to life indirectly, obliquely, or symbolically; from works in which the propagandistic intent is clear and expressed overtly to those in which—as in Shakespeare's plays—the dramatic counterpoint provides a convincing illusion of objectivity.

These distinctions are correct so far as they go, but crude and inadequate—first, because they propose a blunt antithesis of "naïve" and "mature," polar terms; and secondly, because, by simplification, they do injustice to the experience of the mature reader.

A passage from Charles Mauron seems typical of much contemporary aesthetic theory.[19] "What appears to be most surprising in a work of art," he writes, "is its power of stimulating us gratuitously, with no possible reflex. In [practical life] we scarcely look or listen at all, except in view of some future activity. Now the unreality of the work of art debars us straight off from any action of this kind. The first words the artist seems to say to us are: 'Look, listen, but don't move.'" Art, that is, is a form of contemplation; and its moral value, if one seeks a moral value, is its negative assistance to the good life—its staying of men's biological passions by interrupting their instinctive movement from impulse to action. The proper comment upon this Schopenhauerian theory is again to say: true—for the mature reader—but too simple. We must add to "no possible reflex" "but a possible future reaction"; to "straight off" a "but eventually"; and to "don't move" a "just now." If we say, as I think we ought, that Mauron has correctly described the aesthetic experience in that which differentiates it from practical life, we must say that in differentiating it we must not forget what unites it. With the mature reader—and this concept carries us from the descriptive to the normative, the response to literature is not permanent withdrawal from action or aesthetic escape from life but an immediate contemplation which helps the reader to considered action instead of instinctive behavior. Within the ordered structure of novel or play or poem, human experience is represented and interpreted. In any work of art, some pattern is imposed upon the matter, some significance selects and organizes; in the greatest works, the imagination, moral as well as aesthetic, offers patterns of moral possibility, of adjustments by revolt and by submission, of humanly discreditable successes and humanly admirable failures. We have the opportunity, denied us in ordinary life, of seeing the inner life and motivations of our fellows; and we have the chance to watch sequences of cause and effect work themselves uninterrupted by irrelevance. Literature provides us with a series of hypothetical situations, a series of dramatic propositions, in which we are asked provisionally to accept the "if," the condition, and to follow through to the conclusion, passing judgment on the inevitability of the sequence before we weight the plausibility or the necessity of the condition.[20]

Our account of the formal and the ideological methods of criticism would be incomplete if we failed to make explicit that each, in practice, is likely to make assumptions with reference to the other. Thus ideological critics are likely to take it for granted that poetry should possess the grandeur of generality and the aes-

thetic character of ready communicability; while formal
critics, by preference concerned with a complex poetry
which, by its metaphorical condensation, requires close
study and the service of analytic criticism, are likely to
take for granted a moral scheme in which subtlety is
superior to simplicity and a social scheme in which there
is protected leisure for the development of personal
complexity.

Neither of these correlations, however, can be taken
as self-evident. Not all whose primary interest in criticism (and in literature) is ideological, would require
that poetry reach an audience of widest dimensions;
and some critics who prefer difficult poetry to simple
are democrats or socialists. Art, they hold, is not a suit-
able medium for the promotion of economic or political
ends: [21] in a society to come, in which all have leisure,
all will have leisure for contemplation; and even when
leisure is scant, men will expend it upon those kinds of
activity which they value or are taught to value, of
which aesthetic experience should be a chief.

It would certainly be a disservice to criticism to make
the aesthetic method and the ideological divide the work
between them by assuming that the business of the one
is with *form* in the sense of external technique, of the
other with *content* as political or moral doctrine completely separable from the mode of embodiment. We
must rather take these two methods as complementary
emphases. Formal criticism will then study the total
structure of a literary work, including conceptual statements as parts of the structure; ideological criticism will
concern itself with the explication and judgment of a
work's philosophical attitude, explicit and implicit, including the expressive character of its structure and its
tone. Properly conducted, the two will interpenetrate.

§ III

Whether formal or ideological, whether theoretical or practical, criticism is rarely content to describe or elucidate: it tends toward an ultimate judgment, though that judgment would be premature were it not the conclusion of careful analysis, and though the judgment may be implied rather than made systematically explicit.

Normative criticism exercises judgment through the application of standards or ultimate criteria. Every man, of course, makes use of standards, albeit some are rudimentary; others, unarticulated; most, confused. Therefore when critics urge other readers to "have" standards, they are presumably urging them to clarify and systematize their principles of judgment or inviting them to "raise" their standards—to be more exacting, to require more of each work of literature and each experience of a literary work. It follows that critics themselves must be persons uncommonly aware of their own principles of judgment, whose own principles (whether or not they care to give them extended public exposition) are exacting and coherent.

A discussion of literary standards, their kinds and their coördination, may well take its start from the celebrated passage in which Longinus considers the tests by means of which a work comes to be accredited as classic.

"If then a passage after being heard several times does not impress with a sense of its greatness a man of good judgment and much experience in literature . . . but the more he considers it the less admirable it appears, it cannot be genuinely excellent, because it does not outlast the moment in which it is heard. But what is rightly

great will bear close inspection, attracts us with an irresistible fascination, and imprints itself deeply in our
memories. Consider a passage fully and genuinely excellent only when it pleases all men in all ages. When
men of different occupations, habits, ideals, and ages all
agree that a verse is excellent, such unanimity of opinion on the part of diverse critics secures strong and un-
shakable confidence in the object they admire." [22]

Longinus evokes a norm and a judge. The standards
are readers' standards—intensity and duration. The
work attracts with "irresistible fascination," and its appeal is not readily exhaustible: first surviving the repeated scrupulous readings of a single reader, it then
attains the approval of "all men in all ages." The classic,
that is, is defined by its capacity to survive its moment
and to interest and attract men for whom it has not immediate timeliness and topicality. Whether the "passage" attracts all readers for the same reasons Longinus
does not consider, nor is he concerned to scrutinize the
possible limits of "all ages": his "always" is an honorific
prediction based upon classic status from a relatively remote past up to the present.

It is not clear whether he makes a distinction in kind
between the hypothetic preliminary judge and the readers "of different occupations, habits, ideals, and ages."
He may mean that the estimate of the proper critic will,
eventually, be ratified by the experience of relatively in-
articulate readers. In any case, his prime evaluator is
"a man of good judgment and much experience in literature"—that is, a man of general intellectual powers who
is, at the same time, a connoisseur of the special art.
Classical antiquity agrees that the judge of literature is
not any man but a man especially qualified: he is the

wise man, or the good man, or the aesthetic expert, or
the man who best combines in himself moral and aesthetic qualifications.

Antiquity never seriously considered a universal fran-
chise in the nomination of masterpieces. It appealed to
the verdict of cultivated men within the civilized, the
Graeco-Roman, world. And till the end of the eighteenth
century, not only the judges but the masterpieces as well
were drawn from western Europe, classical and Christian.

In the eighteenth century, the reading public was
augmented by the addition of women and the middle
classes; and the literature upon which generalizations
must be made was extended beyond the "classical" to
include mediaeval literature and folk literature, Germanic and Celtic literature, and the literature of the
Orient. These extensions patently complicate the situation of criticism: the widening of the audience makes
the contemporary critic chary of predicting for "all men"
"always," while the accumulation of reputable books in
many tongues makes him fearful that he may have
missed acquaintance with some of the masterpieces. A
criticism of use and distinction may, of course, be based
upon a comparatively limited reading in a single important literature—Greek, French, or English—and may
frankly address itself to a specific and limited audience
sharing interests and standards with the critic. But
practical criticism ideally aims at basing upon an experience of the world's literary greatness the judgment it
passes upon a given new book or writer; and, till our induction is complete, our critical generalizations remain
tentative.

Who is to be the judge? the commoner, the aristocrat,
the saint, or the literary expert? This question is gener-

ally evaded—and answered—by saying that the work increases in value according to the inclusiveness of its appeal. Thus T. S. Eliot believes that the poet "naturally prefers to write for as large and miscellaneous an audience as possible"; and the critic points out the levels of significance in a play by Shakespeare. "For the simplest auditors there is the plot, for the more thoughtful the character and conflict of character, for the more literary the words and phrasing, for the more musically sensitive the rhythm, and for auditors of greater understanding and sensitiveness a meaning which reveals itself gradually." [23] The norm is here implied by the description: the masterpiece embodies values so rich and so various that each kind of reader, though neglecting much that is offered, receives the satisfaction he desires. [24]

It is generally possible, of course, to define the audience intended by a writer, even when that audience is the writer himself or ideal extensions of himself. And the preliminary judgment should certainly be that of the audience for which a work is designed: the "pulp" story succeeds if it sells; the Broadway comedy if it makes many laugh. But the final judgment must surely be that of the most widely experienced and inclusive and exacting judge. The man who, like Santayana, appreciatively comprehends Dickens, Proust, and Dante is the critical superior of him who comprehends only Dickens. Of the cultivated man, we may say that our common human nature, our instincts and passions, are his as well as another's, but that, including *was uns alle bändigt, das Gemeine,* he transcends it.

The Longinian appeal to the judge is supplemented by an analysis of criteria; and this analysis includes— and attempts, inadequately, to relate—both the psychic endowments of the writer and the stylistic characters of his work. Thus of the "five sources" of excellence, the first two are greatness of soul and mind, and "vigorous and inspired emotion"; the last three are effective figures —phonetic and imaginative, proper diction, and "fitting and dignified arrangement," or structure.[25] In strictest speech, of course, the writer's qualities and the devices of his art cannot be separated. The former are known only through their embodiment in the latter, and any other conception falls into the dangerous error of conceiving metaphor and even language as decorative and extraneous to the literary work. But it is permissible and practically useful to disengage the total impression made by a work, an impression characterized in psychological or moral terminology, from the stylistic and structural study of the means by which that impression is conveyed.

To turn from the examination of Longinus' theory of value to attempt a statement for our own time, we may distinguish five kinds of standards: persons (the judge or critic); masterpieces (by comparison with which we judge the relative merit of men or works); formal characters of structure and style in works of literature; the psychological effects of literature upon the reader; and the philosophical attitude or *Weltanschauung* of the author.

Of the first, we may here resume that, since values require an evaluator, and since persons differ in convictions, attainments, and sensibility, the final appeal, in case of dispute, will have to be to a personal arbitrament, whether it be conceived as that of "all men" or the best man or the expert.

Masterpieces are often thought of as standards— models for lesser or younger writers who by analysis of

the masters' methods and by imitation of their compositions are initiated into their craft; [26] but the masterpieces also serve the critic as normative points of reference: [27] Homer, Dante, Milton, Molière, Shakespeare,
Dostoevsky. Of an untried work, we ask, "Is it as good
as —?" Arnold's "touch-stones" are short passages chosen
for their character as concentrated specimens of poetry;
but large works as a whole, in structure and composition, make a massed impression which can be disengaged from their particularity of "fable" or dramatis
personae, and that total impression serves as standard
for new or hitherto unfamiliar works.

The masterpiece itself, the "classic," has attested its
importance by a reputation which, though it may have
been interrupted by periods during which the work was
not known or did not engage critical attention, has sur-
vived enough changes of taste to give warrant of comparative permanence. It may not always have been
cherished for the same reasons. With the masterpieces,
as with certain institutions, it is probable that loyalty to
them survives many changes of taste and formulation.[28]
There is the diversity of the audience at a single time
and place; there is also, as studies of literary reputations
make clear, a diversity, from age to age, of readers' expectations. Admiration for Shakespeare persists; but the
neoclassicist stressed his wisdom, the romanticist studied
his characters, the critics of the twentieth century are
concerned with his metaphors, his poetry, his stage-
craft.[29] Each age similarly finds elements to which it
takes exception, as the neoclassicist objected to Shakespeare's puns, his low comedy, and his "bombast"; but
each age, striking Shakespeare's balance, finds him for
itself as well as, hypothetically and honorifically, "for all
time."

The formal values have constituted one of the approaches to objectivity most practiced by aestheticians from the end of the eighteenth century to the present. It has been supposed that some forms (simple, like tones, colors, shapes, and lines; and complex, like particular structures) are universally pleasing to human beings; that, for literature, some sounds are phonetically agreeable in themselves. Fechner and other German aestheticians have attempted the statement of the supreme categories of form, of which Fechner's trio—unified connection of the manifold, consistency, and clearness—may be taken as representative.[30]

Any list of formal categories inevitably sounds thin in comparison with the concrete richness of particular literary works, their richness even as purely aesthetic structures. That is the necessary case, unfortunately, with any treatment of the arts in terms of abstracted universal patterns: it can be countered only by the reader's remembering that they are abstracted and must be returned to the specific contents in which, existentially, they operate. Final categories of form will be categories of organization, presupposing always that which is organized; and most of them also imply the presence, in a lesser degree, of their complementary antithesis. Thus novelty is praised, but the novelty is never total and would be neither praised nor comprehended if it were: it is novelty within a framework of tradition and continuity; while, on the other hand, the tradition is not praised if it is mere repetition, and that which is not mere repetition has its element of novelty. A work is praised for its unity, but implied is a diversity to be unified; for its variety, but the variety implies a continuity to be varied. Similarly coherence, or consistency, implies some refractorily various matter which is to be brought, through mastery, into an agreeable order.

The ultimate aesthetic criteria, it would appear, are richness and purity. Wagner's operas and Shakespeare's plays are praised for their inclusiveness (the opera combines poetry, music, and drama; the plays combine tragedy and comedy); Haydn's string quartets and Racine's tragedies are praised because they are unmixed (the music is without the words or ideas or program; the tragedy is pure stylized tragedy). Imagist poetry is "pure"; Donne's poetry is "rich." [31] Richness and purity, however, are also correlative, since the richness is always within some boundaries, has some exclusions, and since the purity is always relative to the purity of some other work, actual or hypothetical. It follows that, as Prall has pointed out, the "standards are the degrees, not the qualities,[32] or, more strictly perhaps, the proportions of contrary qualities. Schools of criticism, and critical generations, vary (in a pendular fashion, it is often supposed) in the relative proportions they desire of unity and variety, consistency and contrast, complexity and simplicity.

The quantitative aspects of form have engaged intermittent attention since the time of Aristotle, who preferred the tragedy to the epic on the ground that in the former "the end of the imitation is attained in less space, and the more concentrated is the more pleasing . . . ," and of Poe, who, on psychological grounds, gave the lyric and the short story decided superiority over the epic and the novel.[33] Yet the praise of brevity is countered by the traditional praise of length in its character of "sustained power." Traditionally, a criterion of an artist's greatness has been his power successfully to command the large form—the epic, the symphony or opera, the mural or "historical painting." Poe does not succeed in showing that a long poem is a contradiction, but he does succeed in demonstrating that a special kind of effect, a "special pleasure," as Aristotle would say,[34] is the consequence of an intense brevity. Of course length and brevity do not constitute single and self-sufficient criteria: the long must be brief considering its richness, the brief long by its implication. Both require architecture; and, since the longest novel cannot contain all that might go into it, both require selection and concentration. But the brief is capable of a superior intensity; for the long, there is possible the power of duration: each has its special pleasure. The traditional distinction between "major" and "minor" genres and the preference for the epic writer appear based upon the comparative rarity of sustained power, the general inclusiveness of the major writer, and the general inclusiveness of the major work.[35]

From formal standards to psychological, the transition may be made through the theory of literary "kinds." [36] The most persistent and rigorous thinking in generic terms was done by the neoclassicists; but the neoclassical hierarchy of genres, for all its apparent absolutism, never arrived at a logical ordering of definitions. Boileau's canon, for example, includes the pastoral, the elegy, the ode, the epigram, satire, tragedy, comedy, and the epic.[37] What is the basis for this constitution of types? Are they differentiated by their subject matter, their structure, their verse form, their magnitude, or their emotional tone? Patently all of these, in varying degree, play parts. But for the most plausible attempt to systematize the basis of genre we still must return to consider Aristotle's conception of tragedy as aiming at a "special pleasure," that of exciting and then moderating pity and fear. The formal structure of each genre, ancient or modern, can plausibly be argued to be governed by the special emotional attitude it expresses and seeks to arouse in the reader; and there are corroborations of this view in the current use of "epic" as well as "elegiac" and "satiric" as adjectives expressive of emotional attitudes. This consideration has special force if, after the manner of criticism, one deals with the genres in terms of present response rather than in terms of historical origins. "L'histoire, sans laquelle la psychologie marcherait d'échec en échec, nous dira qu'il y a tel genre qui est né de nécessités cultuelles, politiques ou techniques, etc. Mais ces nuances n'en contribuent pas moins maintenant où les raisons génétiques de l'existence de ces genres ne sont plus d'actualité . . . C'est *maintenant* que nous groupons nos genres, c'est donc l'emploi *actuel* des moules que nous devons consulter pour connaître la principale fonction de chacun d'entre eux." [38]

The standard for genre so conceived will be a conception of how, most powerfully and artistically, one has been affected by a specific work of that genre (as Aristotle seems to regard the *Oedipus* as the most satisfactory example of what tragedy can do) or a hypothetical conception of what the genre should do, a conception which can never be wholly unrelated to what it has done. Tragedy, says Aristotle, "ought to produce, not any chance pleasure, but the pleasure proper to it"; and this conception of the "proper" pleasure is the standard for the judgment of specific performances. Its central pleasure of catharsis is attached to other emotional pleasures through which catharsis is effected: the "power" of tragedy, its "vividness of impression in reading as well as in representation," its "concentrated effect," which is "more pleasurable than one which is spread over a long time and so diluted." [39] The form is determined by, and evaluated by, the kind of pleasure at which it aims and provisionally judged by the efficiency with which it provides that pleasure.

Some aesthetic critics of our day appear to scrutinize a literary work by purely formal criteria, as though the organization of a poem could be appraised without reference to its proposed effect upon the reader. So neoclassical critics sometimes talked as if they possessed principles which could be applied without consideration of the audience to which a work addressed itself. But Addison, Pope, and Johnson ridicule the play which, though no one cares to see it, observes all the "rules"— rules made but to promote their end. So Corneille, Racine, Molière, Boileau, and La Fontaine reiterate that the great rule among artistic rules is that of pleasing. [40] No available psychology seems of much assistance to the literary critic; [41] but the lack of a scientific instrument at once precise and relevant must not prevent the contemporary critic from seeing, as Aristotle saw, that the formal organization of literature aims at the production of a calculated response. The "chief things by means of which tragedy moves the feelings of the audience are parts of the plot. . . ." "Since it is necessary for the poet to provide this pleasure [proper to tragedy] by means of pity and fear through imitation, it is clear that this effect must be worked into the incidents." [42] When the audience for literature and what it desires from literature can be taken for granted, analyses of form are provided with an assumed reference to the purpose of the art; in periods when expectations are uncertain, it is necessary for the critic to define these controls of form with some exactness. Whatever else they are, shifts in poetic method are alterations in the kind of experience which is to be communicated or in the size or sensibility of the audience addressed.[43]

Of course, psychological standards often appear without explicit reference to their "objective correlatives." [44] We characterize works as "moving," "vivid," "powerful," "sincere," "vital," and as "subtle" or "delicate" or "pathetic." The first adjective seems, like "interesting," a mere note of our attention to a work. "Moving" equates "emotionally significant"; it requires to be followed by explications: moving toward what attitude or action, how powerfully moving, moving for how long? The ultimate psychological criteria are often said to be intensity and duration: "vivid" seems a clear instance of intensity; "powerful" and "vital" both appear to betoken a combination of intensity and duration.

Certain psychological terms are appropriate either to passages in a longer work or to the total appraisal of a work; and a work on a large scale generally is inclusive of a range of emotions, including contrasts of powerful and delicate, heroic and amatory, just as a large-scale form transcends by including many smaller units of form. The obvious cases of emotional inclusiveness are the great novels—*Vanity Fair, The Brothers Karamazov, The Magic Mountain,* in which episodes and sequences deploy their several emotional tones, like the contrasting and supplementing andantes and allegros of a symphony; but poetry of that kind inadequately called lyric—the poetry of Donne, Baudelaire, Rilke, Eliot— has its own emotional inclusiveness in which the elements, instead of being deployed over symphonic space, are pressed into tension and stratified concentration.

The last category of standards is philosophical. "The

great question as to a poet or a novelist is, How does he feel about life? What, in the last analysis, is his philosophy? When vigorous writers have reached maturity we are at liberty to look in their works for some expression of a total view of the world they have been so actively observing. This is the most interesting thing their works offer us." The speaker is Henry James, in his essay on the novels of Turgènieff.[45] In recent times, the office of "right popular philosopher"—as Sidney calls the "poet"—has been chiefly exercised by the novelists, such novelists as Dostoevsky, Hardy, Lawrence, Mann, and Kafka. But, whether he "thinks" for himself or like the philosophical poets of the past accepts the system of a great metaphysician, and even when he does not deal in conceptual statements, the modern poet also offers imaginative equivalents of philosophical attitudes; and, if his sensibility is coherent, it can be translated into conceptual statements and philosophically judged.[46]

Philosophical standards can be applied with varying degrees of appropriateness, refinement, and rigor. The recent theoretical and practical essays of communist critics, Russian and American, are important for their attempted development of methods for studying the relation of literature to society, methods which avoid resort to "vulgar sociology" or to disposition of a great author by extracting and labelling his political doctrine. Grib's *Balzac*, Plekhanov's *Ibsen*, Farrell's *Literary Criticism* are instances of intelligent scrupulosity. In a similar spirit, though with a very different doctrine, some of Eliot's recent prose pieces, notably *After Strange Gods*, seek to "apply moral principles to literature quite explicitly" without forgetting the nature of literature; and Yvor Winters' *Primitivism and Decadence* concerns itself with "The manner in which the moral intelligence actually gets into poetry." [47]

With the philosophical judgment of literature, as with the critical judgment of philosophy, there are provisional estimates. "When the doctrine, theory, belief, or 'view of life' presented in a poem is one which the mind of the reader can accept as coherent, mature, and founded on the facts of experience, it interposes no obstacle to the reader's enjoyment, whether it be one that he accept, or deny, approve or deprecate." [48] These provisional criteria are exacting enough: they are intended to exclude works which show their authors unaware of sickness, stupidity, ugliness, self, and society; but in excluding the adolescent, the sentimental, and the evasive they leave intact not only the great novels and plays and "epic" poetry but short poems as well which, by inclusion and implication, express attitudes possible to maturity.

Eliot is raising specifically the question of how far agreement with the beliefs of a poet is necessary to appreciation of the poetry; but Eliot's hypothetical reader is obviously one whose own mind is "coherent and mature" and whose experience has been wide and deep enough to assume his receiving no basic surprise from the mode in which another envisages it—in short, who is a potential critic; and the question raised is thoroughly relevant to the criticism of poetry.

How many, and what, theories of life are there which a critic can accept as coherent and mature? The question might be answered in terms which would receive rather general assent; and most of them would prove to be patterns traditional from at least the time of the Greeks: scepticism, naturalism, humanism, religion. [49]

But two questions will supervene. Are these philosophies equally "mature and coherent"? And should not these judgments apply themselves to the method by which writers have reached their view of life and the subtlety or profundity with which they entertain them as well as to the conclusions themselves?

The answer to the first question appears to be that no critic who is himself a scrupulous and integrated mind can regard Catholicism and Marxism—to cite a pair of contemporary options—as equally tenable readings of reality. Privately, he must have arrived at the decision that one exceeds the other in maturity and coherence; and, as between two hypothetically equal writers, the one a Catholic and the other a Marxist, he must consider the "true believer" to be the greater, though this certainly need not mean that the critic will use his author, whether "orthodox" or "heretical," as the occasion for doctrinal homily.

To the second question, the answer is clearly, yes. The sagest conclusions can be superficially adopted and verbally parroted, while dubious or false statements may be uttered in poems, novels, and plays the psychological and moral substance of which is deeply sound. The wisdom of a writer must affect not only his intellect but his sensibility; it must appear in his control as well as his statement; and it must be a wisdom which he has won and which he therefore deserves, which he has felt and can therefore imaginatively sustain.[50]

We may now attempt to adjust the normative species to one another: The final judgment of literature will have to be a human judgment, and a selective human judgment—that of a special kind of man. The appraisal is to be made by a man widely and deeply experienced in life and letters, who can utilize in the evaluation of new work his acquaintance with the existing master-pieces of the art without precluding the possibility of a new work the greatness of which will be different in kind and hence enlarge the canon of greatness. In his judgment of a work, he will envisage its audience, estimate its writer's intentions and the efficiency of the means aimed at their realization. Skilful at analysis of its structure and at comparison of its aesthetic organization with that of other works, he will interpret its worth as an object for contemplation; and, since every work imaginatively implies a philosophic attitude the scope and depth of which is inseparable from its stature, his own best apprehension of reality must pass comprehensive judgment upon the "world" of his writer.

The perfect critic has, of course, never existed, though he must be conceived as a standard for the criticism of standards and critics. Happily, imperfect critics and criticism can be of salutary use in an imperfect scheme of things; and critics whose temperaments and aptitudes lead them to specialize in the application of one standard or another, one method or another, can be seen as collaborators rather than rivals. The total act of judgment, assuredly, must be conceived of as one in which, coherently related and flexibly applied, all the standards unite.

§ IV

Criticism sustains close relations to linguistic study, to literary history, and to imaginative writing.

Literature is an art whose medium is words, words used (as I. A. Richards has made us all conscious) in a different mode from that of scientific discourse.[51] The latter wishes to define all its terms and either to devise new counters or, using those already current for practical or hortatory purpose, to sterilize them of their emotive force; its ideal would be a fixed word for each concept, and a terminology so conceptual as to suffer translation without shrinkage. Poetry, on the other hand, is, by common consent, not to be paraphrased: its "meaning" is not reducible to what prose statement can draw off. Its language ("poetic diction" in the exact sense) is compact, rich, connotative.

By the same token, poetry is untranslatable; and (considerations of European trade or Continental travel apart) the chief—and indeed probably the only humanistic—argument for the study of the classical tongues, and of French, German, and Italian, is the inseparability of poetry from its phonetic-semantic form. If the "general ideas" or the "plot" be all that is desired from a book, the reader's desires can be satisfied by a translation. But if the critic of poetry or of other imaginative literature is ambitious to concern himself with the exact and total meaning of the text before him, including its most specifically aesthetic aspects, he will have not only to read his Racine in French and his Goethe in German but to possess a more than glossarial knowledge of the language which they at once inherited and helped to make.

Of course the importance of language to poetry holds equally for literature in one's own tongue. A poet knows the ancestry of his words, their range of semantic play, their phonetic allies; and the critic must correspondingly acquire, both through general studies in the history of language and through specific scrutiny of the diction in the poem immediately before him, an analogous sense of the depth as well as the latitude of words.   To evade the words—to forget that they are things as well as symbols—is to miss or seriously to truncate the literary experience.[52]

Of literary history, whether defined with precision or taken loosely, some critics would deny the relevance to criticism; indeed, some might go so far as to deny the necessity for acquaintance with the literature of the past. In reply, it may at once be said that criticism naturally begins with the explication and evaluation of contemporary literature—which is simply to say that criticism begins at home, with what is most sharply immediate for us. It may further be granted that here is the readiest ground for the exercise of native and self-sufficient sensibility: one may well suspect a critic who, like some academicians, never ventures a judgment on contemporary literature, or for whom it is all deplorably bad or fascinatingly exciting.[53] But genuine criticism of our literary past—which neither merely repeats stock verdicts, nor yields to the intimidatory "Tout est dit," nor, by rebellion, reverses the stock verdict, but examines the inheritance steadily and freshly—is probably the most exacting of all critical labors. And, moreover, though a provisional or interim criticism may usefully pass judgment on a contemporary work by comparing it with other works of its year or generation, a comprehensive criticism of current performance requires acquaintance with and reference to the past.

Between literary history in its strict sense and criticism, the relation appears to be this: That which is at once *history* and *of literature* must take form as a chronologically arranged study of an aesthetic sequence (as distinct from the biographical or social references of literature or its ideological content); it must concern itself with the cycle—the rise, equilibrium, and fall of a genre or style. But this involves, at every moment, the use of critical criteria—in the definition of the genre (and what belongs or does not belong within it), in the estimate of what elements (added or enhanced or better arranged) are to constitute "progress," and of what constitutes the norm or height of the genre toward which it advances, from which it falls away. It is thus a serious error to speak of literary history as concerned only with facts, for only a system of values can determine what facts are relevant. The literary historian must either be a critic as well, or borrow his standards from traditional estimates or from practising critics.

Criticism is not historical in its ultimate method. Characteristically, its comparisons and contrasts (like Arnold's touch-stones or Eliot's juxtapositions of plays and passages from poems) propose significant relationships, ideological or aesthetic, between works composed in widely separated periods. Criticism ideally assumes a system of values which, if not à priori, is at least timeless. It may include within its total judgment the "historic estimate," the assignment of value relative to a closed past sequence; but it does not stop with such appraisal. Its final judgment, taking into account all that has been written up to the present, and, granting favoritism neither to past nor to present, proposes a hierarchic arrangement.

Moreover, criticism, operating habitually through the essay and focussing habitually on a single work or the work of a single author, is free to deploy itself more variously than literary history and, treating literature as the complex art that it is, to make use of more than aesthetic criteria, to treat its text with something like the range and fulness of reference which its character demands.

Between criticism and imaginative writing the relation is at once more close and less. Obviously the former is explication and judgment of the latter. But this need not mean that only those who can "do" may criticize.[54] The masters have no strict intention of limiting their audiences to fellow-writers; and the critic may put himself forward as a representative reader, a reader of uncommonly wide and rich experience, both of life and letters, analyzing works of literature and his responses to them for the benefit of other less practiced and less articulate readers; or the critic may be a philosopher or a psychologist or a sociologist, concerned with the interrelations of aesthetic and other forms of value.

Indeed, as critic of other men's work, the poet or novelist has his own liabilities: if it be true that the critic is sometimes a frustrate artist and tempted therefore to jealousy of his successfully creative contemporaries, it is also true that successful poets are not invariably just to those other successful poets, alive or dead, who are their rivals for public attention. Further, practicing artists appear to require, for their own salvation, a certain narrow orthodoxy concerning the nature of "true" poetry or the "real" novel which may lead to a needlessly stringent reduction in the kinds of pleasure and profit allowable to a reader. And, lastly, not every writer possesses the sort of intelligence which produces criticism, but only the kind of writer who, to quote Valéry, "carries a critic within him and who associates him intimately with his work." [55]

Most critics, however, have been practitioners of poetry, drama, or the novel—practitioners of varying eminence, to be sure—turning aside temporarily from their work to define their own creative intentions, or to defend the whole cause of imaginative literature against the philosopher who has charged it with untruth, or the philistine who has charged it with inutility, or the puritan who has charged it with immorality.

In any case, a poet may be presumed to know better than a sheer layman, what kind of intentions another poet might propose. A poet knows what makes people write poetry (or at least what makes him write), and he knows how the imagination works (at least how his works). If the proper reading of poetry begins with the reconstruction of the poet's meaning, then it is important to be able to experience poetry as the poet experiences it. If, furthermore, the total meaning of poetry cannot be disengaged from its technical devices, then to write verses oneself is a chief help to the comprehension of other men's.

It follows that, for the aesthetic criticism of literature, some proficiency in the writing of its forms (the poem, the play, the novel) is highly salutary. One reads in a new way, with a fresh attention, when he studies the craft of a writer in the hope that it will aid his own; and that practical concentration leaves a permanent perceptiveness of how a writer sees and how he translates what he sees into words.

Linguistics, literary history, and imaginative writing certainly do not exhaust the disciplines requisite to criticism. Philosophy, both historical and theoretical, is doubly necessary: because great literature has always been philosophical and its interpreters must comprehend philosophy without poetry in order to comprehend the nature of that difficult and precious compound, philosophical poetry; and because critics themselves need all the discipline in logical method, in definition, and in system of which, without disadvantage to their sensibility, they are capable. The study of the plastic arts and music provides aid not only in proposing the analogies between the aesthetic mediums but in disengaging their differences of function and purpose. The social "sciences," more recent in their development, are aids to the study of the world out of which author and book come and the world which the book addresses.

There is, one is tempted to say, no kind of learning a critic cannot use if his learning does not overbalance his taste and his judgment. Indeed, the exactions are so stringent that great critics have been more rare than great poets; the full task of criticism is so manifold that most critics of the past have been limited in their scope and those of the future are likely to carry this specialization further. The chief improvement modern criticism can make is a superior awareness, on the part of the specific critic, of what he is attempting: whether he is passing a moral or a political judgment or an aesthetic, what his criteria are and whence he derives them—in short, such a methodological clarity and coherence as were patently present in Aristotle's *Poetics* and the relevant and complementary sections of the *Politics* and have been patently absent from too much criticism, even by eminent names, between his time and ours.[56]

The case for criticism does not rest upon the claim that it is an exactly objective science.[57] It aims, to be sure, at such exactness and objectivity as it can command: it will increasingly eschew the vague and the impressionistic. But it will not undertake a specious simplification of its problems or attempt to make itself scientific at the expense of sacrificing concern with the values characteristic of the literary experience. The exactness to be desired is a precision in analyzing the structure of the literary work, the naming with a consistent terminology of the features apprehended, the careful discrimination of its effects upon the reader. The relative objectivity desirable is to be attained, in formal criticism, by making the specific work of literature the object of attention, so that the interpretation tendered may be verified by the reader's scrutiny of the text; in ideological criticism by the reference of judgment to some system of moral or political philosophy.[58]

But the case for criticism rests upon its being, in relation to literature, what philosophy is in relation to a wider world of discourse, an unusually persistent concern for the fullest apprehension and comprehension and appropriation of literature: in some degree subjective, since it deals with values, and values exist for persons; in some degree objective, since it analyzes and compares works to which all can refer for corroboration of the critic's exegesis, and applies standards which are more than personal; concrete in its concern with specific poems, with poetry in the particular; abstract as it attempts such large and general statements of aesthetic and philosophical principles as can be educed from the close study of specific works and the relations between them.

The future for criticism, and for the "higher study" of literature of which it is the focus, depends upon our cultivation of increased awareness of aim and method; it depends upon our loyalty to the double responsibilities of concrete analysis and speculative theory; it depends finally, upon our constant recollection that literature is life in art, and that the total act of literary criticism is a total judgment, aesthetic and philosophical.

5

IMAGINATIVE WRITING

Wilbur L. Schramm

When EMERSON commended to Alcott the "adroit New York broker," Colonel Perkins, Alcott replied that he gave his hand "with some reluctance to mere merchant or banker." "What is so comic, I pray," asked Emerson, recording the incident in his journal, "as the mutual condescension with which Alcott and Colonel Perkins would give the hand to each other?"

For more than half a century, writer and scholar in America have given each other the hand only with the mutual condescension which Emerson found so amusing. Such a relation is unnatural and damaging: it tends to impoverish books and the study of books alike. Increasingly of late, writers as well as scholars have risen to deplore the situation, challenging the universities to search their consciences and deny, if they can, that they have played a major part in bringing about a division disturbing to the prospects of both American scholarship and American literature.[1]

The university has become the scholar's fortress. As man of letters, the scholar busies himself in the past, rather than the present; prefers the example and company of scientist and social scientist to the example and company of the artist. As administrator, the scholar assigns the teaching of "composition" to the young assistants; relegates contemporary literature to an incidental "luxury" or "popular" course, in either case rather frivolous. As productive writer, the scholar leaves little trodden the road approaching literature as an art, though the highways of history of literature, biography, politics, economics, science, and moral philosophy of literature are worn deep with the steps of pilgrims seeking palms in the learned journals. The official viewpoint, Max Eastman said, has come to be that a poet in history is divine, but a poet in the next room is a joke.

The scholar's attitude is neither mysterious nor indefensible. Professor Beers of Yale recognized and sought to explain it as early as 1900. "It is natural that one whose mind has been braced, whose taste has been cultivated to a nice severity by the study of the masterpieces of the world's literature should be impatient of the popular acclaim which greets the last new novel," he said, bravely assuming that all scholars master the great books before they become specialists. Furthermore, "Scholarship makes a man fastidious, difficult, exacting of himself as of others, and checks the impulse to produce." Finally, "It is much safer to praise an old book than a new. The old book has been duly labelled. Contemporary merit is uncertain as yet; authorities have not yet stamped it with their approval. A dull man gets a certain advantage over a clever man, if he is able to compare him to his disadvantage, with some cleverer man who is already dead." [2] This, we may assume, is what Pope was satirizing when he wrote,

> He who, to seem more deep than you or I,
> Extols old bards or Merlin's prophecy,
> Mistake him not; he envies, not admires,
> And to debase the sons, exalts the sires.

Characterized more kindly, the literary scholar is a scientist, avid for truth, scrupulous in using his inductive tool, anxious to eliminate the personal equation from his researches. Therefore, he avoids the problems of artistic judgment, which are hard to document and hint at subjectivity. He avoids the study of contemporary books because all the evidence concerning them is not yet apparent. His integrity is admirable. Yet it has made the graduate school no place for young men who want to write poetry and fiction, as Allen Tate, poet and university teacher, indicated when he said: "We study literature today from various historical points of view, as if nobody ever again intended to write any more of it. The official academic point of view is that all the literature has been written, and is now a branch of history. If a poem is only an instance of its history, the young writer is not going to find out how to study the poem; he will only know how to study its historical background." [3]

But the university need not assume all the responsibility for the divorce of writer from scholar. The same respect for inductive method which has led the scholar to footnoted objectivity in his study of books, has led the writer away from college halls toward an inductive quest of "experience"—by which he has meant observed, rather than distilled or interpreted, action. Philip Rahv has argued shrewdly that the central impulse of American writing from *Leaves of Grass* to *Winesburg, Ohio* and until recently, has been this cult of experience, and that the more characteristically American the writer, the more deeply he has been absorbed in the cult.[4] In this mood, the writer has learned to use as his most damning adjective, *academic,* which is to say, *dead.* He has become accustomed to prefer the company of un-learned men to that of learned; to regard the university as an antithesis of life, rather than a place for living; and in his own education to substitute "real life" for thought-upon-life enriched by a knowledge of the other humanities and the mind of the past. On the whole, the harvest of a month on the road was considered by a typical young realist of the nineteen twenties to be greater than the harvest of a semester with Plato or Whitehead. Therefore the writers have left themselves vulnerable to such a blast as Professor Douglas Bush loosed against them some years ago:

American novelists, whatever their native talents, seem to be largely uneducated, like their public. Mr. Dreiser writes as if he had not read much Eng-lish, Mr. Anderson as if he had read little but his own works. Mr. Lewis' background is that of a re-bellious sophomore who has read Mr. Mencken. . . . How much contemporary American fiction is only reporting, good or bad,—and how often do the reviewers call it such? Mr. Cabell's ironic sophisti-cation and suave erudition have given him a place apart, as an exotic, but Mr. Cabell's goods, it may be suspected, are mostly in the shopwindow. On the whole, literary cultivation is so far to seek that Mr. Elmer Davis, who can write about Catullus—though without absorbing his subject's love of pure diction—seems, not being a professor of Latin, al-most a freak in nature.[5]

So far apart have the scholar and the writer grown that they are able to explain their mutual aversion in al-most identical words: the scholar dismissing the whole of contemporary literature by saying, "You can't *know* anything about a book until it is a hundred years old!"; the writer taunting the scholar by reminding him, *"You can't know anything about a book until it is a hundred years old!"* The sight of explainers and practitioners of an art thus looking down on each other would be comical, were it not ominous. And chiefly the situation challenges the universities: having helped to foment an unwise divorce, can they now contribute toward bringing the parties closer together? [6] If the universities are to answer this challenge convincingly they must review *in toto* the relation of scholar to writer, and in particular they must reconsider the question, has imaginative writing a place beside the honorable disciplines of language, literary history, and literary criticism in the graduate school?

§ II

Scholars have not been overfond of admitting that imaginative writing is itself an honorable discipline. Romantic notions of inspiration have lingered rather too long, and the wind harp has remained as a symbol of the belief that creation of art is somehow inexplicable—it is supernatural or subrational—it is play, scholarship is work—it is dreams, scholarship is fact and logic. So far as it goes, this conception of the making of art may be true enough; but it would never be recognized by a practicing novelist or poet as an account of what happens in the production of a novel or a poem. The practicing writer knows that Izaak Walton's epigram holds good when its order is reversed: "As no man is born an angler, so no man is born an artist." The art of imaginative writing must be achieved. The complete writer, like the complete angler, must learn his craft.

Let us recall briefly, by developing a few fairly self-evident propositions, what the craft includes.

1. The creative process involves both hard thinking and imaginative insight.

We have already referred to the favorite lay theory of artistic creation, the "inspiration" theory, the "fine frenzy" with which the poet

> gives to airy nothing
> A local habitation and a name.

This conception has brought forth the idea that the artist is abnormal; is related rather more closely to the madman than to the solid citizen; has access to magic hidden from the ordinary man; indeed, is more newsworthy when he behaves like the ordinary man than when he behaves like Oscar Wilde. But if this conception may be traced to Plato (with footnotes by the Romantic Movement) it must be acknowledged that there is a better text in Plato. The seventh book of the *Republic* explains how a man may attain to a true perception of the Form or Ideal, which is the ultimate and most desirable reality. The seeker after reality must first devote himself to arduous study of the exact sciences of measuring, weighing, and counting. After long study, he will be rewarded suddenly by an intuition, a mystical vision apart from his previous logical processes, in which he will perceive the Form. In this passage, Plato is speaking of the philosopher, rather than the artist, but it will be remembered that in the *Phaedrus* Plato contends that the Form of Beauty is the only one which appears on earth as it really is; the Forms of Justice, Wisdom, Goodness reveal themselves only partly to man, but in the best art the Form of Beauty exists pure.[7]

In this conception, at least, modern psychology has tended to corroborate Plato. As far as it has been possible to determine from the introspection of artists, the process of creating art is essentially the same as the process of creating a new formula, a new philosophic synthesis, or any other new birth in the world of ideas. There is first a period of hard thinking, during which the mind explores the problem; then a period of relaxation, during which the rational processes of the mind are withdrawn from this particular problem; then the flash of insight which reveals the solution, organizes the symbols, or directs the thinking; and finally another period of hard thinking, during which the formula is tested, the work of art shaped and developed. Discussing this process in *The Art of Thought,* Graham Wallas calls the four stages Preparation, Incubation, Illumination, and Verification. Such a division may seem too violent, but artists themselves have not found it offensive, and it serves to call attention to the fact that in the making of art there is a calculable as well as an incalculable element. If the poet must "loaf and invite his soul," he must also invite his mind.

2. Art is concerned with reality.

When an artist is asked toward what his insight is directed, he is likely to answer, *reality,* for from time immemorial the subject of art, no less than the subject of science or philosophy, has been considered to be the real and the true.

Now the layman has usually been willing to concede a certain elementary relation between art and reality. The artist's mind must be well-stocked with usable knowledge, symbolized at least by a dictionary and the World Almanac on the desk. Stephen Vincent Benét must have known something about Daniel Webster before he wrote the delightful series of stories introduced by *The Devil and Daniel Webster*, and a knowledge of farm life must logically have preceded the making both of Virgil's *Georgics* and of Grant Wood's *Dinner for Threshers*. Furthermore, the artist must observe closely, his senses must be schooled to keenness; this has been thought akin to "reporting" and has been called by some unwary persons "realism." "Facts" and "reporting" have been popularly accepted in the twentieth century as the artist's window on reality, and the resultant conception of art has been a half-truth as dangerously facile as the older half-truth about "divine madness." As the older leads to a too naïve understanding of "inspiration," so the newer leads to a too naïve understanding of "imitation." As one encourages the undervaluing of intellection, so the other encourages the undervaluing of imagination.

When Michelangelo's *Moses* or Da Vinci's *Last Supper* or Shakespeare's character of Othello is praised for being real, the praise is manifestly not for a faithful copying of some object in nature. The reality of such art is not the kind which might be captured from life by a camera, even by a motion camera miraculously designed to enclose all the human senses. The true function of the mind in making art is to perceive and shape a reality which the artist believes to be more real than the actual.

In a certain sense, art is about the mind, rather than about nature. There is no direct connection between reality—however that term is defined—and art; all routes traverse the mind. Every impression of reality is

held in the mind before it is put into the form of art. It
is filtered through the senses, then shaped, modified,
enriched by the accumulated backgrounds and attitudes
of the individual. This is the process to which T. S. Eliot
referred when he called poetry "a *concentration,* and a
new thing resulting from that concentration, of a great
number of experiences . . . not the assertion that something is true, but the making of that truth more fully
real to us." *Concentration* is as good a one-word description of art as any. The artist brings his antecedent
experience and his world view to bear on a special problem, to enrich a stimulus; the lightning flash of intuition
helps to fuse the core of his thinking, to make diamonds
out of carbon; the final lucubration polishes and cuts the
diamonds to the utmost concentration of beauty and
genuineness.

In the process, the original sensory stimulus may be
left far behind, as it was, for instance, in Keats's sonnet
on the grasshopper. Whether Keats's sensory impression
or the later activity of his mind was more important to
the composition of the poem we have mentioned,
whether Shakespeare's reading in Holinshed and the old
Leir play was more important than the activity of his
mind in framing the character of Lear, whether Thomas
Benton's model for the young woman in *Susannah and
the Elders* contributed more to that picture than did the
activity of Mr. Benton's mind, are questions that need
not concern us here. Yet we cannot fail to notice that
the impressions which we think of as the originative impulses from life are really only the starting points of a
long creative process, during which the mind is occupied in gathering related materials, intensifying them,
perceiving a pattern within accidents.

For an objectivist, it is very hard to think of the proc-

ess of making art as other than a penetration to some
kind of "essences." Plato called them Forms; Clive Bell,
Significant Forms. Mr. Eliot talks of a new thing arising
out of concentration; Paul Engle, of an "intense wisdom." For myself, I have been inclined to look on art, in
the words of C. E. M. Joad, as "a window through which
we gaze upon reality." Sometimes the glass is dim, sometimes bright; but always the view is toward some essential meaning and form significant apart from the inci-
dentals of an object in nature.

3. Art is symbols.

For our purposes, it makes no difference whether the
artist is called a maker (which was the sense of the
word ποιήτης in Greece) or a communicator, as many
persons prefer to call him today. My own preference is
for the first of these terms. The true obligation of the
artist, it would seem, is to make a work of art. The poet
should make a good poem; the obligation of the reader,
if he wishes to participate in the poet's experience, is to
read the poem with sympathy and intelligence.

If the obligation of the artist is making, and the obligation of the audience is intelligent contemplation of
what is made, then somewhere between the two participants must exist an organism which is not necessarily
equal to the state of mind out of which it grew or the
state of mind engendered by contemplating it. Something exists apart from either maker or reader. That
something is a symbol or a group of symbols standing
for whatever reality is being imitated.

All the arts function in terms of symbol. Thus, on the
most elementary level music uses sound; painting, color.
Musical sound is varied in many patterns of timbre,
rhythm, pitch, loudness; color in patterns of shade, line,
mass. On the highest level of composition, the composer

and the painter organize their symbols still more delicately—Beethoven to stand for noble grief in the second movement of the Eroica symphony, Da Vinci to represent his conception of the head of Christ. Yet the actual work of art is only oil and pigment, or instructions for sending sound waves through the air. The realities are symbolized and must be recovered from the symbols by recreative activity.

Like the other arts, literature is "equal to, not true." Its medium is words. Its peculiar symbol is the name. The smallest name is the word; the largest, the work. Between these lie the metaphor and the other resources of figurative and pictorial language, which must represent the deepest and most subtle realities in a sort of shorthand:

> For all the history of grief
> An empty doorway and a maple leaf—

Goethe pointed out that the poet (and every writer is a poet in the sense that he is a namer) is like a child who wanders around an unfamiliar world bestowing names, calling the lampshade a skirt for the light, noticing that the setting sun is lying down to sleep on the hill, characterizing a person by such a pungent sentence as that which Robert Frost quotes from a boy's conversation: "He is the kind of person who wounds with his shield." The child will probably forget these names and grow up to use the hackneyed tags adults rely upon, but if he is to grow up a writer each sunrise must remain "herrlich wie am ersten Tag." He must apply this fresh quality of observation to a world infinitely more subtle and complex, call upon a storehouse of naming material infinitely more subtle and complete than "on the first day." He must scrape the barnacles off old names and let the salt get to them. He must take name-mummies, unwrap them, breathe life and personality into them. He must become an expert in language, though not in the linguist's way, and he must pursue the quest of the right word in the right place as untiringly as the historical scholar pursues facts and the linkage of facts.

For the writer must enter into competition with the greatest namers who have ever lived. He can, of course, choose his own field of competition—the hard clear understatement of much modern fiction—the "monstrous ingenuities" of modern metaphysical and symbolistic poetry—practices as diverse as that of Hemingway from Joyce, and Auden from Housman. Indeed Housman contended, in the face of the greatest outpouring of metaphorical poetry since the seventeenth century, that metaphor and simile are unnecessary to poetry; that they are sometimes pleasant adjuncts, useful illustrations, but not organic to the art. The greatest poets of our time have not agreed with Housman; they have preferred to meet the challenge of Donne's naming, rather than Wordsworth's. But they, no less than Housman, have felt the weight of a tradition on their work. Shakespeare and Homer used these symbols! When a writer undertakes to name realities, he acknowledges an obligation to make his symbols rich, to embody the full subtlety of his thinking and perceiving. He accepts a challenge to his very highest cognitive and imaginative powers.

4. Art is structure.

The preceding pages have doubtless given an impression of atomism, as though matter and manner, ideas and writing, force and wisdom were to be built piece by piece into a work of literature. Nothing could be farther from the truth. The secret of good art is fusion, concentration, intensity. If intense wisdom is to be poetry, there must be no line of demarcation between the wisdom and the intensity. Indeed, the intensity derives rather from the wedding of form to matter, reality to symbol. If there is any part of a piece of writing which may be discussed in purely technical terms, that is an unsuccessful part of the writing. If there is any part for which the "prose meaning" is equivalent to the whole meaning, that also is an unsuccessful part. The materials must fuse, and not merely as quartz and feldspar fuse to make granite, but as iron and carbon unite to make steel.

Essential in the making of art, then, is the combination of symbols so that they fuse into the great symbol which is the work of art. Poetry is not necessarily a poem. The child is scarcely fashioning a poem when it says, "He is the kind of person who wounds with his shield"; the woman who talks vividly of an incident at her bridge club is not thereby writing a novel. Between the figure and the poem, the incident and the novel, lie the problems of structure. These problems are first met, during the writer's apprenticeship (his period of "measuring, weighing, and counting"), as exercises in *structures*. The writer studies, practices, acquires supple hands. Then he undertakes the specific problems of *structure,* different for each work of art, yet similar in essence: to devise the right pattern, the one manner which is perfectly accordant with the matter. This manner must exist not as a servant but as an equal collaborator, receiving as well as contributing, so that manner and matter together make something greater than either. "Essential form," the editor of *New Directions* called it, and Edward J. O'Brien spoke of it in terms any writer can appreciate when he referred to a successful story—

a union of memorable matter and manner within the space of a few thousand words—as a "little miracle."

Yet the solution is laborious, rather than miraculous. No matter how inevitable and predestined the result may seem, no matter how smoothly the surface covers the labor that went into it, still the effect is won by long and arduous selection, emphasis, organization. The peculiar circumstance that the work of art exists apart from its maker is a challenge to the craftsman. He must select his small units carefully, rejecting the unfit and calling on better substitutes, repeating again and again the process of reorganization, seeking the best formation, lavishing endless care toward grace and intensity. The process has been compared to a general's preparation of his army for battle. Except for the artist whose main purpose is didactic, the parallels are not exact. But every general in words knows sadly well the truth of Horace's line, *nescit vox missa reverti.*

The discipline we have been describing is comparable both in quality and in severity with the discipline of any other advanced literary study. The graduate student would not find a good play, or novel, or book of verse an easy substitute for the usual thesis or dissertation. Such a piece of imaginative writing would have to be based upon close, accurate observation and information; it would have to be composed with a feeling for words as expert as that of the linguist; it would require a series of judgments not unlike those of the literary critic, and by virtue of selection and organization would require quite as much "logic" as a difficult study in literary history. If it were to have either breadth or depth it would require a keen perception of both timely and timeless elements in the world around the author, and funda-

mental decisions upon aesthetic, social, and philosophical questions. A specialized discipline it would indeed
require, but the kind of specialization which broadens,
which turns the practitioner's mind outward as well as
inward, toward the great questions of life as well as the
minutiae of behavior and appearance. Every serious
piece of imaginative writing must ultimately answer
Touchstone's question, "Hast any philosophy in thee,
shepherd?" Does the writing in some way illuminate
life? Is it a clear window on reality? Because the writer
takes all experience and all knowledge to be his province,
the discipline of imaginative writing—perhaps more certainly than any other branch of higher education—must
draw upon the intellectual wealth of the whole university, must include whatever will help the apprentice toward truth.

§ III

If it be granted that imaginative writing is an honorable
discipline which should deepen and sharpen the minds
of those students who pursue it seriously and faithfully,
then a further question presents itself: What has imaginative writing to contribute to other advanced disciplines? Since the university is a tight little community
of interrelated and interdependent units, the problem is
a practical one. And the proponents of imaginative writing can return a practical answer.

For one thing, writing as a scholarly discipline would
tend to raise the level of *all* writing done by scholars.
Now, scholars have never been reticent about criticizing
the quality of the writing in fiction and poetry. The
novels of such a man as Theodore Dreiser currently pro-

vide happy hunting grounds for scholars who sail through the books harpooning the floundering sentences and the lumbering whales of paragraphs; indeed, most of them have been so busy in this sport they have failed to notice that Mr. Dreiser in the course of his fumbling has made a massive study of the human will. One is greatly tempted to pay the debt in kind by discussing the quality of the writing in learned journals and scholarly books. Woodrow Wilson once remarked wryly of scholarly work, "It is painfully evident, upon experiment, that not many of the books which come teeming from our presses every year are meant to be read," [8] and the same comment has been made all too frequently upon academic journals. But considering the purpose which has informed American scholarly writing, and the conditions under which the writing has been produced, its quality has not been discreditable. One distinguished American scholar thus defends his colleagues: "Granted that Americans . . . do not generally err on the side of the literary graces, a learned journal is not the place for pleasant *causeries*. . . . The cost of publication alone compels strict attention to business, and because an article is dry —to those ignorant of the subject—it scarcely follows that the author is dry also." [9] Scholarly style is a sort of utilitarian style, and learned periodicals are technical journals composed in a series of signs clear and exciting to specialists in the profession, if not always to others. But scholarly writing is not so good that it might not be better, and the imaginative writer could show the scholar how to make it better. The scholar just quoted is not, of course, assuming that the way to transform utilitarian technical writing into writing worthy of the literature it discusses is to graft on a set of "literary graces," thus coloring it the shade of tea-time talk and lengthening it beyond the bounds of necessity. The change would have to be much more fundamental and would in fact be more likely to reduce than increase the length of the writing. Without adding or subtracting anything whatsoever, scholars could greatly improve their writing by giving some attention to a matter which must distress those learned men who have picked Mr. Dreiser to shreds: that is, the extreme insensitivity to the word, which is characteristic of much learned writing. I suspect that the presence of imaginative writing practised as an art in the graduate school would affect the other writing done in the school as the presence of a few fine tennis players in a club operates to improve the tennis of the whole club, or as the presence of two fine physicians in a Minnesota village drew other fine physicians, made better practitioners of apprentices, and ultimately built in Rochester one of the greatest medical centers of the world.

I confess to being disturbed, however, over the implication, in the quotation we have been discussing, that style may be dissociated from the man. This does not seem to be true of serious imaginative writing or of "good" writing in any form, and I am inclined to think that the way our learned journals read tells us, after all, something about our learned writers. If their publications read like technical journals, may it not be that our scholars are becoming more like technicians, less like artists? If literary scholars write like scientists—although, scientists insist, not half so well—may it not mean that they also think like scientists? I wonder whether too many literary scholars have not come to treat literature as laboratory work, as a social phenomenon or a scientific specimen? So far as this approach goes, of course, it is highly admirable; straight scientific thinking is always admirable. But when an art is treated only as a science, much of the art is left out. The scholar who studies an art must be more than a scientific historian; he must learn to see also with an artist's eyes. As Allen Tate puts it, the two ways in which we may read "correspond to the two ways in which we may be interested in a piece of architecture. If the building has Corinthian columns, we can trace the origin and development of Corinthian columns; we are interested as historians. But if we are architects, we may or may not know much about the history of the Corinthian style; we must, however, know all about the construction of the building, down to the last nail or peg in the beams. We have got to know this if we are going to put up buildings ourselves; we have got to know this if we are going to have even an elementary conception of what a building is." [10] The imaginative and critical discipline of reading a poem as though writing it would be salutary for the scholar who tends to treat literature as a piece of history. And I cannot help thinking that the introduction of the discipline of writing into the graduate school, whether it were participated in or merely observed at close hand, would help to discourage studies of literature as specimen or phenomenon and encourage studies of literature as *art*.

To literary scholars literature has proved interesting chiefly as a *kinetic* thing, influencing and being influenced, playing a part in the development of ideas, forms, institutions. The chief questions scholars have answered have been factual ones (*what* is the right text?), temporal ones (*when* was it written?), or causative ones (*why* or *how* was it written as it was?). With value judgments, which consider a particular work of art for the moment as a *static* thing and measure it by qualitative standards, they have been less concerned. Both the critic and the writer are chiefly concerned with this latter view of literature. The writer is little exercised over the determining factors on his own writing—whether he comes at the end of a Romantic Movement or whether his work shows the influence of the *Symbolistes*. His concern is to write well. His problem is to make a constructive analysis and judgment of a particular work of art.

The writer must therefore be a critic before he can be a good writer, even as the critic must be an artist before he can be a good critic. The writer, of course, need not be a systematic critic. He need not affiliate with a school or group, or raise a neatly jointed structure on the foundations of Aristotle, Longinus, and Sainte-Beuve. He need not put into public circulation his opinions of other men's works. But he must learn to look at art with an artist's eyes. He must read other men's work with the intelligent understanding of a fellow craftsman, in order to see how others have met the common problems of the craft and to estimate the effectiveness of their solution. Above all, he must learn to read his own work with uncompromising severity. He teaches himself to write by a process of constant self-criticism. If he is a thoughtful writer he will soon proceed from artistic evaluation to a judgment of ideas as well, for he will perceive the need of both art and wisdom. And thus he will join with his natural ally, the critic, to shift the balance of interest in the graduate study of literature away from history and research, back toward art and philosophy, toward an interest in the true as well as the new, toward what William Butler Yeats called a view of literature as "an object of contemplation."

It is reasonable to suppose, furthermore, that the study

of writing should make for better teachers. The love of reading literature (as art, rather than history) and the closely related desire to write it are the motives which animate most scholars and teachers of literature in their youth. In those years literature is thrillingly *alive*. Too often in later years it chills and ossifies and is finally placed on museum shelves. The early fructifying motives ought to continue long enough deeply to affect academic careers. A prospective teacher of literature in any language ought not to lose his love of reading and his keen interest in the literature being written around him. He ought to be able to interpret his art, insofar as possible, from the viewpoint of a participant, rather than a spectator. He should be a poet, even though he no longer writes poetry.[11] Many of our best teachers and scholars are men who have kept writing for years, and it is only necessary to recall the names of Sidney, Jonson, Boileau, Dryden, Goethe, Coleridge, Sainte-Beuve, France, Arnold, Lowell, More, and Eliot to realize that most of our greatest scholar-critics have also been writers. Other things being equal, a man can speak with far more confidence and infinitely greater understanding of his art if he has seen it from the inside.

After all, is not the ideal professor of literature, as we envisage him, a combination of the attributes of scholar, critic, and writer? The scholar seeks out, arranges, clarifies the facts; the critic takes charge of value judgments; the writer interprets the art. When the three fuse in one man, they produce the sort of teacher that George Edward Woodberry was, and Bliss Perry, or Lowell and Longfellow, Erasmus and Plato. They produce, that is to say, the complete teacher, the man whose outlook on literature will always be fresh and vigorous, who will see the work as a whole and treat it thus, whose interpretation will be sound because it proceeds from the intimate view of the artist and the buttressed facts of the scholar, whose judgment will be sane because it is based on systematic thinking, who, at the same time he calls on history and philosophy and science for what help they can give, will ever be keenly conscious that literature is primarily an art. This is a high goal, but not unattainable.

And if the study of imaginative writing will make for better teaching, it will make for better future scholars. Teachers who are themselves trained in the discipline of writing and reading as artists, may reasonably be expected to train scholars who will be better equipped to understand, explain, and judge an art.

§ IV

But what of the artist? Dare a talented youth risk injury to his career by studying in libraries and seminars?

Let us understand several things clearly at the outset.

In the first place, I have no intention of maintaining that every potential writer can profit by university training. Probably none of us would have sent Shakespeare to graduate school, even if we could have persuaded him. He seemed to need nothing from the university; possibly such training might have made him a Jonson. Advanced study of literature might have made François Villon a different writer, probably not a better one. By way of parallel evidence, one might set down a long list of authors who have had university training and apparently profited nothing from it; I can see no evidence, for example, that Thomas Wolfe (whose work one critic has unkindly called "a chaotic recapitulation of the cult of experience as a whole, traversing it in all directions and ending nowhere") gained direction or illumination from his advanced study. I can conceive even of a talent so delicately balanced at the time of entrance into the university that the new discipline might create a clerk rather than a poet. I do not believe this would be a common occurrence, and I shall maintain in pages to follow that the university has something to offer nearly every writer. Still, the thesis that the university is a necessary training ground for the writer is even less tenable than the thesis that the university is a necessary training ground for a learned man.

It is equally obvious that no university could undertake to turn out writers as it produces physicians, lawyers, chemists, and teachers. One cannot teach a man to write, or, for that matter, to practice any profession. The teacher directs, aids, encourages; the student learns by his own effort. But the initial endowments of a serious writer of poetry or fiction are somewhat more rigorous and specialized than those of the other professions mentioned. The creative imagination is rather rarer in first-year graduate students than the intelligence, gift of discourse, pleasing personality, and interest in people which go to make good secondary school teachers. Furthermore, the progress of a writer is less easily measured and his capability less surely predicted. When a university graduates a man with an M.D., it can confidently say: This man knows enough of the human body to minister to its ills; he can prescribe medicine when that is necessary; he can remove an appendix and amputate a limb; he can speak with authority on questions of health and disease; and all this he can do on demand. But when a university graduates a writer it can hardly say: This man knows enough about literature as an art to produce it on demand; he can salve your feelings with a sonnet; in the evenings he can stir you with another *Hamlet;* he can untighten your nerves with a new *Huckleberry Finn.* In the case of a lawyer or a chemist or a surgeon or a teacher, the university can even predict with some assurance the future career of the graduate. He has been a B student; he will probably be an adequate chemist, reliable but not brilliant. He has been an A student and has produced a brilliant thesis; he is capable of filling a highly paid research job. But pity the poor university which tries thus to grade its writers. It may discover, as others have, that its O'Neills are those who flunk out at the end of the freshman year. For the paths to the professions are not parallel. The university can set a certain number of assignments, a certain number of examinations, for its lawyers, doctors, chemists, and be quite sure at the end that the student is capable of practising law, medicine, chemistry. For the prospective writer it can speak of promise, but only hope for fulfillment.

In graduate work, spur tracks leave the university at the end of each semester. Some students of writing might be expected to derive what benefit they can, and leave before receiving the master's degree. Others would be shunted off after being made Master of Arts or Master of Fine Arts.[12] Only those with special capacity and aptitude for scholarship, and ordinarily with the intention of becoming college teachers, would proceed to the Ph.D. This is not the same as saying that advanced study or teaching spoils a writer for writing, provided that he has a capacity for advanced study or teaching. Dorothy Canfield Fisher has a Ph.D. degree. Archibald MacLeish and John Galsworthy went through law school. John Crowe Ransom, Robert Penn Warren, and Paul Engle all spent several years at Oxford in advanced study beyond the American A.B. or A.M., and now teach in American universities. Thomas Wolfe took graduate work and taught English. T. S. Eliot spent several years in the advanced study of metaphysics and related subjects at Harvard. A. E. Housman was one of the most learned men of his day and a conscientious teacher of Latin at Cambridge; his editions of Latin authors are models of scholarship. Hervey Allen spent two graduate years at Harvard, taught several years, wrote a scholarly book on Poe. Wallace Stegner and Howard Baker both earned doctorates in English, still prefer to teach while they write. Thomas Mann, Wystan Auden, and Louis MacNeice are a few of the writers who have come from Europe to teach in American universities. There is nothing in the facts to prove that an intelligent program of advanced study or a congenial teaching position need divert a writer's talent or throttle his production. Not all writers should enter the university, and only a few should do so with the intention of becoming teachers, but those few will find ample freedom to meet their peculiar needs and develop their abilities.

This clearly understood, let us consider what the university offers the writer.

For one thing, it offers vocational training. Only a very few persons in any age can support themselves by serious writing; most writers must have a vocation outside their main interest, as Sinclair Lewis has pointed out in a trenchant article. Of course, the work must be selected with great care to fit the writer. Work with the hands has always proved a desirable complementary part of a writer's life, provided the work is not too arduous or prolonged. Journalism has long been a favorite vocation of prospective writers. It is a natural choice and there is a great deal to be said for it; certainly it helps the young man to gather material, to come into contact with many kinds of life and many problems, to know intimately many persons whom he might otherwise never meet. On the other hand, the constant excitement of the city room, the necessity of meeting deadlines, the jargon of newspapers, do not make for the best writing or the most usable leisure. Probably more writers support themselves by "pot-boiling" than by any other means. They write for the pulp magazines or the cheap serials; they ghostwrite; they grind out factual articles as impersonally as one grinds coffee; and when the chore is done, when the rent is paid and the grocer satisfied, they supposedly have time and inclination to work on the book which really interests them. This may become big business. At one time Upton Sinclair wrote a complete issue of a magazine each week, and a dime novel each fortnight; he kept three stenographers busy, dictating to one while the others transcribed. What effect this had on his novels may be only conjectured; in general, the pot-boiler's routine, the constant writing-down to an audience, the necessity of writing what one does not believe in a manner one does not admire, the realization that the most of one's writing is false and that one is using an art as an artifice, is not a good discipline for a man who has the ability to produce distinguished work. It is patently less desirable than any of the supplementary vocations the literary graduate school has to offer, of which the chief are teaching, editing, and professional criticism.

Rather too much has been said about the remoteness of teaching from life. The impression has been given that the act of entering the academic profession is a retreat from life, and that the act of teaching is the antithesis of life. Teaching is concerned with theory, living with action; and literature must deal with life: thus the argument goes. Yet there may well be theory behind action;

an unexamined life, Socrates said, is not worth living. Indeed, any intelligent teaching will connect theory with life. The teacher need not be one "who multiplieth words without knowledge," or

> The bookful blockhead, ignorantly read,
> With loads of learned lumber in his head.

A psychologist devising a dependable method of measuring public opinion is not ordinarily thought of as remote from life. An organic chemist striving to synthesize a vitamin is remote from life only in the sense that he may prefer his laboratory to the bridge club. The philosopher—favorite butt of the philistine's jokes—is hardly more remote from life when he synthesizes guides for human conduct than is the drunk practicing one kind of human conduct by lying on the sidewalk. It will be remembered that Wilson, Masaryk, Beneš, Moscicki, Clemenceau, Daladier, Herriot came from the classroom into politics, and that several of them later returned to the university. Robert Frost apparently did not find that his residence and teaching at Amherst, Michigan, and Harvard divorced him from life and drew the red blood from his poetry; nor have the numerous other writer-teachers found it necessary to withdraw from life. They have found a profession which offers unrivalled opportunities of leisure and contemplation. They have enjoyed the opportunity of living in a climate of ideas, and have appeared to enjoy meeting with young minds and fresh sensibilities. As far as I know, they are content with their choice, and I can see no evidence that academic experience has worked to their detriment.

There is less current objection to the careers of editing and professional criticism. Editorship of a magazine is, indeed, a natural progression for the writer-scholar. The *Atlantic Monthly* has had a distinguished list of such editors; among them Lowell, Howells, Aldrich, Page, and Perry. Henry Adams edited the *North American Review*, and Paul Elmer More the *Nation*. Poe, Harte, Gilder, Emerson are names that instantly occur when one tries to remember the writer-editors of the last century. In our own time T. S. Eliot has edited the *Criterion*, Willa Cather and Theodore Dreiser have served terms as editors of national magazines, and Robert Penn Warren and John Crowe Ransom have founded two of America's most distinguished small quarterlies. Archibald MacLeish was an editor of *Fortune* before he became Librarian of Congress. The editor of the *Virginia Quarterly* is a writer-teacher. The first two editors of *The Saturday Review of Literature* (Henry Seidel Canby, Bernard DeVoto) were writer-teachers and authors of scholarly volumes on American authors. An even larger list might be made of writers and writer-teachers who have supported themselves wholly or in part by means of reviews and critical articles. For the serious writer who gives a great deal of thought to the principles of his art and learns to read as an artist while learning to write as an artist, the exercise of professional criticism is easy and congenial.

§ V

Beyond vocational training, and far more important, the university offers the writer something which, carefully defining the word, we might call *experience*. We have already suggested that it is common to scoff at the university as a source of experience, for the word has come to have a physical connotation, and a whole generation of writers has avidly sought the kind of experience to be found in brothels and barrooms, garrets and South Sea islands, hobo jungles, the rods of freight trains, and the wagons of the Okies. To such as these, the university offers several kinds of experience they have been inclined to neglect.

It offers, for one thing, the opportunity of apprenticeship. In the Renaissance young artists gathered in small groups around great men and taught themselves and each other how to paint. For the American writer this gathering together has always been difficult. It has been approximated in certain literary small towns or communities like Concord, but rather late in the lives of the writers concerned. It has been approached by certain admiring groups gathered at city salons or cocktail parties, by expatriate groups in Paris cafés, sometimes by persons gathered around the editor of a little magazine. But on the whole the young writer has found these poor substitutes for what the young painter found in the society of his master and his fellow students. Not until recently has it been realized that the university offers the opportunity to associate intimately with other young writers, and, when a broadening acquaintance seems desirable, the opportunity of acquaintance with keen young men in the other arts, in the humanities and the sciences. It offers the opportunity of trial publication— by reading to a group, by seeing one's play on the stage of the theater (university theater plants are now among the finest in the country), and by printing in the university magazine. Many universities now have magazines of national circulation, such as the *Sewanee Review*, the *Southern Review*, the *Kenyon Review*, and *American Prefaces*, in which the student writer may compete with other young writers throughout the country. But most of all the university offers stimulation: living in the company of young persons who want to write, working in an atmosphere where good poetry, fiction, criticism, are constantly being written and published, coöperating in authorship by discussing and criticizing manuscripts. How well this system of group apprenticeship can work was shown brilliantly by the writers who gathered in the nineteen twenties around John Crowe Ransom at Vanderbilt. The group included Donald Davidson, Allen Tate, Merrill Moore, Laura Riding, Robert Penn Warren, Andrew Lytle, and John Donald Wade, all of whom came to Vanderbilt as students or teachers, all of whom have since produced work of distinction, many of whom have become editors or teachers writing in universities. Not every university can hope to produce so many able poets, fill its magazine with verse of such quality as that which the Vanderbilt writers poured into *The Fugitive*, or expect that its writers will produce a political and cultural credo (such as the Southern agrarianism of *I'll Take My Stand*) in addition to their imaginative work. Indeed, Vanderbilt itself has never had another such flowering. But many universities can reproduce or approximate the conditions under which the Vanderbilt group flourished. I should not be surprised if in the future many of our best writers were to come out of apprentice groups gathered at the universities.

The university is an especially sanative place for the gathering of apprentice writers because of another kind of experience it offers. Long ago Sir Philip Sidney described it neatly: "this purifying of wit, this enriching of memory, enabling of judgment, and enlarging of conceit, which commonly we call learning." The university spreads out before the writer a grand panorama of the mind of the past, an X-ray view of the present. The great minds are there in books, and the great physical discoveries in formulas, models, and demonstrations. The sweep of history may be viewed, and the development of man. The challenging ideas of the world may be considered in terms of theoretical validity (philosophy) and practical application (history). The university offers leisure for this kind of thinking. It offers a mountain-top studio from which the writer may gain some perspective on the hurly-burly outside, and understand it better, and make up his mind. Why this exercise should be referred to scornfully as fleeing from life, I do not know: the quarterback is not regarded as fleeing from football when he looks over the opposing team before calling the next play; the student of music is not called impractical when he extends his studies beyond the opera he is to sing at his debut, nor is the student of law when he comes to the university to learn about law and its place in man's activities. Books may be ordinary or great according to whether their authors are able to look with perspective on the world, and, like the quarterback, see the whole field, not merely the few feet of turf in the immediate vicinity of the feet.

Freud, Marx, Spengler, Nietzsche, Pavlov, Veblen, Pareto—one hears their names a great deal today. Such men, it is said, rule the world. One hears about them, in fact, more than one reads them, and that is the reason for the weird versions of Freudian psychology which appear frequently in our literature. Yet, if these men are worth talking about, they are worth reading—carefully and thoughtfully, and in relation to the great thinkers who have preceded them, to Darwin, for example, and Hegel and Kant, Locke, Hobbes, Bacon, Machiavelli,

Saint Thomas, Aristotle, and Plato. They are worth pondering, and their use for the present and the individual is worth deciding. There is a great deal of literature that is worth pondering, too—not only the literature of America and England today, but the literatures of other languages (*Wer fremde Sprachen nicht kennt, weiss nichts von seiner eigenen!*) and the literatures of other times; there are many live names in the dead Greek and Latin. I am not worried over a prospective author's reading too much in other men's books, I am worried rather over his reading too little. Professor Bush's remarks concerning contemporary American authors carry a sting: "Not many American poets have any close contact with literature and tradition, and their poetry is so much the poorer. If it be said that learning is not part of any imaginative author's craft, literary history says otherwise." [13]

The truth is, we have come to think of the author as an "expresser," and have lost sight of the fact that "man thinking"—in the production of great literature—precedes "man expressing." Our literature is distinguished by facility, force, brilliance, accuracy, but not particularly by wisdom. In general, modern writers have been good "realists," masters of sense-impressions, good recorders. They have been satisfied with the limited horizons of today and the special method of experimental science. "A poem should be motionless in time," said Archibald MacLeish; but they have been content to be timely, rather than timeless. As thinkers they have too often been easy dupes for half-cooked theories and fashionable attitudes. Unaware of the great questions, they have too often wasted their strength on little ones. Faced with the challenge of a naturalistic philosophy, they have floundered around like buffalo in quicksand, reversing themselves, disbelieving the existence of the quicksand, worshipping the quicksand, seeking frantically and blindly for something solid on which to put their feet. They have not been able to speak to men in the ancient connotation of the Roman word for poet, *Vates,* which is to say, seer, prophet; or for men in the sense of W. H. Auden's definition of the poet as the voice of Man. They have not pursued the truth beyond immediacy.

"It is a pleasure to stand upon the shore and to see the ships tost upon the sea," wrote Francis Bacon, "a pleasure to stand in the window of a castle, and to see a Battle, and the adventures thereof below: but no pleasure is comparable to the standing upon the vantage-ground of Truth (an Hill not to be commanded, and where the air is always clear and serene)." The writers of our time have tasted fully of the inferior pleasures Bacon points to, but all too inadequately of the incomparable pleasure. To such as these the university offers the company of associates devoted to the quest of the true, and of its allies, the right and the best; the opportunity to learn what are the chief modern problems in which these central quests may be expected to repeat themselves; to order their thinking, enrich their memory, clarify their judgment, and enlarge their power of comparison so that they may better perceive truth within the modern problems. Will such experience ruin a promising writer? The answer certainly is that it will not ruin a writer worth saving. If a writer is ruined by the university, if he grows into the kind of pedant Milton called "deep versed in books, and shallow in himself," he must have found a discipline quite different from that which we have been describing. In that case it behooves the university to examine what it is teaching.

§ VI

The practical questions remain. How is writing to be taught—insofar as it can be taught? How is the university to function in order best to encourage the growth of poets and poet-scholars and writer-teachers? These are trenchant questions, deserving of more pages than I can give them, more experiments than American universities have made.

But the main outlines of the necessary program are already clear. Let us open the riches of the university to the young writer. Let us be sure that the university takes seriously both the great books of the past and the important books of the present, that the student has leisure and opportunity to read them, think about them, talk about them with older men who have given years to understanding. Let us represent the other arts in the university by examples of their historical development and their present practice. Let us have natural scientists and social students ready to turn their particular kinds of light on the present. Let us have critics and historical scholars working beside the writer, practicing their particular approaches to his art.

Let us not make a great effort to "prime the pump" by offering rich prizes for student writing. All too often such prizes distract the apprentice writer from the main goals of his advanced study, which are to enrich his mind from the university's storehouse, to sharpen his mind on worthy cutting-stones, and to learn to write well. Let us accept the young writer not as a professional in quest of prizes, but as a student in quest of improvement; let us offer him, instead of prizes, the recognition of degrees and the spur of publication. Let us try to make the writer a part of the university, rather than a separate entity; let us encourage him to partake of disciplines other than his own; but let us honor *his* discipline, and not look askance at the novel or book of poems (if publishable in quality) which he submits as a thesis or dissertation.

And let us not create an elaborate system of courses in imaginative writing, but rather keep the mechanism as simple as possible. The "teaching" of writing, as has already been suggested, is essentially a relationship of apprentice and master. The most important requirement is that the "master" be a wise man who has been or is a practicing artist and has learned to read with an artist's eyes. The master need not be a famous writer; sometimes it is better if he is not, for then he may have more geniality and patience for his apprentices, more sympathy for modes other than the one he himself practices. The student should have the counsel of the master and, when needed, the stimulation of a group of other young writers. If the student writes plays, he will need a theater, and counsel on technical problems. He will be stimulated by a magazine near at hand, in which he may aspire to publish and in the editing of which he may be able to take some part. But this is peripheral; the essentials are the master, the apprentice, the group, and around them the intellectual wealth of the university.

The university which treats writing thus may expect to see many related problems solve themselves. A greater number of its students will almost surely be interested in literature, a smaller number in the history of problems related to literature, than in the typical university today. Some of its research students will find time to take courses in fiction or poetry or critical writing because they "want to see literature from the inside, once." Con-

versely, some of the best students of writing will register
for classes in philosophy to discuss what Plato had to
say about communism and dictatorship and justice, or
for seminars in *Hamlet* to see "what really happens
there." The scholar, critic, and artist will be encouraged
to work side by side, each learning from, each teaching
the other. The fine arts—including literature—will be
stimulated to study each other to mutual advantage. Advanced students will produce poems, plays, stories, novels, some of them very good. The students who are grad-
uated from the university, whether or not they have published good writing, will have had a chance to see much
in literature, as well as learn much *about* it. And the
university may confidently expect that a large number of
its teachers and scholars, present and prospective, will
set as their goal that healthy condition of scholarship
which in an older period could produce a man like
Lowell—linguistic scholar, literary historian, critic, and
writer.

§ VII

Harvard meant a good deal to American literature one
hundred years ago; now it means about as much as the
New York subway. And I have heard it said regretfully
in England that Oxford and Cambridge, with their long
tradition of University poets—Spenser, Donne, Herrick,
Herbert, Milton, Dryden, Gray, Wordsworth, Coleridge,
Byron, Tennyson, Hopkins—have likewise fallen greatly
in their importance to current literature. The universities
were the better for having had in their midst the men
just mentioned. The writers themselves felt no incom-
patibility between the idea of a learned writer and the

idea of a writer who can speak vigorously of and to his own times. They did not find that the university stunted their literary growth, drew the teeth from their satire, flattened their muscles, emasculated their emotions, taught them to graft on "literary graces," and led them away from "life." Rather they were strengthened for the task ahead. Of the academic discipline they underwent they were inclined to say as William James said of the teaching of philosophy in his university, that "by its poetry it appeals to literary minds; by its logic it stiffens them up and remedies their softness." [14] And as the universities and the poets gained, literature gained.

The worst we might expect from a reunion of writer and scholar within the university would be a continuance of the mutual distrust which now estranges them, in which case the artist would soon slip away from the university and the experiment would be judged a failure. But there is every reason to expect that the reunion, intelligently accomplished, will result in a richer study of art in the universities, and in literature which has illuminated sense-recording with the lamp of a wise and liberal philosophy.

For if the discipline of imaginative writing within the university can be conceived as having a supreme goal, it is to encourage the growth of philosopher-poets who unite, in the highest terms, the attributes of man thinking and man expressing. Such a poet was Dante; such a one was Sophocles; such were Homer and Milton and Goethe and those others of the great writers who still speak with flaming tongues to men. The universities do not know how to make a Dante, nor how to make a wise man or a great poet, nor how to put the two in the same body. Indeed, they believe that wisdom and poetry are achieved, not made. But they can offer freely the conditions under which wisdom and the art of poetry may be achieved. They can put it within the student's power to reunite philosophy and art. They cannot expect their young writer to be a Dante, but they can hold before him the standard of Dante. And they can go a long way toward destroying the false popular contradiction between literature and life, learning and living, even to the point when we may hope to say of our literature, as Sidney of the poetry he defended, that it is real in the deepest sense, that it is not "an art of lies, but of true doctrine; not of effeminateness, but of notable stirring of courage; not of abusing men's wits, but of strengthening man's wit."

NOTES

ONE: THE STUDY OF LETTERS

1. Literary scholars have, of course, a perfect right to do this, and they are capable, on occasion, of dealing with outside fields more largely or more penetratingly than professional scholars in those fields. The point in the text is simply that the inclination of scholars to move out of rather than more deeply into their own subject is a symptom of a dubious state of affairs in their own subject.

2. Abraham Flexner, *Universities: American, English, German,* 1930, *passim.*—In Great Britain, at the beginning of the present century, literary research had already borrowed from science a positivistic turn. Interpreting actual usage, John Burnet said in 1904: "It is 'research' to study the manuscripts of an author's text, but it is not 'research' to interpret his meaning or to show the significance of the form in which he clothes it. The aesthetic interpretation of a tragedy or the philosophic interpretation of a Platonic dialogue is not 'research'; the investigation of scolia and lexica is. . . . In the minds of its loudest advocates, everything that is merely external and subsidiary is a fit object for 'research,' while the study of the things themselves is the province of the *littérateur* and the dilettante. . . .

"Scholarship in the old-fashioned sense is a thing of slow growth; it implies ripe knowledge and a trained judgment. 'Research,' on the other hand, is certainly laborious; but, in its lower forms, it requires little knowledge and makes few calls upon the higher powers of the mind" (*Essays and Addresses,* 1929, 35).

In 1936, after quoting the passage above, E. R. Dodds in his inaugural lecture as Regius Professor of Greek remarked: "I confess that when I have myself engaged in technical research I have done so partly as a release from the painfulness of thinking."

In the United States today, *research,* in the best sense, implies the use of scientific methods of investigation, regardless of the subject of study, directed to a specific end whose value is clearly conceived. More commonly—especially when accented on the first syllable—the word implies diligent study, more or less scientific in method, directed to an end whose value may or may not be well understood. In its lowest sense the word means merely the systematic presentation of information already easily accessible, as in the "research paper" written by college freshmen.

Thus we have all but lost what appears to be the basic meaning of *research,* namely, any careful inquiry that moves from the known to the unknown by means of techniques suited to the subject. From this definition it follows, for instance, that the literary critic engaged in critical inquiry is engaged in research. It may be that an effort should be made, eventually, to bring this basic meaning into general currency. At present, however, we must recognize that the scientific connotation of the word *research*, as of the word *investigation* as well, will remain fixed for some time to come. In this situation the literary scholar will do well to seek other terms for his labors, such as *inquiry*, which is neutral, and *scholarship*, which is humanistic.

3. ὅταν οὖν ὑπ' ἀνδρὸς ἔμφρονος καὶ ἐμπείρου λόγων . . . (Longinus, *De Sublimitate*, ed. A. O. Prickard, 1906, Sec. VII.) The translation in the text is that of W. Rhys Roberts. Prickard translates: "a man of sense and literary experience."—The scholar is not the same as the learned man or *erudit*, for, as Donaldson put it, "not all learned men are accomplished scholars, though any accomplished scholar may, if he chooses to devote the time to the necessary studies, become a learned man" (*Classical Scholarship and Classical Learning*, 1856, p. 149).

4. There is a sketch of Renaissance scholarship with special reference to Erasmus in Norman Foerster's *Toward Standards*, 1930, ch. I.

5. The beginnings, however, were mainly English. See the book by René Wellek on *The Rise of English Literary History*, 1941.

6. Lecturing in Berlin on the *Nibelungenlied*, A. W. Schlegel declared: "Let no one believe that such poems can be made out of nothing. There must be great deeds, before there can be great poems. Poetry and history are intimately connected, especially epic poetry is often only another and truer reflex of events than prose documents. And thus the present age may look here into the mirror of an heroic past, if, by looking, it is not made to feel too painfully its own nothingness." Since the romantic revolt, many German scholars have tended greatly to exaggerate the literary worth of the *Nibelungenlied* for sentimental reasons, as many English and American scholars have done in the case of *Beowulf*. In an address given in 1923, J. W. Mackail reported the belief of enthusiasts for English studies that "*Beowulf* is more important, both for linguistic and for literary study, than *Paradise Lost*, and (as I have heard it boldly put) that English, as a subject of serious study, came to an end in the fourteenth century" (*Classical Studies*, 1925, p. 81). Andreas Heusler (*Die altgermanische Dichtung*, 1926) represents a more critical approach.

7. R. W. Livingstone, *Greek Ideals and Modern Life*, 1935, p. 25. "The eighteenth century may have done justice to Greek poetry. The nineteenth was to realize that Greece had also created an ideal of life which remains as a permanent light of humanity" (pp. 26–27).

8. The effort to make literary scholarship scientific had the support of a parallel effort in other branches of the humanities, notably in the "sister field" of history. "Most of the scholarly history written in the United States from 1875 to the present," says W. Stull Holt, "has

been conceived in terms of objective facts. The value put on the facts as an end in themselves; the emphasis given to the establishment of facts; the fear of making any statements without a supporting document; the belief, sometimes avowed, that complete objectivity could be attained merely by honest effort; the denial of any philosophy and theory of history in the prepossession that historians should, or could, be without prepossessions—all testify to the same conclusion" ("The Idea of Scientific History in America," *Journal of the History of Ideas*, I [1940], 361).

9. In Germany, the nineteenth-century pattern had gone out of favor in the first decade of the twentieth century. After the positivistic school represented by Scherer came the *geisteswissenschaftliche* school associated especially with Dilthey; *Das Erlebnis und die Dichtung*, 1906, marks the change of approach. This reversal of emphasis from the analytical to the synthetical was not repeated in American scholarship.—Certain attempts at renewal of vitality in other European countries are indicated by René Wellek in chapter III.

10. William A. Nitze, as president in 1929, had also pointed this out, declaring: "Henceforth our object is research," and in 1940 he called upon the Association to preserve civilization by upholding "scientific research."

Early in the 1920's it had even been proposed that the Modern Language Association hold its meetings with the American Association for the Advancement of Science.

11. The General Topics in 1939 and 1940 included Relations of Literature and Science, Relations of Literature and Society, Poetic Form and General Aesthetics, and Critical Study of Romanticism.

12. It should be noted that these qualities are not timeless "in the sense that they have always been [or, he might have added, "should always have been"] apprehended and judged in the same way by different readers." As Professor Crane has kindly further explained in a letter, his conception of timeless qualities means that "the values we are interested in as critics are values expressed by the works themselves as these are understood by the aid of appropriate universal principles which, if ever true, continue to be true irrespective of the date of their enunciation; it does not mean that the objects of criticism can ever be taken as constants in the nature of things independently of the critic's determination of the particular kind of principles he wishes to use in talking about them."

13. Professor Crane conceives that a metaphysics is needed to provide criteria of the relevance of the principles that may be discussed, but that criticism will have its own explicit content of definitions and principles and in this respect will be quite distinct from metaphysics.

14. However, Horace's view, which became proverbial, was not religious but ethical and/or aesthetic—to instruct or delight or both. The Horatian formula persists to this day, e.g., in Robert Frost, who

says that a poem "begins in delight and ends in wisdom," and Paul Engle, who describes its function as "a wise excitement or an intense wisdom."

15. This is discussed at length in Norman Foerster's *The American State University*, 1937, and *The Future of the Liberal College*, 1938.

16. The suggestion may be hazarded that the ideal college preparation of the prospective doctoral candidate in English consists of a liberal education with Latin or Greek as the major subject, several years of French or German, several year courses in English, and studies in history, philosophy, fine arts, and natural science. This is recommended despite the unsatisfactory manner in which the classics are taught in many colleges.

17. Modern language candidates should, at the least, present evidence of a knowledge of Latin (Vergil, Horace) or Greek (Homer) acquired in the years of graduate study if not earlier. Secondary school and college training in the Classics was a normal part of the equipment of modern language scholars when the German system was adopted in this country. Upon this basis it was possible to erect a large requirement in the other early languages out of which the modern vernaculars developed. Today the latter requirement is in process of reduction, while the Classical background has virtually disappeared. There would seem to be room, as well as necessity, for a substantial requirement in Classics. If a choice must be made between the two Classical languages, one may venture to predict that, despite the historical importance of Latin, we shall eventually turn to Greek as providing the finest literary culture available for the training of scholars.

18. Under imaginative literature may be included also a range of strongly imaginative works, such as *Religio Medici, The French Revolution, Culture and Anarchy,* Emerson's *Essays,* which at the same time have close relations to utilitarian writing and therefore require a somewhat different kind of interpretation and evaluation.

19. The term "natural sense" appears, e.g., in Addison (*Tatler,* No. 165, April 29, 1710). The young lady of this charming paper "had that natural sense which makes her a better judge than a thousand critics" like the pedantic Sir Timothy Tittle.—Today, many a professor of literature is aware, or should be, that his own wife is more gifted in natural literary aptitude than he is. However, as a distinguished scholar has realistically observed, "For the traditional methods of studying literature taste is desirable but not essential; there are men of great reputation who possess little of it."

20. Like any other admirable method, the *explication de textes* is capable of subversion. In the hands of an instructor or student who is less imaginative than learned, it may offer a new area for the depredations of the natural pedant. Used sensitively, every part of the method is valuable, including practice in intelligent oral reading.

21. One example: Grant Showerman used to say that Classical students do not know the *Iliad,* though they know all about research upon it.

22. *"Der Kritiker muss nach dem Lorbeer geweint haben!"*

23. *The Higher Study of English,* 1906, p. 23.

24. With undue severity yet not without reason, President H. D. Gideonse speaks of the unstimulating atmosphere, even in our great centers of scholarship, "generated by the mechanization of the process of thought itself. Men and women with great human potentialities have lapsed into that state of resentful coma known as research, while a battle-front bleakness hangs over the intellectual landscape" (Inaugural Address, *Bulletin of the Association of American Colleges,* December, 1939, p. 495).

25. "English in Modern Education," *School and Society,* April 21, 1917, p. 459.

26. Abraham Flexner, *op. cit.,* pp. 20–21.

TWO: LANGUAGE

1. Thurman W. Arnold, *The Symbols of Government,* 1935, and *The Folklore of Capitalism,* 1937.

2. P. W. Bridgman, *The Logic of Modern Physics,* 1927.

3. C. K. Ogden and I. A. Richards, *The Meaning of Meaning,* 1923; fourth edition, 1936.

4. Alfred Korzybski, *Science and Sanity,* 1933.

5. Stuart Chase, *The Tyranny of Words,* 1938.

6. Leonard Bloomfield, *Language,* 1933, a revision of his *Introduction to the Study of Language,* 1914; Edgar H. Sturtevant, *Linguistic Change,* 1917. To these should now be added Louis H. Gray, *Foundations of Language,* 1939.

7. Applied linguistics enters the field of freshman English in S. I. Hayakawa's *Language in Action,* 1939. According to the Preface, it is designed "to provide an orientation towards language based upon modern linguistic, scientific, and literary theory." This experimental textbook is chiefly an adaptation of Korzybski—the sounder and more intelligible part of his work—and Ogden and Richards, though others, including the linguists Sapir and Bloomfield, are mentioned in the bibliographical note. Tentative as the author declares it to be, it is in the main a good book, making the best use of its originals and avoiding most of their aberrations. The variation of word-meaning according to context is admirably driven home. But is it not a bit remarkable that all the illustrations are drawn from strictly contemporary English? To be sure, these are essential; the student is primarily concerned with the language as he must use it. But cannot the fact of variation in meaning be equally well enforced by examples of historical change? Why not study a few words that have undergone semantic change since Shakespeare or Chaucer? Would not this call the student's attention to a new aspect of the same subject and be concretely useful in his study of literature as well?

8. Leonard Bloomfield, *Language,* 1933, p. 79.

9. Hans Kurath, and others, *Linguistic Atlas of New England,* 1939, and *Handbook of the Linguistic Geography of New England,* 1939.

10. Edward Prokosch, *A Comparative Germanic Grammar,* 1939, pp. 47–55.

11. W. F. Twaddell, *On Defining the Phoneme*, No. 16, Language Monographs Published by the Linguistic Society of America, 1935. He proposes to use the term as "an abstractional fiction," "a unit defined for a convenient description of phonological relations." Thus, p. 55, "There are as many different phonemes in a language as there are consecutive relations of significant phonetic differentiation (plus one) in each articulatory range." The phonological system of a language would be the sum of all the phonological relations obtaining in it.

12. George L. Trager, in a review of N. Van Wijk's *Phonologie*, *Language*, 16 (1940), 247–50. Trager refers to his own "La Systématique des Phonèmes du Polonais," *Acta Linguistica*, I, No. 3 (1939), for an example of "correct phonemic analysis and tabulation."

13. Ferdinand de Saussure, *Cours de linguistique générale*, 1916, p. 205.

14. Leonard Bloomfield, *Language*, 1933, p. 351.

15. Otto Jespersen, *Linguistica*, 1933, p. 225.

16. *Ibid.*, pp. 205–06.

17. Edward Prokosch, *A Comparative Germanic Grammar*, pp. 56–57.

18. Edgar H. Sturtevant, in a review of H. L. Koppelmann's *Ursachen des Lautwandels*, *Language*, 16 (1940), 236.

19. George O. Curme, *Syntax* (Volume III of *A Grammar of the English Language* by Hans Kurath and George O. Curme), 1931, Preface.

20. Sterling A Leonard, *Current English Usage*, 1932; and Albert H. Marckwardt and Fred G. Walcott, *Facts about Current English Usage*, 1938. Both are Publications of the National Council of Teachers of English.

21. Charles Carpenter Fries, *The Inflections and Syntax of Present-Day American English*, 1939; and a more complete presentation of the same material in his *American English Grammar*, 1940. Both are under the auspices of the National Council of Teachers of English. The last chapter of the *Grammar* is entitled "Some Inferences from this Study for a Workable Program in English Language for the Schools."

22. A Walde, *Etymologisches Wörterbuch der Indo-germanischen Sprachen*, edited by J. Pokorny, 1930–32.

23. H. Hirt, *Die Indogermanen*, 1905. For recent studies, see the works cited in Edward Prokosch, *A Comparative Germanic Grammar*, 1939, pp. 299–300.

24. A Meillet, *Esquisse d'une histoire de la langue latine*, 1928, especially pp. 165 ff.

25. Karl Vossler, *Frankreichs Kultur im Spiegel seiner Sprachentwicklung,* edition of 1921.

26. Gustaf Stern, *Meaning and Change of Meaning, with special reference to the English language,* 1932. His view of the functions of speech is summarized on pp. 20–21.

27. Edgar H. Sturtevant, *A Comparative Grammar of the Hittite Language,* 1933, and various articles in the periodical *Language* since 1933.

28. Eric Partridge, *A Dictionary of Slang and Unconventional English,* 1937, is the standard work for English. For a survey of the immense literature of the subject in the Romance languages, see Iorgu Jordan, *An Introduction to Romance Linguistics,* revised and translated by John Orr, 1937, pp. 355–74.

29. J. Gilliéron, *Généalogie des mots qui designent l'abeille* (*Bibliothèque de l'Ecole des hautes études; Sciences historiques et philologiques,* 225), 1918; and his *Pathologie et thérapeutique verbales* (*Collection linguistique publiée par la Société de linguistique de Paris,* 11), 1921.

30. Zellig S. Harris in a review of Louis H. Gray's *Foundations of Language, Language,* 16 (1940), 221.

31. George O. Curme, *Syntax,* 1931, and *Parts of Speech and Accidence,* 1935 (Volumes III and II, respectively, of *A Grammar of the English Language* by Hans Kurath and George O. Curme); Otto Jespersen, *Linguistica,* 1933, pp. 304–45 and *Essentials of English Grammar,* 1933.

32. Edward Sapir, *Language,* 1921, p. 7.

33. W. F. Twaddell, *On Defining the Phoneme,* No. 16, Language Monographs Published by the Linguistic Society of America, 1935, p. 9, ftn. 8.

34. Leonard Bloomfield, *Linguistic Aspects of Science,* Vol. I, No. 4, *International Encyclopedia of Unified Science,* 1940, p. 13.

35. *Ibid.,* pp. 8–9.

36. Zellig S. Harris in a review of Louis H. Gray's *Foundations of Language, Language,* 16 (1940), p. 227.

37. *Ibid.,* p. 228.

38. *Ibid.,* p. 228.

39. *Ibid.,* p. 228.

40. *Ibid.,* p. 227.

41. Karl Vossler, *Frankreichs Kultur im Spiegel Seiner Sprachentwicklung,* edition of 1921, p. 37.

42. *Ibid.,* p. 191. For Vossler's views in general see, e.g., his *Positivismus und Idealismus in der Sprachwissenschaft,* 1904, and *Geist*

und Kultur in der Sprache, 1925 (translated into English by O. Oeser as *The Spirit of Language in Civilization,* 1932).

43. E.g., *Aufsätze zur romanischen Syntax und Stilistik,* 1918; *Stilstudien,* 1928.

44. For a general presentation of the views of Charles Bally, see the essays collected in his *Le langage et la vie,* edition of 1935. His principal work in stylistics is the *Traité de stylistique française,* 1921. See also his *Linguistique générale et linguistique française,* 1932.

Considerable interest has been aroused in France by the elaborate psychological study of the French language in Jacques Damourette and Edouard Pichon, *Des mots à la pensée: Essai de grammaire de la langue française,* 1911—.

45. I. A. Richards, *Practical Criticism,* 1920, *The Philosophy of Rhetoric,* 1936, *Interpretation in Teaching* [1940]; R. P. Blackmur, *The Double Agent,* 1935, *The Expense of Greatness,* 1940; T. S. Eliot, *Selected Essays,* 1932; William Empson, *Seven Types of Ambiguity,* 1930.

THREE: LITERARY HISTORY

1. W. P. Ker, *Thomas Warton*, 1910, p. 6; also in his *Essays*, 1922, I, 100.

2. *The Book of Margery Kempe*, 1936. Medwall's play was discovered in 1919. A facsimile edition was edited by S. De Ricci (1920) and there is a critical edition by F. S. Boas and A. W. Reed (1926).

3. Leslie Hotson, *The Death of Christopher Marlowe*, 1925. *Shakespeare vs. Shallow*, 1931. The many discoveries concerning James Boswell and his circle should be mentioned.

4. The methods of the "bibliographical" approach are discussed in the following publications: Dover Wilson's "textual introduction" to his (and Sir A. Quiller-Couch's) edition of the *Tempest* (1921); Percy Simpson, "The Bibliographical Study of Shakespeare" in *Oxford Bibliographical Society Publications* (Vol. I. 1923); R. B. McKerrow's *An Introduction to Bibliography* (1927) and his *Prolegomena for the Oxford Shakespeare: A Study in Editorial Method* (1939).

5. W. W. Greg, "Hamlet's Hallucination" in *Modern Language Review* XII (1917), pp. 393–421. "Re-enter Ghost: A Reply to Mr. J. D. Wilson," *Ibid.*, XIV (1919), pp. 353–369, and "What Happens in Hamlet?" *Ibid.*, XXXI (1936), pp. 145–54.

6. *The Place of English Literature in the Modern University*, 1913, reprinted in *Elizabethan and Other Essays*, 1929, p. 7.

7. A short description of the method is in Robert Vigneron's *Explication de Textes, and its Adaptation to the Teaching of Modern Languages*, 1928.

8. *Wechselseitige Erhellung der Künste* (Berlin), 1917. *Gehalt und Gestalt im Kunstwerk des Dichters* (Berlin), 1925. *Das Wortkunstwerk* (Leipzig), 1926.

9. An account of the Russian movement (with bibliography) by Nina Gourfinkel can be found in *Le Monde Slave*, VI (1929), p. 234 ("Les Nouvelles Méthodes d' histoire littéraire en Russie"). Some account of the Prague "structuralism" in my paper "The Theory of Literary History" in *Travaux du Cercle Linguistique de Prague*, VI (1936), p. 173.

10. Besides the writings of I. A. Richards, see W. Empson, *Seven Types of Ambiguity*, 1930, and Geoffrey Tillotson, *On the Poetry of Pope*, 1938.

11. I am thinking of the writings of Cleanth Brooks, J. C. Ransom, Allen Tate, R. P. Warren, Yvor Winters. With some modifications, the same approach can be found in R. P. Blackmur and Kenneth Burke. Chard Powers Smith, *Pattern and Variation in Poetry* (1932) is an independent attempt to find one principle for the analysis of poetry.

12. J. Vachek's article "What is Phonology?" in *English Studies,* XV (1933), p. 89, gives further bibliography. The most important discussion by an American is W. F. Twaddell's *On Defining the Phoneme,* 1935.

13. L. C. Knights, *How many Children had Lady Macbeth?* (1933) states the case against the confusion of drama and life well. The divergent writings of George Wilson Knight, L. L. Schücking, and E. E. Stoll all use the approach through dramatic technique rather than psychology.

14. E.g., Joseph Warren Beach, *The Twentieth Century Novel: Studies in Technique,* 1932, Percy Lubbock, *The Art of Fiction,* 1921, and E. M. Forster, *Aspects of the Novel,* 1927, are outstanding. In Russia, Viktor Shklovskij's *Teorija Prozy* (Moscow), 1925, is a most remarkable application of the formal approach to narrative art.

15. F. W. Bateson, in answer to F. R. Leavis's criticism of his book *English Poetry and the English Language* in *Scrutiny,* IV (1935), p. 181.

16. F. R. Leavis's reply, *ibid.,* p. 187.

17. Especially Wilhelm Dilthey, *Das Erlebnis und die Dichtung* (Leipzig), 1907, and Friedrich Gundolf, *Goethe* (Berlin), 1916.

18. E. M. Tillyard, *Milton,* 1930, p. 237.

19. See the interesting discussion between Tillyard and C. S. Lewis in *The Personal Heresy: A Controversy,* 1934, p. 7.

20. *Principles of Literary Criticism,* London, 1925, p. 125. Cf. *ibid.,* p. 248.

21. F. W. Bateson, *English Poetry and the English Language,* Oxford, 1934, p. 7.

22. E. Greenlaw, *The Province of Literary History,* 1931, p. 35.

23. A. O. Lovejoy, *The Great Chain of Being,* 1936, p. iv.

24. E.g., A. O. Lovejoy, *The Great Chain of Being,* 1936; Étienne Henri Gilson, *Les Idées et les lettres* (Paris), 1932; Ernst Cassirer, *Idee und Gestalt* (Berlin), 1921; *Freiheit und Form* (Berlin), 1916. The writings of Dilthey collected in *Gesammelte Schriften,* 12 vols. (Leipzig), 1923–36.

25. Ernst Kohn-Bramstedt, *Aristocracy and the Middle Classes in Germany* (1937), p. 12.

26. Cf. the criticism by R. S. Crane in *Philological Quarterly,* XIV (1935), p. 152.

27. *The History of English Poetry*, Vol. I, 1774, p. ii.

28. Preface to *English Writers*, 1864.

29. *English Literature and Society in the Eighteenth Century*, 1904, pp. 14 and 22.

30. *A History of English Poetry*, 1895, Vol. I, p. xv.

31. *A Short History of Modern English Literature*, 1897, Preface.

32. See letter to F. C. Roe, March 19, 1924, quoted by Evan Charteris, *The Life and Letters of Sir Edmund Gosse*, 1931, p. 477.

33. See the quotations in Oliver Elton's lecture on Saintsbury before the British Academy, *Proceedings*, Vol. XIX (1933).

34. *A Survey of English Literature, 1780–1830*, 1912, Vol. I, p. vii.

35. See *L' Évolution psychologique de la littérature en Angleterre* (Paris), 1920, and the second half of E. Legouis and L. Cazamian, *Histoire de la littérature anglaise* (Paris), 1924.

36. A fuller discussion of this question is in Roman Ingarden's *Das literarische Kunstwerk* (Halle), 1931, and in my "Theory of Literary History" in *Travaux du Cercle Linguistique de Prague*, VI (1936), p. 173.

37. *Thomas Warton*, 1910, in *Essays*, 1922, I, 100.

38. "Tradition and Individual Talent," an essay in *The Sacred Wood*, 1920, p. 42.

39. Cf. the brilliant, though sometimes over-ingenious analyses in William Empson's *Seven Types of Ambiguity*, 1930.

40. See note 35.

41. Cf. especially *L' Évolution des genres dans l'historie de la littérature* (Paris), 1890; John Addington Symonds, *Shakspere's Predecessors in the English Drama*, 1884, and "On the Application of Evolutionary Principles to Art and Literature" in *Essays Speculative and Suggestive*, 1890, Vol. I, pp. 42–84.

42. Aleksandr Veselovskij, *Tri glavy iz istoricheskoy poetiki* (St. Petersburg), 1890.

43. (Munich), 1925. Another good history of a genre is Karl Viëtor's *Geschichte der deutschen Ode* (Munich), 1923.

44. See especially C. S. Lewis, *The Allegory of Love*, 1936 and Howard Baker, *Induction to Tragedy*, 1939.

45. Thus, attempts at "defining" periods are doomed to failure. A fuller discussion is given in my paper "Periods and Movements in Literary History" in *The English Institute Annual, 1940*, 1941, pp. 73–93.

46. Jan Máchal, *Slovanské Literatury* (Prague), 1922–29, in Czech. L. Olschki, *Die Romanischen Literaturen des Mittelalters* (Berlin), 1928.

47. Gerard O'Leary's *English Literary History and Bibliography* (London, 1928), is a small unpretentious sketch of English literary historiography. My study of *The Rise of English Literary History*, 1941, covers the period up to the end of the eighteenth century. Sigmund von Lempicki's *Geschichte der deutschen Literaturwissenschaft* (Göttingen), 1920, is a parallel history up to Herder. Sketches of the history of German literary history in the nineteenth century can be found in Erich Rothacker's *Einleitung in die Geisteswissenschaften* (Tübingen), 1920, and in Emil Ermatinger's *Philosophie der Literaturwissenschaft* (Berlin), 1930. The volume, edited by Ermatinger, contains an article "Die philosophisch-weltanschauliche Entwicklung der literaturhistorischen Methoden" by Franz Schultz.

FOUR: LITERARY CRITICISM

1. Cf. Ronald Crane's "History versus Criticism in the University Study of Literature," *English Journal* (College Edition), XXIV (1935), 663 ff.; John Crowe Ransom's "Criticism, Inc.," *The World's Body*, 1938; and the symposia jointly entitled "Literature and the Professors": *Kenyon Review*, II (1940), 403 ff. and *Southern Review*, VI (1940), 225 ff.

2. A generic phrase to stand for critical studies of particular books and authors—essays like Kenneth Burke's "Mann and Gide," books like Albert Thibaudet's *La Poésie de Mallarmé*, 1926—is a convenience; for this purpose I have appropriated the title of I. A. Richards' *Practical Criticism*, 1929, a book already a classic of literary pedagogy; but I use the phrase in a sense different from that of Mr. Richards.

3. In the *Lives of the English Poets*, Johnson offers first a biographical sketch, including the "natural history" of the poet's compositions (their creative genesis and their public reception), together with some ideological judgment upon them; then, separately, he provides a reasoned aesthetic criticism of the poetry, considering each major work in turn and concluding with a general estimate of its value.

4. Treatment of "the poem as an object in itself" is furnished by Cleanth Brooks, Jr., and R. P. Warren, in their *Understanding Poetry* (1938), an anthology interspersed with brilliant little essays in practical criticism.

5. Cf. David Daiches, *The Novel and the Modern World*, 1939, p. 213.

6. Cf. Aristotle, *Poetics*, I. Subsequent quotations are from the recent translation by Allan H. Gilbert, included in his *Literary Criticism: Plato to Aristotle*, 1940.

7. John Steinbeck, having published a sociological report on migratory workers, then composed *The Grapes of Wrath*.

8. *Of Education; Areopagitica.*

9. Cf. Yvor Winters, *Primitivism and Decadence*, 1937, "The Morality of Poetry," especially pp. 3–4. The moral attitude "is defined only by the entire poem, not by the logical content alone; it is a matter not only of logical content but of feeling as well."

10. Croce, *The Essence of Aesthetic*, 1921, pp. 53–7; and cf. the spirited attack on the literary study of "constants" in Martin Schütze's *Academic Illusions*, 1933, especially pp. 253 ff.

11. *The Essence of Aesthetic*, pp. 35–44.

12. Ransom, *The World's Body*, pp. 346–7.

13. A Polish critic, Kridl, writes: "La méthode littéraire à élaborer aurait pour point de départ le fait que l'œuvre littéraire est un organisme, un ensemble, une unité dont on ne peut pas séparer certains éléments, tels que par exemple (le fond et la forme) et les traiter à part. Chaque élément doit être étudié dans sa *fonction littéraire*. Ainsi ce qu'on appelle, par exemple, (l'idéologie) de l'œuvre n'existe pas en dehors d'elle (ou existe en forme d'abstraction), y remplit une fonction littéraire particulière comme tout autre élément. Il la faut donc étudier dans cette fonction. *Helicon*, II (1940), 215.

14. Cf. the preface to Ernst Kohn-Bramstedt's *Aristocracy and the Middle Classes in Germany*, 1937.

15. Jacques Maritain, *Art et Scholastique*, 1927, and Mortimer J. Adler, *Art and Prudence*, 1937.

16. T. S. Eliot, *Essays Ancient and Modern*, 1936, p. 93. The passage quoted comes from the essay "Religion and Literature."

17. Cleanth Brooks, *Modern Poetry and the Tradition*, 1939; R. P. Blackmur, *The Double Agent*, 1935; Ralph Fox, *The Novel and the People*, 1937; Philip Henderson, *The Novel Today*, 1936; L. C. Knights, *Drama and Society in the Age of Jonson*, 1937. An able example of ideological criticism applied to a single writer is T. A. Jackson's *Charles Dickens: The Progress of a Radical*, 1938.

18. Cf. Leon Trotsky's attack on the formalist school of Russian critics, in his brilliant *Literature and Revolution*, 1925, especially p. 169.

19. Charles Mauron, *Aesthetics and Psychology*, 1935, p. 31.

20. This thesis is best developed in the writings of Kenneth Burke: *Counter-Statement*, 1931, *Permanence and Change*, 1935, and *Attitudes toward History*, 1937.

21. Max Eastman, in *The Literary Mind*, 1931, and *Art and the Life of Action*, 1934, is perhaps the best example. Politically a socialist, as an aesthetician he follows Kant, Schopenhauer, and Croce in regarding the arts as offering forms for contemplation, not incitations to action; and as a critic he wishes poetry to clear itself of ideological pretensions. The "value proper to all art," Eastman writes, "is the universal value of an increased consciousness."

22. I quote Longinus in the new translation by Allan H. Gilbert (*Literary Criticism: Plato to Dryden*, pp. 152–3); cf. the version by Rhys Roberts, *Longinus on the Sublime*, 1907, pp. 55–7.

23. Eliot, *The Use of Poetry and the Use of Criticism,* 1933, p. 153.

24. Eliot's analysis ought not to be understood to imply any *either-or:* the fully competent auditor will comprehend *Lear* at all its levels; the meaning "which reveals itself gradually" is compounded of them all.

25. Gilbert, *op. cit.,* p. 153.

26. Cf. the statements of Sir Joshua Reynolds for neoclassical theory at its best. "Instead of copying the touches of those great masters, copy only their conceptions," writes Reynolds (*Discourses* [ed. Burnet, 1842], p. 25). "Instead of treading in their footsteps, endeavor only to keep the same road. Labor to invent on their general principles. Possess yourself with their spirit."

27. Thus Pope advises the critic:
"Be Homer's works your study and delight . . .
 Thence form your judgment, thence your maxims bring . . ."

28. Cf. Ralph Barton Perry, *General Theory of Value,* 1926, p. 648, and George Boas, *A Primer for Critics,* 1937, pp. 62, 137.

29. For a "reputation" study of a painting, cf. Boas, "The Mona Lisa in the History of Taste," *Journal of the History of Ideas,* I (1940), 207–24.

30. Katherine Gilbert and Helmut Kuhn, *A History of Esthetics,* 1939, p. 529.

31. When one reaches poetry, however, the case is complicated by the complex nature of literature, the least "pure" of the arts, as music (in such non-referential forms as the fugue and the sonata) is the most "pure." When poetry undertakes to be "pure," it is likely to fall to imitation of painting's purity or music's, forsaking the special nature of poetry.

32. D. W. Prall, *Aesthetic Judgment,* p. 324.

33. *Poetics,* Chapter XXVI (Gilbert, *op. cit.,* p. 114); Poe, "The Poetic Principle," "The Philosophy of Composition," and the review of Hawthorne's *Twice-Told Tales.*

34. One "should not seek every pleasure from tragedy, but only that proper to it" (*Poetics,* Chapter XIV). It is "necessary that poems produce not any pleasure they happen to . . . [Tragedy] is superior to the epic because it attains its end better" (*Ibid.,* Chapter XXVI). Aristotle discusses the pleasures of brevity and length in considering the relative worth of the tragedy and the epic. The epic has the advantage of "magnificence of effect, variety for the hearer, and the weaving of dissimilar episodes into the action . . ." (*Ibid.,* Chapter XXIV).

35. To take traditional examples: Virgil and Milton, writers of the epic, had earlier composed successful poems in the minor genres; and *Paradise Lost* contains within itself autobiographical equivalents to

the lyric (the openings of Books III and VII) and the equivalent of a tragedy (Book IX). Shakespeare wrote sonnets as well as comedies and tragedies; and his tragedies include description, epigrams, satire, and lyrics.

36. A systematic and not purely historical discussion of this subject, important for criticism as well as literary history, has yet to be written; but the papers presented at the Third International Congress of Literary History and published in *Helicon*, Vol. II, p. 117 and ff. as "Les Genres Littéraires" show the very great current interest in the problem and indicate the lines at present taken by European theorists. Cf. also Kenneth Burke's brilliant prolegomena to a new theory of genre, in his "Poetic Categories," *Attitudes towards History*, 1937, I, 41–119.

37. *L'Art Poetique*, Cantos 2 and 3.

38. Hankiss, "Les genres littèraires et leur base psychologique," *Helicon*, II, 127.

39. *Poetics*, Chapter XXVI.

40. Henri Peyre, *Qu'est-ce le classicisme?*, 1933, p. 83.

41. I derive little help for the practical criticism of poetry from I. A. Richards' "Analysis of a Poem" (*Principles of Literary Criticism* [2nd Edition, 1926], pp. 114 ff.), which undertakes to apply psychology "in its present conjectural state" to the elucidation of poetry's function, or from Norman Maier's and H. Willard Reninger's *A Psychological Approach to Literary Criticism*, 1933. More useful, within its limits, is June Downey's *Creative Imagination: Studies in the Psychology of Literature*, 1929; but apparently critics must still chiefly, with whatever corrective from such sensible works as William James' *Principles of Psychology*, 1890, construct their own tentative psychology of literary response.

42. *Poetics*, Chapters VI and XIV.

43. The just perception of this prompted Wordsworth to write his preface to *Lyrical Ballads*. "It is supposed that by the act of writing in verse an author makes a formal engagement that he will gratify certain known habits of association . . . This exponent or symbol held forth by metrical language must in different eras of literature have excited very different expectations . . . it will undoubtedly appear to many persons that I have not fulfilled the terms of an engagement thus voluntarily contracted." Then he offers the theory of his practice.

44. "The only way of expressing emotion in the form of art is by finding an 'objective correlative'; in other words, a set of objects, a chain of events which shall be the formula of that particular emotion; such that when the external facts, which must terminate in sensory experience, are given the emotion is immediately evoked." T. S. Eliot, *Selected Essays*, 1932, pp. 124–5.

45. Henry James, *French Poets and Novelists,* 1884, p. 243.

46. Cf. Robert Petsch, "Die Analyse des Dichtwerkes," *Philosophie der Literaturwissenschaft* (ed. Emil Ermatinger, 1930), p. 259. "Der geistige Gehalt der Dichtung unterscheidet sich von der philosophischen oder auch unterwissenschaftlichen Welt-und Lebensanschauung vor allem durch den Mangel fester Systematik und begrifflicher Klarheit; dennoch herrscht auch bei ihm eine deutlich wahrnehmbare, nur nicht starre Ordnung und eine durchsichtige Klarheit, nur von anderer Art."

47. The first two pieces are published by the Critics Group, N. Y., in their series which also include *Literature and Marxism: A Controversy by Soviet Critics,* edited by Angel Flores, 1938. James T. Farrell's *A Note in Literary Criticism,* 1936, is a leftist criticism of such leftist critics as Michael Gold and Granville Hicks. "I think," writes Farrell, "that literature must be viewed both as a branch of the fine arts and as an instrument of social influence."
To Eliot's *After Strange Gods,* 1934, and Yvor Winters' *Primitivism and Decadence,* 1937, and *Maule's Curse,* 1938, should be added Ramon Fernandez's *Messages, Premierè Série,* 1926, and G. R. Elliott's *Cycle of Modern Poetry,* 1929, together with the opening essay of the latter's *Humanism and Imagination,* 1938.

48. Eliot, *The Use of Poetry and the Use of Criticism,* 1933, p. 96.

49. Cf. the judicious discussion of "Artistic greatness" in Theodore Meyer Greene's *The Arts and the Art of Criticism,* 1940, pp. 471–8, especially 474–5 on "generic patterns of insight and belief."

50. Cf. Morton Zabel's discussion of E. A. Robinson's "stoicism" (*Literary Opinion in America* [ed. Zabel, 1937], pp. 399–404). Zabel possesses special taste and talent for the analysis of how a poet comes by his philosophic faith and how that faith is textured and substanced.

51. I. A. Richards, "The Two Uses of Language," *Principles of Literary Criticism* (2nd edition, 1926), pp. 261 ff. Cf. also Richards' *Philosophy of Rhetoric,* 1936.

52. Cf. George Rylands' *Words and Poetry,* 1928, and such special studies as Geoffrey Tillotson's *The Poetry of Pope,* 1938, and R. B. Blackmur's "New Thresholds, New Anatomies. Notes on a Text by Hart Crane," *The Double Agent,* pp. 121 ff.

53. "The aesthetician who claims to know what it is that makes Shakespeare a poet is tacitly claiming to know whether Miss Stein is a poet, and if not, why not. The philosopher-aesthetician who sticks to classical artists [i.e., accepted masters] is pretty sure to locate the essence of art not in what makes them artists but in what makes them classical, that is acceptable to the academic mind." R. G. Collingwood, *Principles of Art,* pp. 4–0.

54. This is a restriction which writers have often wanted to make; Ben Jonson, for example, writes: "To judge of poets is only the faculty of poets; and not of all poets, but of the best."

55. Joining the offices of critic and poet affects the poetry as well as the criticism. Those poets and novelists who have written technical criticism—such men as Jonson, Poe, James, Valéry, and Eliot—have been writers uncommonly sure of their own effects.

56. George Boas' *Primer for Critics,* a brilliant book modestly named, attempts, with more success than any other work known to me, to schematize the assumptions of critical schools. "We are not claiming to have written an account of critical theory which will be historically true, but merely one which will have logical truth." (*Primer,* p. 87).

57. Criticism, as a pedagogic discipline, can be taught as philosophy and the fine arts are taught: historical information can be imparted to all; the principles held by theoreticians of the past can be explicated; those students who have an interest in and an aptitude for analysis, comparison, and judgment of literary works can be encouraged and directed—by widening their attention and references, by helping them to make their systems of judgment self-coherent. That is, students can be taught a provisional what to think, but they are centrally to be trained in how to think.

58. Sometimes the critic expounds his own extra-aesthetic beliefs, as Arnold did in *Literature and Dogma* and *Culture and Anarchy;* Eliot, on the other hand, aligns himself with Anglo-Catholicism and Distributism but, fearing that he may do injustice to his cause by inexpert defense, refers us to his "authorities."

FIVE: IMAGINATIVE WRITING

1. E.g.: "For whatever reasons, the universities in the United States no longer put such a shoulder to the wheel of creative literature as they put there half a century or so ago. No poet of the relative eminence of Longfellow, no wit of the relative eminence of Holmes, no critic of the relative eminence of Lowell, is now a professor. . . . Creative writers and scholars alike seem often to forget that beyond the gulf from each of them there is another side concerned with letters. The scholars spend their talents, often admirable, on antiquarian research, but rarely know or care enough to encourage, interpret, or preserve the best that is being done from year to year. The creative writers know or care little about learning which alone can impart certain of the most solid merits to masterpieces. In creative circles it is regarded as singular that Robert Frost intermittently and Robert Herrick persistently hold professorships; in professorial circles it is commonly thought best, when an active poet or novelist is added to the staff of a university, to keep him below the salt with the instructors or among the side shows with the extension lecturers. . . . Doubtless the men of imagination will go on hacking at their own sweet wills, and the men of erudition will go on carefully gathering up the chips when they are dry. It seems a pity." Carl Van Doren, *Many Minds,* 1924, p. 67.

2. H. A. Beers, *Points at Issue,* 1904, pp. 42–47.

3. See Allen Tate's article, We Read as We Write," *Princeton Alumni Weekly,* XL, 22 (March 8, 1940), 505–6.

4. "The Cult of Experience," *Partisan Review,* VII, 6, 412–424.

5. "Scholars and Others," *Sewanee Review,* XXXVI (October, 1929), 481–482.

6. In the last few years such universities as Harvard, Iowa, Vanderbilt, Michigan, North Carolina, Louisiana, and Princeton have recognized and accepted the challenge. Most of these universities and many others now offer seminars in writing which enforce professional standards of accomplishment. Beyond these seminars, efforts to encourage imaginative writing within the university have been various: prizes to stimulate production; lectureships for distinguished writers; part-time teaching fellowships for promising young authors; national literary magazines edited and published within the university; advanced degrees which emphasize the discipline of imaginative writing.

The problem which has motivated such experiments is necessarily

236

that with which this chapter is concerned: the relation of university to writer. It is a somewhat different problem from that of the three preceding chapters. In the case of linguistics and literary history, the relation of scholar to university has been defined by long usage, and the chief desideratum is an analysis of the disciplines and their practice. Literary criticism has also been recognized—though seldom employed—as an advanced discipline, and the matters of chief concern are the ways and means of its use. Imaginative writing, on the other hand, has not been generally recognized as a discipline to be practiced beside the other three in the university; scarce, indeed, are the advanced degrees which may be approached through the main road of writing. Therefore, the central task of this chapter is not to analyze the discipline of imaginative writing, but to estimate what the writer and the university can contribute to each other.

7. It will be remembered also that at another point Plato denies a vision of the Ideal to the artist, because he will not undertake the preliminary hard thinking—an observation with modern implications.

8. *Atlantic Monthly,* lxxx, 320.

9. Douglas Bush, *op. cit.,* p. 480.

10. Allen Tate, *loc. cit.* Mr. Tate adds: "If a young man wishes to teach himself to be a poet, he has got to find out what a poem is . . . we are trying to find out what words can do, and we read certain poems, stories, and novels, not for historical information, but to see whether we can find any flaws in the way they are written; insofar as it is possible we try to read a poem as if we were writing it."

11. Admission of imaginative writing to the graduate school as a discipline on even terms with the other disciplines raises another important practical question. What attainment in imaginative writing is desirable for students who have no special aptitude in this direction? In particular, how much time can those who will become specialists in language, literary history, or literary criticism afford to give, in the earlier stages of graduate work, to the study of writing as part of their general training?

The answer may be hazarded that a single course in writing, undertaken in the right spirit, or equivalent work done independently, will amply reward such students with a kind of literary insight hardly attainable in any other way. Ideally, to be sure, prospective graduate students in letters should practice imaginative writing in their undergraduate years and bring the insight thus gained to the aid of their advanced studies, just as they should acquire a reading knowledge of Latin, French, and German before entering upon graduate work.

12. The degree of Master of Fine Arts, whether in music, the graphic arts, or literature, is ordinarily distinguished from the Master of Arts degree by being reserved for a candidate whose chief interest is in the art rather than the history or theory of his subject and who has proved distinct ability in artistic creation. The "thesis" may be a

musical composition, a painting or sculpture, a novel or a book of poems; and somewhat greater emphasis is placed on the thesis than in the case of the M.A.

13. Douglas Bush, *op. cit.*

14. *Some Problems of Philosophy,* 1911, p. 7.

A BIBLIOGRAPHY

This is a chronological list of some twentieth-century studies dealing primarily with the aims and methods of literary scholarship. As a rule it does not include the more restricted studies cited in the chapters (II–V) on the several disciplines.

—René Wellek.

1904—

VOSSLER, KARL. *Positivismus und Idealismus in der Sprachwissenschaft.* 98 pp. Heidelberg. An attack by a Crocean idealist on the theory and methods of the *Junggrammatiker;* best statement of Vossler's point of view.

1907—

ELTON, OLIVER. The Meaning of Literary History, *Modern Studies,* pp. 122–156. London. A discussion of methods, with special attention to Courthope and Saintsbury.

1908—

BABBITT, IRVING. *Literature and the American College: Essays in Defense of the Humanities.* 262 pp. Boston. An attack on the Ph.D. degree as currently administered, and on the dehumanization of the American college.

UNGER, RUDOLF. *Philosophische Probleme in der neueren Literaturwissenschaft.* Munich. Unger's first plea for the application of Dilthey's philosophy to the study of literature.

1909—

MURRAY, GILBERT. *The Interpretation of Ancient Greek Literature. An Inaugural Lecture.* 23 pp. Oxford. A plan for Greek studies with a broad background.

1911—

ELSTER, ERNST. *Prinzipien der Literaturwissenschaft.* Vol. I 481 pp. Vol. II 292 pp. Halle. (Vol. I appeared in 1897.) A learned theory of literary scholarship which was largely based on the principles of Wundt's psychology.

MANN, MAURYCY. Rozwój syntezy literackiej od jej początków do Gervinusa. *Rozprawy Akademii Umiejętności*, Serja III, Tom III, pp. 230–360. Kraków. A Polish sketch of the history of literary history from the beginnings to Gervinus.

SHOREY, PAUL. American Scholarship, *Nation*, XCII, pp. 466–469. (Reprinted in *Fifty Years of American Idealism*, ed. G. Pollak. pp. 401–413. Boston, 1915.) Shorey doubts adequacy of prevalent German scholarship and deplores its influence in America.

1913—

LEE, SIR SIDNEY. *The Place of English Literature in the Modern University.* London. (Reprinted in *Elizabethan and Other Essays*, pp. 1–18. Oxford, 1929.) Inaugural at East London College of the University of London.

SHERMAN, STUART P. Professor Kittredge and the Teaching of English, *Nation*, XCVII, pp. 227–230. (Reprinted in *Shaping Men and Women*. pp. 65–86. Garden City, 1928.) Points out the dangers of the philological method.

1914—

NADLER, JOSEF. Die Wissenschaftslehre der Literaturgeschichte, *Euphorion,* XXI, pp. 1–63. An elaborate
defense of an approach to literature through the study
of race, region, and heredity.

1915—

COOPER, LANE. *Methods and Aims in the Study of Literature. A Series of Extracts and Illustrations.* 239 pp.
Boston. (New edition, Ithaca, 1940.) Miscellaneous
extracts illustrating methods in general, the practice
of great writers in composing, the studies of poets,
method in the poetry of love, etc.

MOULTON, R. G. *The Modern Study of Literature.* 530
pp. Chicago. Stresses the evolution of literature, the
unity of world-literature, and the central importance
of interpretation.

QUILLER-COUCH, SIR ARTHUR. English Literature in Our
Universities, *On the Art of Writing,* pp. 230–277.
Cambridge. Inaugural at Cambridge University.

1916—

SAUSSURE, FERDINAND DE. *Cours de linguistique générale.*
337 pp. Paris and Lausanne. (Third edition, 1931.) A
standard introduction to general linguistics; represents view of French school of early twentieth century.

1920—

LEMPICKI, SIGMUND VON. *Geschichte der deutschen
Literaturwissenschaft.* 468 pp. Göttingen. A history of
German literary scholarship up to and including
Herder, by a Polish scholar.

ROTHACKER, ERICH. *Einleitung in die Geisteswissenschaften.* 288 pp. Tübingen. (Second edition, Tü-

bingen, 1930.) Contains a sketch of the history of German literary history in the nineteenth century.

1921—

McKerrow, Ronald B. *A Note on the Teaching of English Language and Literature.* English Association Pamphlet, No. 49. 32 pp. Advocates the study of the history of ideas.

Merker, Paul. *Neue Aufgaben der deutschen Literaturgeschichte.* 82 pp. Leipzig. A survey of the state of German literary scholarship with suggestions of new problems.

Van Tieghem, Paul. La synthèse en histoire littéraire: Littérature comparée et litterature générale, *Revue de synthèse historique,* XXXI, pp. 1–27. Best statement of the distinction between general and comparative literature.

1922—

Jespersen, Otto. *Language: Its Nature, Development, and Origin.* 448 pp. London. Comprehensive account; perspective adequate for the general reader as well as the student of linguistics.

Morize, André. *Problems and Methods of Literary History.* 314 pp. Boston. A textbook for graduate students in French, largely concerned with questions of bibliography, textual criticism, sources and influences.

1923—

Cassirer, Ernst. *Philosophie der symbolischen Formen. Erster Teil, die Sprache.* 293 pp. Berlin. A philosophical study of language as a symbol system.

Mahrholz, Werner. *Literaturgeschichte und Literaturwissenschaft.* 244 pp. Berlin. (Second ed., 244 pp., Leipzig, 1932.)

Pos, H. D. *Kritische Studien über philologische Methode.* 138 pp. Heidelberg. A discussion of the philosophical problems involved in textual criticism, interpretation, etc.

RUDLER, GUSTAVE. *Les techniques de la critique et de l'histoire littéraires en littérature française moderne.* 204 pp. Oxford.

VOSSLER, KARL. *Gesammelte Aufsätze zur Sprachphilosophie.* 272 pp. Munich. Contains article on the relation between the history of literature and the history of language.

WALZEL, OSKAR. *Gehalt und Gestalt im dichterischen Kunstwerk.* 408 pp. Berlin-Babelsberg. A full discussion of numerous methods in the study of a literary work of art, with stress on the relationships with the arts of design.

1924—

AUDIAT, PIERRE. *La Biographie de l'œuvre littéraire; esquisse d'une méthode critique.* 274 pp. Paris. Purely psychological approach to the study of the work of art.

FEUILLERAT, ALBERT. Scholarship and Literary Criticism, *Yale Review*, XIV, pp. 309–324. Deplores the current divorce of literary history and criticism.

JESPERSEN, OTTO. *The Philosophy of Grammar.* 359 pp. London. A critical discussion of traditional classifications and terminology; exposition of Jespersen's system.

PEDERSEN, HOLGER. *Sprogvidenskaben i det Nittende Aarhundrede: Metoder og Resultater.* Copenhagen. English translation by John Webster Spargo, *Linguistic Science in the Nineteenth Century: Methods and Results.* 360 pp. Cambridge (Mass.), 1931. A standard historical survey of all branches of linquistics: the emergence of scientific study of language in the early nineteenth century; successive steps in the formation of principles and method; results and achievements.

Stand und Aufgaben der Sprachwissenschaft. Fest-

schrift für Wilhelm Streitberg. 683 pp. Heidelberg.
Chapters by nineteen German linguists on the state of
research at that time in a number of special fields.

UNGER, RUDOLF. *Literaturgeschichte als Problem-
geschichte. Zur Frage geisteshistorischer Synthese.* 30
pp. Berlin. Recommends the study of the attitude of
writers to the main problems of life and death rather
than technical philosophical questions.

1925—

LANSON, GUSTAVE. *Méthodes de l'histoire littéraire.* 52
pp. Paris. Lectures on the scientific spirit and the
method of literary history, on *l'explication de textes,*
etc.

MEILLET, A. *La méthode comparative en linguistique
historique.* 776 pp. Oslo and Cambridge, Mass. Exposition of methodology of comparative linguistics.

RICHARDS, I. A. *The Principles of Literary Criticism.* 290
pp. London. Mr. Richards' most important book on his
psychological approach to criticism.

TOMASHEVSKIJ, B. *Teorija literatury.* Leningrad. Best
statement of the Russian "formalistic" approach to
the study of literature.

1926—

CYSARZ, HERBERT. *Literaturgeschichte als Geisteswissen-
schaft.* 304 pp. Halle. Fullest statement of the theory
of German "Geistesgeschichte," but frequently ver-
bose and obscure.

PETERSEN, JULIUS. *Die Wesenbestimmung der deutschen
Romantik: eine Einführung in die moderne Literaturwissenschaft.* 205 pp. Leipzig. Discusses the different methods of German literary scholarship in its
attempts to define the nature of Romanticism.

UNGER, RUDOLF. Literaturgeschichte und Geistesgeschichte, *Deutsche Vierteljahrschrift für Literaturwissenschaft und Geistesgeschichte,* IV, pp. 177–193. The

relationship between literary history and a general history of the human mind.

1927—

ENGELGARDT, B. *Formal'ny metod v istorii literatury.* Leningrad. The Russian formalistic method and its use in literary history.

RICKERT, EDITH. *New Methods for the Study of Literature.* 275 pp. Chicago. Recommends the study of artistic form with statistical devices, graphs, etc.

STOLL, E. E. Certain Fallacies and Irrelevancies in the Literary Scholarship of the Day, *Studies in Philology,* XXIV, pp. 485–508. Attacks the search for parallels at any price and considers the study of the structure and value of the poem as central.

WILAMOWITZ-MOELLENDORFF, ULRICH. Geschichte der Philologie, Gercke, A. and Norden, S., *Einleitung in die Altertumswissenschaft,* Vol. I, pp. 1–80. Leipzig and Berlin. A sketch of the history of classical philology.

1928—

BENDA, OSKAR. *Der gegenwärtige Stand der deutschen Literaturwissenschaft.* 66 pp. Vienna. A survey of the state of German literary scholarship.

DRAGOMIRESCOU, MICHEL. *La sciénce de la littérature.* Vol. I, 192 pp. Vol. II, 218 pp. Vol. III, 211 pp. Vol. IV, 246 pp. (Vols. III and IV were published in 1929.) A full discussion of general aesthetics, the aesthetics of literature, methodology, culminating in an analysis of the "masterpiece."

LOMBARD, ALFONSE. *La crise de l'histoire littéraire.* 22 pp. Neufchâtel.

O'LEARY, J. G. *English Literary History and Bibliography.* 192 pp. London. A sketch of English literary historiography with bibliographies.

1929—

BAUGH, ALBERT C. Graduate Work in English, *English Journal* (College Edition), XVIII, pp. 135–146. Deplores the decline of interest in original research and advocates a sharp distinction between M.A. and Ph.D.

CANBY, H. S. The American Scholar. *American Estimates,* pp. 129–143. New York. Draws a sharp line between literary scholarship and science and objects to the stress on fact-finding.

CAZAMIAN, LOUIS. The Aims and Methods of Higher Literary Studies, *Rice Institute Pamphlet,* Vol. XVI, pp. 1–45. Also in *Criticism in the Making,* pp. 3–63. New York. Contains three papers on The Lure of Sources; the Object of Criticism; Eugenius: or Everybody His Own Critic. Developing the critical faculty is more important than historical knowledge.

FOERSTER, NORMAN. *The American Scholar. A Study in Litterae Inhumaniores.* 66 pp. Chapel Hill.

GOURFINKEL, NINA. Les nouvelles méthodes d'histoire littéraire en Russie, *Le Monde Slave,* VI, pp. 234–263. An account of the Russian formalists with bibliographical references.

KANTOROWICZ, HERMANN. Grundbegriffe der Literaturgeschichte, *Logos,* XVIII, pp. 102 ff. A discussion of the philosophical conceptions underlying the history of literature.

Mélanges linguistiques dédiés au premier congrès des philologues slaves. 245 pp. Prague. Travaux du Cercle Linguistique de Prague No. 1. Contains the theses of the Prague Linguistic School.

1930—

BRAY, RENÉ. Les tendances nouvelles de l'histoire littéraire, *Revue d'histoire littéraire de la France,* XXXVII, pp. 542–557. Deplores dissipation into political history, history of ideas and the study of insignificant figures. The historian of literature should be also a critic.

ERMATINGER, EMIL. ED. *Die Philosophie der Literaturwissenschaft*. 478 pp. Berlin. Contains articles by F. Schultz on the history of German literary scholarship in the nineteenth century, by H. Cysarz on periods in literature, by J. Petersen on literary generations, by F. Medicus on a comparative history of the arts, by R. Petsch on the analysis of the work of art, by E. Ermatinger on laws in literary history, by J. Nadler on the history of style, by M. Wundt on literature and philosophy, by F. Strich on general and comparative literature, etc.

GEISSENDOERFER, TH. A Critical Bibliography of Recent Methods in German Literary Research, *Journal of English and Germanic Philology*, XXIX, pp. 390–419.

JONES, HOWARD MUMFORD. Graduate English Study: Its Rational, *Sewanee Review*, XXXVIII, pp. 464–476; continued in 1931, XXXIX, pp. 68–79, 200–206. Graduate work should develop a time-sense and a knowledge of bibliographical methodology.

VAN TIEGHEM, PHILIPPE. *Tendances nouvelles en histoire littéraire*. 66 pp. Études Françaises, No. 22, Paris. The Russian formalists, Dragomirescou and Cysarz, discussed. A short bibliography on methods included.

1931—

BOAS, GEORGE. *A Primer for Critics*. 153 pp. Baltimore. Discussions of problems of value, standards of criticism, etc.

BÖCKMANN, PAUL. Von den Aufgaben einer geisteswissenschaftlichen Literaturbetrachtung, *Deutsche Vierteljahrschrift für Literaturwissenschaft und Geistesgeschichte*, IX, pp. 448–471. A synthesis of methods recommended with stress on interpretation rather than causal explanation.

FOERSTER, NORMAN. Language and Literature, *Trends in Graduate Work*, pp. 111–119. *University of Iowa Studies, Series on Aims and Progress of Research*, No. 33. Iowa City. An address, November, 1930, on the program of a school of letters established in that year. A passage has been incorporated in the first chapter of the present book.

GREENLAW, EDWIN. *The Province of Literary History*. 183 pp. Baltimore. Literary history should embrace the whole history of civilization. Much incidental discussion of history of scholarship.

INGARDEN, ROMAN. *Das literarische Kunstwerk*. 389 pp. Halle. Analysis of the structure of a work of art, its "ontological situs," etc. Ingarden is a Polish pupil of the German philosopher of "phenomenology," Edmund Husserl.

VAN TIEGHEM, PAUL. *La littérature comparée*. 222 pp. Paris. Statement of the theory and methods of comparative literature with a sketch of its history.

VAN TIEGHEM, PAUL. Le premier congrès international d'histoire littéraire et la crise des méthodes, *Modern Philology*, XXXIX, pp. 129–148. A report on the first congress of literary history at Budapest in 1931.

1932—

HANFORD, JAMES HOLLY. Edwin Greenlaw and the Study of Literature, *Studies in Philology*, XXI, pp. 141–148. Criticizes Greenlaw's theory.

IORDAN, IORGU. *Introducere în studiul limbilor romanice. Evoluţia şi starea actuală a lingvisticii romanice*. Iasi (Rumania). Revised, translated and in parts recast by John Orr, *An Introduction to Romance Linguistics*. 403 pp. London, 1937. An account of the views, theories, methods, and works of the various schools in this field (which is broadly interpreted and often involves principles and methods of general linguistics). Full bibliographical guidance (in text and footnotes). At once a handbook and a history of the subject.

Le Premier Congrès international d'histoire littéraire, Budapest (1931), *Bulletin of the International Committee of Historical Sciences,* IV, No. 14, pp. 1–144. Paris. Contains papers on methods of literary history by P. van Tieghem, F. Baldensperger, Th. Thienemann, B. Croce, B. Faÿ, M. Dragomirescou, L. Eckhoff, E. Ermatinger, J. Nadler, J. Hankiss, L. Russo, A. Eckhardt, L. Sorrento, O. Walzel, L. L. Schücking, H. Cysarz, G. Ascoli, W. Folkierski.

1933—

BLOOMFIELD, LEONARD. *Language.* 564 pp. New York. The standard text in English on the principles and methods of linguistics.

CASTRO, PAUL SILVA. *Estado Actual de los Métodos de la Historia Literaria.* 171 pp. Santiago, Chile. Translations into Spanish of articles by Van Tieghem, Croce, Dragomirescou, Hankiss, Nadler, Schücking, etc.

JESPERSEN, OTTO. *Linguistica: Selected Papers in English, French and German.* 461 pp. Copenhagen. Latest statements of the views of the Danish linguist on methods, theories, and special topics.

SCHÜTZE, MARTIN. *Academic Illusions in the Field of Letters and the Arts.* 328 pp. Chicago. A criticism of German "Geistesgeschichte" and of the current factualism. A theory of "integral variables" is proposed which would make the interpretation of the work of art the center of literary studies.

1934—

BATESON, F. W. *English Poetry and the English Language.* 129 pp. Oxford. Contains an introduction discussing the methods of literary history. Rejects the sociological approach and advocates a study of literary history through the development of poetic language.

JONES, HOWARD MUMFORD. Literary Scholarship and Contemporary Criticism, *English Journal* (College Edition), XXIII, pp. 740–766. A defense of scholarship against the attacks of creative writers and critics. The primary purpose of the scholar is historical, not aesthetic.

LOWES, JOHN LIVINGSTON. The Modern Language Association and Humane Scholarship, *PMLA*, XLVIII Supplement, pp. 1399–1408. Sketches the history of the Modern Language Association and advocates attention to wider problems than mere research.

1935—

BLACKMUR, R. P. The Critic's Job of Work. *The Double Agent: Essays in Craft of Elucidation*, pp. 269–302. New York. Distinguishes the philosophical, sociological, the tendentious, the semasiological and the psychological approaches to criticism.

CRANE, RONALD S. History versus Criticism in the University Study of Literature, *English Journal* (College Edition), XXIV, pp. 645–667. A sharp distinction is drawn between literary history and criticism and the systematic study of criticism is recommended.

VAN KRANENDONK, A. S. New Methods for the Study of Literature, *English Studies*, XVII, pp. 129–140. Advocates a combination of literary history and literary criticism.

WARREN, AUSTIN. The Scholar and the Critic: An Essay in Mediation, *The New Frontier*, II, pp. 17–22. [Also in *University of Toronto Quarterly*, VI (1937), pp. 267–277.]

1936—

DODDS, E. R. *Humanism and Technique in Greek Studies. An Inaugural Lecture.* 17 pp. Oxford. Advocates a broadening of Greek scholarship from merely textual problems to a study of Greek civilization from a humanist point of view.

FOERSTER, NORMAN. Literary Scholarship and Criticism, *English Journal* (College Edition), XXV, pp. 224–232.

JAEGER, WERNER. Classical Philology and Humanism, *Transactions of the American Philological Association*, LXVII, pp. 363–374. The modern technical scholarship should be reconciled with the old tradition of humanism as a cultural ideal.

KRIDL, MANFRED. *Wstęp do badań nad dziełem literackiem*. 213 pp. Wilno. A Polish introduction to the study of the literary work of art.

LOVEJOY, A. O. *The Great Chain of Being*. 382 pp. Cambridge, Mass. Contains an introduction on "The Study of the History of Ideas."

SCHÜTZE, MARTIN. Towards a Modern Humanism, *PMLA*, LI, pp. 284–299. An amplification of some points in Mr. Schütze's book. The work of art must be studied in its integral unity; a history must be written with a ruling principle of evaluation.

THOMSON, J. A. K. The Present and Future of Classical Scholarship, *Essays in Honour of Gilbert Murray*, pp. 279–291. "Scholarship is both an art and a science; an art based upon science. To divorce one from the other is fatal."

WELLEK, RENÉ. The Theory of Literary History, *Travaux du Cercle Linguistique de Prague*, VI, pp. 173–192. An earlier statement of the point of view explained in Chapter III. Somewhat fuller on the epistemological questions.

1937—

INGARDEN, ROMAN. *O poznawaniu dzieła literackiego*. Lwów. Ingarden's restatement of the theory propounded in the earlier book.

KOHN-BRAMSTEDT, ERNST. *Aristocracy and the Middle Classes in Germany. Social Types in German Literature, 1830–1900.* 362 pp. London. The introduction contains a discussion of the sociological approach.

POTTER, STEPHEN. *The Muse in Chains. A Study in Education.* 287 pp. London. A spirited attack on academic teaching and sketch of the history of teaching English in Great Britain.

RANSOM, JOHN CROWE. Criticism, Inc., *Virginia Quarterly Review,* XIII, pp. 586–602. (Reprinted in *The World's Body,* pp. 327–350. New York, 1938.) A plea for collaborative criticism in the universities and for criticism which shall be really "literary."

1938—

COFFMAN, GEORGE R. Some Recent Trends in English Literary Scholarship, with special reference to Mediaeval Backgrounds, *Studies in Philology,* XXXV, pp. 500–514. Discusses the relations of literary history and philosophy with special reference to Lovejoy.

LOVEJOY, A. O. The Historiography of Ideas, *Proceedings of the American Philosophical Society,* LXXVIII, pp. 529–543. A restatement of Lovejoy's "history of ideas."

SPENCER, THEODORE. An Ideal for Graduate Education in English Literature, *English Journal* (College Edition), XXVII, pp. 33–43. Literature should be studied as product of human mind. Detailed recommendations for curriculum in graduate study of English.

TEETER, LOUIS. Scholarship and the Art of Criticism, *ELH,* V, pp. 173–194. Argues for a double standard of evaluation: critical and historical. These standards are complementary, not exclusive.

WARREN, AUSTIN. The Criticism of Meaning and the Meaning of Criticism, *Sewanee Review,* XLVI, pp. 213–222.

1939—

BLOOMFIELD, LEONARD. Linguistic Aspects of Science. *International Encyclopedia of Unified Science*, Vol. I, No. 4. 58 pp. Chicago. Statement of the mechanist's view of language: its nature, structure, operation and relation to science.

GRAY, LOUIS H. *Foundations of Language.* 530 pp. New York. The most recent textbook of general linguistics; with stress on historical method; survey of languages of the world; bibliography.

OPPEL, HORST. *Die Literaturwissenschaft in der Gegenwart: Methodologie und Wissenschaftslehre.* 182 pp. Stuttgart. A discussion of methods and ideology from the point of view of *Existentialphilosophie.*

PETERSEN, JULIUS. *Die Wissenschaft von der Dichtung. System und Methodenlehre der Literaturwissenschaft.* Vol. I: *Werk und Dichter.* 516 pp. Berlin. The second volume has not been published. The first is devoted to a survey of the methods for the study of the poet and the work of art. Volume II will discuss historical questions.

1940—

BLACKMUR, R. P. A Featherbed for Critics, *The Expense of Greatness,* pp. 277–305. New York. A plea for a recognition of the place of the writer in the university.

BROOKS, CLEANTH; MIZENER, ARTHUR; COX, SIDNEY; SAUNDERS, HADE; TRILLING, LIONEL. Literature and the Professors: A Symposium, *Kenyon Review,* II, pp. 403–442. A number of papers, of uneven value, on the teaching of English in American universities.

HARRIS, ZELLIG S. Review of Gray's *Foundations of Language, Language,* XVI, pp. 216–231. Statement of method of synchronic, structural school of linguists.

LOVEJOY, A. O. Reflections on the History of Ideas, *Journal of the History of Ideas,* I, pp. 1–23. Introductory reflections on the new journal.

Nicolson, Marjorie. The History of Literature and the History of Thought, *English Institute Annual, 1939,* pp. 56–89. New York. A statement in agreement with Lovejoy's point of view.

Ransom, John Crowe; Tate, Allen; Horrell, Joe; Thomas, Wright; Levin, Harry. Literature and the Professors: A Symposium, *Southern Review,* VI, pp. 225–269. A collection of essays, of uneven value, on the problems of teaching literature in American universities.

Tate, Allen. Miss Emily and the Bibliographer, *American Scholar,* IX, 449–460. (Reprinted in *Reason in Madness: Critical Essays.* New York, 1941. pp. 100–116.) A criticism of the historical method in literary scholarship.

1941—

Auden, W. H.; Foerster, Norman; Ransom, John Crowe; Wilson, Edmund. *The Intent of the Critic.* Princeton.

Crane, R. S. Interpretation of Texts and the History of Ideas, *College English,* II, pp. 755–765. A method of contraries is recommended for the writing of histories of ideas, and some dangers of the approach are discussed.

Heilman, Robert Bechtold. Footnotes on Literary History, *Southern Review,* VI, 759–770. A continuation of the debate begun with the 1940 symposium in the same review.

Richter, Werner. Von der Literaturwissenschaft zur Literaturgeschichte, *Monatshefte für deutschen Unterricht,* XXXIII, pp. 7–22. Advocates a return to literary history as an expression of the national mind.

Spitzer, Leo. History of Ideas versus Reading Poetry, *Southern Review,* VI, pp. 584–609. Advocates the analysis of poetic art in preference to the history of ideas.

THORP, WILLARD. The Problem of Greatness in Writing Literary History, *English Institute Annual, 1940,* pp. 94–114. New York. Discusses criteria of choice and emphasis in the writing of literary history.

WELLEK, RENÉ. Periods and Movements in Literary History, *English Institute Annual, 1940,* pp. 73–93. Columbia University Press, New York. A theoretical discussion of the problems of periodisation and development. A few pages anticipate the argument of Chapter III on the question of evolution. They have been reprinted with the permission of the Columbia University Press.

WELLEK, RENÉ. *The Rise of English Literary History.* 275 pp. Chapel Hill. A history of literary history in England up to and including Warton.

INDEX

Adams, Henry, as editor of the *North American Review*, 203

Addison, Joseph, and formal criteria in literary criticism, 162

Adequation, as type of change of meaning, 70

Advancement of Learning, and modern science, 6

Aesthetics, method of criticism, 141 ff.; and literary form, 141 ff.

After Strange Gods. See Eliot

Aldrich, Thomas Bailey, as editor, 203

Alexandrians, and Greek literature, 6

Allen, Hervey, and advanced study, 200

Altertumswissenschaft, in the nineteenth century, 9

Analogy, as type of change of meaning, 70; as type of linguistic change, 56

Anderson, Sherwood, lack of erudition in, 180

Aquinas, Thomas, and Edmund Spenser, 140

Aristocracy and the Middle Classes in Germany. See Kohn-Bramstedt

Aristotle, and formal organization of literature, 162; and literary standards, 146; mentioned, 25, 195, 207; and the *Oedipus*, 161; and his *Poetics*, 140, 141, 147; and literary form, 159, 160; and relation of poetry to

history and philosophy, 138–139; as scholar, 5

Arnold, Matthew, and literary standards, 146, 157, 170; as scholar-critic, 196

Arnold, Thurman W., on use of words, 36; and *The Symbols of Government and The Folklore of Capitalism*, 36

Art, atomism in, 125; attitude of ideological critics toward, 147; combination of symbols in creating, 189; literary, and literary history, 116 ff.; literature as, 116 ff.; and the mind, 183–185; and reality, 183 ff.; relationship between works of, 125 ff.; as symbols, 186 ff.; as structure, 188 ff.; works of, and aesthetic and utilitarian attitudes toward, 147 ff.; and contemporary aesthetic theory, 149–150; difficulty of evaluating, 117 ff.; history of, 120–121

Art of Thought, The. See Wallas

Atlantic Monthly, editors of, 203

Atlas, American, 46

"At Church." *See* Hardy

Auden, Wyden H., and advanced study, 200; and definition of the poet, 208; mentioned, 188

Auxiliaries, and inflectional endings, 58

Babbitt, Irving, on scientific method in American scholarship, 14; and *Literature and the American College*, 14

Bacon, Francis, mentioned, 206; on Truth, 208

Baker, Howard, and advanced study, 200

Bale, John, mentioned, 102

Bally, Charles, and development of special meanings in words, 69; and sound laws, 52; and stylistic view of linguistic methodology, 82–83

Balzac, Honoré de, mentioned, 138

Bateson, F. W., on difference between literary history and literary criticism, 99–100; and *English Poetry and the English Language*, 106–107; and *Language and Poetry*, 87

Baudelaire, Charles, poetry of, 163

Baugh, Albert C., and *History of the English Language*, 65

Beers, H. A., on scholars, 178

Beethoven, Ludvig Van, and artistic symbols, 187

Bell, Clive, and artistic process, 186

Beneš, Eduard, as teacher, 202

Benét, Stephen Vincent, and *The Devil and Daniel Webster*, 184

Bentley, Richard, mentioned, 9, 18

Benton, Thomas Hart, and *Susannah and the Elders*, 185

Beowolf, Klaeber's edition, 4; mentioned, 54, 85, 86

Bibliography, method of, 93; 226 n. 4

Biography, method in study of literary history, 102–104

Blackmur, R. P., and knowledge of linguistics, 88; mentioned, 146

Bloomfield, Leonard, and *Linguistic Aspects of Science*, 78–

79; mentioned, 40; on phoneme, 45

Boileau-Despréaux, Nicolas, and aesthetic criticism, 141; and artistic rule of pleasing, 162; as scholar, 6, 196

Bone, phonology of, 47

Bossu, René le, and aesthetic criticism, 141

Bossuet, Jacques Bénigne, mentioned, 138

Bradley, F. H., mentioned, 138

Bréal, Michel Jules Alfred, and *Essai de Semantique*, 68; mentioned, 39

Bredvold, Louis I., and *Intellectual Milieu of John Dryden*, 4

Bridgman, P. W., on meaning of words, 36–37

Brooks, Cleanth, and criticism of poetry, 146

Brothers Karamazov, The. See Dostoevsky

Brown, John, and *History of the Rise and Progress of Poetry*, 129

Brunetière, Ferdinand, on evolution of literature, 10, 122–123; and history of genres, 127; and *L'Evolution des genres dans l'histoire de la littérature*, 10

Brunot, Ferdinand, mentioned, 73

Brut, Layamon's, mentioned, 86

Bush, Douglas, and *The Renaissance and English Humanism*, 18; on contemporary American writers, 180, 207; mentioned, 19

Byron, George Gordon, mentioned, 103, 211

Cabell, James Branch, lack of erudition in, 180

Cambridge, and University Poets, 211

Canby, Henry Seidel, as editor, 203

Carlyle, Thomas, and German romanticism, 8

Carnoy, Albert J., and *La science du mot*, 69

Cassirer, Ernst, mentioned, 110

Castelvetro, and poetic theory, 140

Cather, Willa, as editor, 203

Catholicism, and Marxism, 166

Catullus, Caius Valerius, 180

Cazamian, Louis, and predictable changes in literature, 122; and literary history, 117

Celts, mentioned, 65

Chadwick, Hector M. and *Growth of Literature*, 129

Chase, Stuart, and semantics, 39; and *The Tyranny of Words*, 39

Chaucer, Geoffrey, and word usage, 42; his pronunciation, 49, 63

Chicago, University of, and scholarship, v

Church, Catholic, 148

Cicero, Marcus Tullius, mentioned, 138

Ciceronians, age of, 26

Classics, knowledge of, and student of literature, 22–23; study of, 220, n. 16, 17

Clemenceau, G. E. B., as teacher, 202

Coleridge, Samuel Taylor, and German romanticism, 8; on imagination, 104; mentioned, 94, 110, 211; as scholar, 196

Communists, and literary standards, 164

Comparative Germanic Grammar, importance of, 4

Conant, James Bryant, on scholar-teachers, 31

Concentration, and art, 185

Concord, mentioned, 204

Cook, Albert S., on philologist, 26–27

Corneille, Pierre, and artistic rule of pleasing, 162; and practical criticism, 136

Courthope, W. J., and *History of English Poetry*, 115–116

Crane, Ronald S., changes graduate study at University of Chicago, 16; his article on "History *versus* Criticism in the University Study of Literature," 16; on literary history, 16–18

Criterion, See T. S. Eliot.

Critic, perfect, 166–167

Criticism, normative, Longinus theory of, 152 ff.

Criticism, teaching of, 235, n. 57

Croce, Benedetto, conception of art, 147–148; mentioned, 80; and theory of analytic criticism, 142; and theory of genre, 127

Curme, George O., mentioned, 42, 73, 77.

Daladier, Edouard, as teacher, 202

Dante, Alighieri, mentioned, 138, 155, 157, 212, 213; his *Divine Comedy*, 139

Darmesteter, A., and study of change of meaning, 68; and *La Vie des mots*, 68

Darwin, Charles Robert, mentioned, 206; his theory of evolution, 123

Davidson, Donald, and Vanderbilt group, 205

Da Vinci, Leonardo, reality of his *Last Supper*, 184; symbols in, 187

Davis, Elmer, lack of erudition in, 180

Day, morphology of, 54–55

De Doctrina Christiana. See Milton

Defoe, Daniel, mentioned, 94

Deutsche Grammatik. See Grimm, Jacob

Devil and Daniel Webster, The.
See Benét
DeVoto, Bernard, as editor, 203
Dickens, Charles, mentioned, 147, 155
Dictionary. See Johnson
Dictionary of American English, 64
Dilthey, William, and literary history, 103; mentioned, 110
Dinner for Threshers. See Wood
Divine Comedy, philosophical interpretation of, 139
Donne, poetry of, and aesthetic criteria, 159; mentioned, 163, 188, 211; his "The Indifferent," 140
Dostoevsky, Feodor M., and *The Brothers Karamazov,* 139; mentioned, 157, 164
Drama, Elizabethan, need for research in, 94
Drama of the Mediaeval Church, importance of, 4
Dreiser, Theodore, as editor, 203; lack of erudition in, 180; as writer, 191–192; and scholars, 193
Dryden, John, and aesthetic criticism, 141; mentioned, 94, 211; and practical criticism, 136; as scholar-critic, 196
Du Bos, Charles, and aesthetic criticism, 141

Eastman, Max, on scholarship, 178
Economics, and ideological criticism, 147; and study of literature, 111–112
Eliot, T. S., and advanced study, 200; as editor of the *Criterion,* 203; and *After Strange Gods,* 164; and literary standards, 146; and linguistics, 88; mentioned, 25, 163, 170, 186; on history of work of art, 119; on

poet's audience, 155; and process of creation in poetry, 185; on appreciation of literature, 165; as scholar-critic, 196
Elton, Oliver, and *Surveys of English Literature,* 116
Emerson, on Alcott, 177; as editor, 203
Empson, William, and linguistics, 88
Engle, Paul, and artistic process, 186; and advanced study, 199
English, cultural, disappearance after Norman Conquest, 66–67
"Equilibrists, The." See Ransom
Erasmus, Desiderius, as scholar, 6; as teacher, 196
Eroica Symphony, artistic symbols in, 187
Esquisse d'une histoire de la langue latine. See Meillet
Essay, critical, 136
Ethics, and critical theory, 136; and literature, 18
Etymology, and dictionaries, 64; and phonology, 63–64; and vocabulary studies, 62–64
Evolution. See also Science, and literary history, 122 ff.
Évolution des genres dans l'histoire de la littérature, L'. See Brunetière
Explication de textes, as aid in developing critical faculty, 24–25, 88, 97, 220, n. 20

Facts about Current English Usage, and syntax, 61
Farrell, James T., and *Literary Criticism,* 164
Fechner, Gustav Theodor, and formal criticism, 158
Feuillerat, Albert, and article on "Scholarship and Literary Criticism," 14–15
Fisher, Dorothy Canfield, and graduate work, 199

Flexner, Dr. Abraham, his use of terms *sciences* and *humanities*, 5; on humanistic disciplines, 30

Flickinger, Roy Casten, and scholarship, 4

Folklore of Capitalism, The. See Arnold, Thurman W.

Foot, phonology of, 48–49

Form, in art, 188 ff.; and literary criticism. *See* Aesthetics

Formalists, Czech, Russian and Polish, 97

Fortune. See MacLeish, Archibald

Fox, Ralph, and criticism of novel, 146–147

France, Anatole, as scholar-critic, 196

Frankreichs Kultur in Spiegel seiner Sprachentwicklung. See Vossler

French, and English language after the Norman Conquest, 66–67

French Dramatic Literature of the Seventeenth Century, and scholarship, 4

Freud, Sigmund, works of, 206

Fries, Charles Carpenter, mentioned, 73; and syntax, 61

Frost, Robert, mentioned, 187; as teacher, 202

Fugitive, The, and the Vanderbilt group, 205

Fulgens and Lucrece, mentioned, 93

Galsworthy, John, and advanced study, 199

"Geistesgeschichte," as approach to study of literature, 113–114; and literary criticism, 134

Geistesgeschichtlichen Grundlagen des Englischen Literaturbarocks, Die. See Meissner

Genres, and national literature, 128–129; theory of, 127

Geography, linguistic, 52, 74–75

Geschichte der deutschen Sprache. See Grimm, Jacob

Geschichte der Kunst im Altertum. See Winckelmann

Geschichte des deutschen Liedes. See Müller

Gilder, Richard Watson, as editor, 203

Gildersleeve, Basil L., and scholarship, 11

Gilliéron, J. and linguistic pathology, 74

Gilson, Étienne H., mentioned, 110

Goethe, Johann Wolfgang, mentioned, 25, 103, 168; on word usage, 187; as philosopher-poet, 212; as scholar-critic, 196

Gosse, Edmund, and *Short Story of Modern English Literature*, 116

Gourmont, Rémy de, and theory of analytic criticism, 142

Graduate student, and creative writing, 179, 190–191, 197 ff., 236–237, n. 6, 237, n. 11; education of, 220, n. 16–17; and literary theory, 24–25; low morale of, vii

Grandgent, Charles Hall, as scholar, 11

Greenlaw, Edwin, and literary history, 109; on reinterpretation of literature, 30; and *Province of Literary History*, 108

Greg, W. W., and "bibliographical" method in literary history, 93; and Hamlet, 95

Greville, Fulke, mentioned, 94

Grib, V., and *Balzac*, 164

Grimm brothers, mentioned, 9; Jacob, and scientific spirit in scholarship, 9; and *Deutsche Grammatik* and *Deutsche Mythologie*, 9

Growth of Literature. See Chadwick

Grundzüge der Phonologie. See Trubetzkoy

Gundolf, Friedrich, and psychological approach in study of literary history, 103

Hallam, Henry, and *Introduction to the Literature of Europe in the Fifteenth, Sixteenth and Seventeenth Centuries,* 115

Hamlet, theme of, 126

Hanley, Professor Miles, and his file of rhymes, 73–74

Hardy, Thomas, novels of, 140; as poet, 164; his "At Church," 140

Harte, Francis Bret, as editor, 203

Harvard, and American literature, 211; experiments in new types of scholarship at, v; James Russell Lowell addresses, 13; mentioned, 14, 18, 27, 202

Hawthorne, Nathaniel, novels of, 140

Haydn, Joseph, mentioned, 159

Hedge, Frederick Henry, and German romanticism, 8

Hegel, Georg Wilhelm Friedrich, mentioned, 110, 206

Hemingway, Ernest, mentioned, 188

Henderson, Philip, and criticism of novel, 146–147

Henry IV, as imaginative work, 138

Herbert, George, mentioned, 211

Herder, von, Johann Gottfried, as prophet of second "Revival of Learning," 8

Herrick, Robert, mentioned, 211

Herriot, Edouard, as teacher, 202

Hirt, H., and ancient Indo-European, 65

Histoire de la littérature anglaise. See Taine

Historiography, literary, 115, 119 ff.

History, of arts, and literary history, 107 ff.; of humanity, 106; relation to scholarship, vi; of languages, 107; of civilization, 108–109; of philosophy, 109–111; of society, 112; political, 91, 114; social, 115–116; of painting, music, and sculpture, 118; of manners, 95, 115; of criticism, 134

History of the English Language. See Baugh

History of English Poetry. See Warton

History of the Rise and Progress of Poetry. See Brown, John

History, relation to scholarship, vi

"History *versus* Criticism in the University Study of Literature." *See* Crane

Hittite, work of Sturtevant in, 72–73

Hobbes, Thomas, mentioned, 206

Hohlfeld, Alexander Rudolf, and scholarship, 11

Holinshed, Raphael, Shakespeare's reading in, 185

Home, phonology of, 47

Homer, mentioned, 9, 25, 119, 120, 138, 157, 188, as philosopher-poet, 212

Horace, Quintus, and poetic theory, 140, and aesthetic criticism, 141

Hotson, Leslie, mentioned, 93

Housman, A. E., and advanced study, 200; on poetry, 188

Howells, William Dean, as editor, 203, works of, 139

Huckleberry Finn, mentioned, 199

Humanism, Babbitt on, 14; of Renaissance, and didactic view of literature, 18

Humanists, of Renaissance, relation to modern scholarship, 6

Humanities, and science, 30–31; and student of literature, 22–23
Hume, David, works of, 137
Huxley, T. H., works of, 137; addresses John Hopkins, 10

I*bsen. See* Plekhanov
Ideen zur Philosophie der Geschichte der Menschheit, 8
Iliad, 120
I'll Take My Stand, and the Vanderbilt group, 205
"Imitation," and critical theory, 141
"Indifferent, The." *See* Donne
Indo-European, development of, 72; inflectional patterns of, 56; as parent language, 49
Ingarden, Roman, and *Das literarische Kunstwerk,* 98
Intellectual Milieu of John Dryden. See Bredvold
Introduction to the Literature of Europe in the Fifteenth, Sixteenth and Seventeenth Centuries. See Hallam

J*ames, Henry,* and critical essay, 136; and literary criticism, 141–142; novels of, 140; and novels of Turgènieff, 164
James, William, on teaching of philosophy, 212
Jespersen, Otto, mentioned, 39, 42, 73, 76, 77, and sound laws, 52
Joad, C. E. M., and artistic process, 186
Jodelle, Étienne, mentioned, 123
Johns Hopkins, and scientific scholarship, 10–11; mentioned, 27
Johnson, Samuel, and aesthetic criticism, 141; and critical essay, 136; and his *Dictionary,* 42; and literary criticism, 162; his *Lives,* 102; mentioned, 94; as scholar, 6

Jonson, Ben, mentioned, 147, 197; as scholar-critic, 196
Joyce, James, mentioned, 188
Jusserand, Jean Jules, and literary history, 116

K*afka, Franz,* as poet, 164
Kant, Immanuel, and art, 147; mentioned, 206; works of, 137
Keats, John, and the creative process, 185; mentioned, 138
Ker, W. P., and literary history, 91, 119
Kinder- und Hausmärchen, mentioned, 9
Kittredge, George Lyman, as scholar, 11; and *Witchcraft in Old and New England,* 108
Klaeber, Friedrich, and *Beowulf,* 4
Knights, L. C., and criticism of drama, 147
Kohn-Bramstedt, Ernst, and *Aristocracy and the Middle Classes in Germany,* 112
Korzybski, Alfred, mentioned, 39; and *Science and Sanity,* 37
Kruisinga, Etsko, and syntax, 59

L*a Fontaine, Jean,* and artistic rule of pleasing, 162
Lancaster, Henry Carrington, as scholar, 4
Language, American, atlas of, 75
Language and Poetry. See Bateson
Latin, development of tense in, 57; inflectional tenses of, 58
Lawrence, D. H., as poet, 164
Layamon, mentioned, 94
Leaves of Grass, mentioned, 179
Lee, Sir Sidney, on literary history, 96
Leir, and Shakespeare's *King Lear,* 185
Leland, John, mentioned, 102
Lewis, Sinclair, lack of erudition in, 180; mentioned, 85; and

other vocations for writers, 200; works of, 139

Linguistic Aspects of Science. See Bloomfield

Literary Criticism. See Farrell

Literature and the American College. See Babbitt

Locke, John, mentioned, 206

Logic of Modern Physics, The. See Bridgman

Longfellow, Henry Wadsworth, and German romanticism, 8; as teacher, 196

Longinus, Dionysius Cassius, mentioned, 195; and theory of values, 152 ff.

Lovejoy, A. O., and "history of ideas," 110; and study of literature, 109

Lowell, James Russell, addresses M.L.A., 13, 14; as editor, 203; and German romanticism, 8; mentioned, 19; as scholar-critic, 196; and scientific scholarship, 13–14; versatility of, 211

Lowes, John Livingston, addresses M.L.A., 15; mentioned, 17; and *Road to Xanadu*, 4, 104; as scholar, 4

Lytle, Andrew, and Vanderbilt group, 205

Máchal, Jan, and *Slavonic Literatures*, 128

Machiavelli, Niccolò di Bernando, 206

McKerrow, R. B., and "bibliographical" method in literary history, 93

MacLeish, Archibald, as editor of *Fortune*, 203; and graduate work, 199; on the poem, 207

MacNeice, Louis, and advanced study, 200

Magazines, scholars as editors of, 202–203; university, and writers, 204–205

Magic Mountain, The. See Mann

Malherbe, François de, as scholar, 6

Manly, John Matthews, as scholar, 4, 11

Mann, Thomas, and advanced study, 200; and *The Magic Mountain*, 139; as poet, 164

Manners, history of, and literary history, 95, 115

Marckwardt, Albert H., and *Facts about Current English Usage*, 61

Maritain, Jacques, and literary standards, 146

Marius. See Pater

Marx, Karl, works of, 206

Masaryk, Thomas G., as teacher, 202

Masterpiece, as standard of criticism, 156–157

Mauron, Charles, and contemporary aesthetic theory, 149–150

Mazzoni, Guido, and poetic theory, 140

Meaning, study of change in, 68 ff.; seven types of changes in, 70 ff.

Meaning and Change of Meaning. See Stern, Gustaf

Meaning of Meaning, The. See Richards

Medwall, Henry, and *Fulgens and Lucrece*, 93

Meillet, A., and *Esquisse d'une histoire de la langue latine*, 65; mentioned, 39; and semantics, 69

Meissner, Paul, and *Die geistesgeschichtlichen Grundlagen des englischen Literaturbarocks*, 114

Mencken, H. L., mentioned, 180

Michelangelo, Buonarrotti, and his *Moses*, 184

Middleton, Thomas, mentioned, 94

Milton, and *De Doctrina Christiana*, 110; mentioned, 13, 42,

86, 104, 157, 211; and *Paradise Lost*, 144–145; on pedant, 208; as philosopher-poet, 212; and poetic theory, 140; and linguistics, 87–88

Modern Language Association, and American Association for the Advancement of Science, 219, n. 10; Lowell addresses, 13; Lowes addresses, 15

Molière, and artistic rule of pleasing, 162; mentioned, 157

Moore, Merrill, and Vanderbilt group, 205

Morality, and literary criticism, 144–145

More, Paul Elmer, and critical essay, 136; as editor of the *Nation*, 203; as scholar-critic, 196

Morize, André, and *Problems and Methods of Literary History*, 94–95

Morley, Henry, and literary history, 115

Morphology, definition and methods of, 54 ff.; and analogical change, 56

Moscicki, Henry K., as teacher, 202

Müller, Günther, and *Geschichte des deutschen Liedes*, 127

Music, history of, and literary history, 118; and literary criticism, 173; and symbols, 186–187

Nation. *See* More, Paul Elmer

Nationalism, and literature, 128–129

Neo-classicism, critical system of, 96

Neo-classicist, and criticism of Shakespeare, 157

New Directions, editor of, on essential form in art, 189

New English Dictionary, mentioned, 64

Newman, John Henry, works of, 137

Nibelungenlied, and Romantic movement, 8

Nietzsche, Friedrich Wilhelm, works of, 206

Nomination, as type of change of meaning, 70

North American Review. See Adams, Henry

Novel, and critical theory, 140; studies of, 99

Novelists, and philosophical category of literary standards, 164

O'Brien, Edward J., on essential form in art, 189–190

Oedipus. See Aristotle

Ogden, C. K., work of, 39

Olschki, Leonardo, and Romance literatures, 128

On Defining the Phoneme. See Twaddell

O'Neill, Eugene, mentioned, 199

On the Sublime, and *Poetics* and *Rhetoric,* 5

Oxford, mentioned, 211

Page, Walter Hines, as editor, 203

Painting, history of, and literary history, 118

Palestrina, da, Giovanni Pierluigi, 120

Paradise Lost and linguistics, 88

Pareto, Vilfredo, works of, 206

Pater, Walter Horatio, and *Marius,* 138; and theory of appreciation, 116

Pater, phonology of, 48

Paul, Hermann, mentioned, 39

Pavlov, Ivan Petrovich, works of, 206

Pedens, phonology of, 48

Peele, George, mentioned, 94

Pericles, mentioned, 76

Permutation, as type of change of meaning, 70

Perry, Bliss, as editor, 203; as teacher, 196

"Personalism," in concept of history, 121

Petrarch, Francesco, as scholar, 6

Philosophy, and critical theory, 142; degree of doctor of, 28; history of, and literary criticism, 134, 172; history of, and literary history, 109–111; and literary standards, 163 ff.; and literature, 140 ff.; and scholarship, vi; and study of literature, 109 ff.

Phoneme, definition of, 45, 223, n. 11, 50; and Linguistic Circle of Prague, 50; and operation of sound laws, 51 ff.

Phonetics, definition of, 43–45; and phonologic history, 49–50

Phonology, definition of, 45 ff.

Plato, and artistic process, 186; his conception of the arts, 148; and creative writing, 182–183; mentioned, 42, 180, 207, 211; as sponsor of ideological critics, 147; as teacher, 196

Plekhanov, Georgy V., and *Ibsen*, 164

Poe, Edgar Allan, as editor, 203; and literary criticism, 141–142, 159, 160; mentioned, 200

Poet, attitude of scholar toward, 178

Poetics, of Aristotle, 5, 140, 141

Poetry, and critical theory, 136–137, 138, 139–141; definition of, 234, n. 53; and formal critics, 150 ff.; and history, 218, n. 6; and ideological critics, 150–151; and literary criticism, 136–137, 140–141; and semantics, 86 ff.; 168 ff.; 171–172

Politics, and humanities, 31–32; and literary criticism, 147, 148; and literature, 146, 111–112; and scholarship, 202

Poliziano, Angelo, as scholar, 6

Pope, Alexander, and literary criticism, 162; on praising "old bards," 178

Poutsma, H., grammar of, 59

Prall, David W., and literary criticism, 159

Primitivism and Decadence. See Winters

Prizes, to encourage student writing, 209

Prokosch, Edward, as scholar, 4; and *Comparative Germanic Grammar*, 50

Province of Literary History. See Greenlaw

Proust, Marcel, and *À la Recherche du Temps Perdu*, 138; mentioned, 155

Psychology, and art, 183 ff.; and critical theory, 135, 136, 142; and linguistic, 79–80, 83–84; and literary standards, 160 ff.; use of, in studying literary history, 103 ff.

Pusey, Edward Bouverie, works of, 137

Puttenham, Pierre de, and aesthetic criticism, 141

Race, idea of, and the study of literature, 112–113, 116–117

Racine, Jean Baptiste, and artistic rule of pleasing, 162; mentioned, 85, 138, 168; and *Phèdre*, 123; tragedies of, 159

Rahv, Philip, on writing, 179

Ranke, von, Leopold, on historiography, 119

Ranson, John Crowe, and advanced study, 199; as editor, 203; and "The Equilibrists," 140–141; and the Vanderbilt group, 205

Reading, value of, 206 ff.

Realism, in American writers, 207

Recherche du Temps Perdu, A la. See Proust

Renaissance and English Human·
ism. *See* Bush

Research, connotation of, 5

Rhetoric, of Aristotle, 5

Richards, I. A., and linguistics,
88; *The Meaning of Meaning,*
37, and meaning, 37, 167;
mentioned, 25, 39; and theory
of poetry, 105

Riding, Laura, and the Vanderbilt group, 205

Rilke, Rainer M., poetry of, 163

Road to Xanadu. See Lowes

Romanticism, and scholarship, 7–
8; and literary history, 96, 127;
and Utilitarianism, 114

Ronsard, de Pierre, and aesthetic
criticism, 141

Russia, and "structuralism," 226,
n. 9

Sainte-Beuve, Charles Augustin,
and critical essay, 136; mentioned, 116, 195; as scholar-
critic, 196

Saintsbury, George, and literary
history, 116, 126

Santayana, George, as critic, 155

Sapir, Edward, and linguistics, 78

*Saturday Review of Literature,
The. See* Canby

Saussure, Ferdinand de, mentioned, 39, 76; and sound laws,
52

Scaliger, and aesthetic criticism,
141

Schlegel, A. W., and Friedrich,
historical sketches of, 128; and
romantic movement, 8

Scholar, definition of, 5

Scholarship, connotation of, 5

Schopenhauer, Arthur, on art,
119, 147–148

Science, and history, 218–219,
n. 8; and linguistics, 40 ff., 65,
71 ff.; and scholarship, vii, 3 ff.,
21–22, 179, 193–194

Science and Sanity. See Korzybski

Science du Mot, La. See Carnoy

Scotus, and Spenser, 140

Sculpture, history of, and literary
history, 118

Semantics, popularization of term,
37

Shakespeare, William, audiences
of, 155, and creative process,
185, and graduate study, 197,
and Classics, 6–7, and *Hamlet,*
126; and *Henry IV,* 138; mentioned, 86, 127, 138, 157, 188;
and *Othello,* 184; plays of, 8,
149, 159; use of words by, 43

Sherer, Edmond, and critical essay, 136

Shortening, as type of change of
meaning, 70

Sidney, Sir Philip, on learning,
205; on poetry, 164, 213

Sinclair, Upton, "pot-boiling" of,
201

Slavonic Literatures. See Máchal

Socrates, mentioned, 22, 202

Sophocles, mentioned, 212

Sound changes, causes of, 53–54

Spencer, Herbert, on scientific
scholarship, 21

Spengler, Oswald, and literary
history, 122, 123–124; works
of, 206

Spenser, Edmund, mentioned,
211; and poetic theory, 140

Spitzer, Leo, and linguistics, 81

Staël, Madame de, and German
romanticism, 8

Standards, literary, 152 ff.

Stegner, Wallace, and advanced
study, 200

Stephen, Leslie, and literary history, 115

Stern, Gustaf, and *Meaning and
Change of Meaning,* 69; and
semantics, 70–71

Structuralists, linguistic methods
of, 75 ff.

Sturtevant, Edgar H., mentioned, 40, 73; and work on Hittite, 72–73

Stylistics, and language, 82–83

Substitution, as type of change of meaning, 70

Susannah and the Elders. See Benton

Symbols of Government, The. See Arnold, Thurman W.

Symbolistes, mentioned, 195

Symonds, John Addington, on evolution of literature, 122; and *Shakspere's Predecessors*, 127

Syntax, discussion of, 58 ff.

Taine, Hippolyte Adolphe, and literary history, 116; and scientific scholarship, 9–10; and *Histoire de la littérature anglaise*, 9

Tasso, Torquato, and poetic theory, 140

Tate, Allen, on scholarship, 179, 194; and Vanderbilt group, 205

Teggart, F. J., and *Theory of History*, 121

Tennyson, Alfred, mentioned, 211

Text of the Canterbury Tales, and scholarship, 4

Thackeray, William Makepeace, novels of, 140

Theory of History. See Teggart

Ticknor, George, and German romanticism, 8

Tillyard, E. M., on critics of *Paradise Lost*, 104–105

Tolstoi, Lev Nikolaevich, Count, and *War and Peace*, 138

Toynbee, Paget J., and scientific scholarship, 122, 124

Trager, George L., and phoneme, 51

Transfer, as type of change of meaning, 70

Trubetzkoy, N. S., and *Grundzüge der Phonologie*, 50–51

Turgènieff, Ivan S., mentioned, 164

Twaddell, W. F., and linguistics, 78; and *On Defining the Phoneme*, 50

Tyndall, John, works of, 137

Tyranny of Words, The. See Chase

Utilitarianism, and literature, 147 ff.; and romanticism, 114

Valéry, Paul, on critics, 171

Value, Longinus theory of, 152 ff.

Vanderbilt group, and apprenticeship system of writing, 205

Vanity Fair, mentioned, 163

Veblen, Thorstein, works of, 206

Vendryes, Joseph, mentioned, 39

Veselovskij, Aleksandr, and history of genres, 127

Vida, Marco Girolamo, and aesthetic criticism, 141

Vie des mots, La. See Darmesteter

Villon, François, and advanced study of literature, 197

Virgil, and his *Georgics*, 184

Vocabulary, study of, 62 ff.

Voltaire, François Marie Arouet de, mentioned, 123, as scholar, 6

Vossler, Karl, and *Frankreichs Kultur im Spiegel seiner Sprachentwicklung*, 81; and linguistics, 80–81; and vocabulary study, 65

Wade, John Donald, and Vanderbilt group, 205

Wagner, Richard, operas of, 159

Walcott, Fred G., and syntax, 61

Walde, A., and etymology, 64

Wallas, Graham, and *The Art of Thought*, 183

Walzel, Oscar, and literary history, 97

War and Peace. See Tolstoi

Warren, Robert Penn, and advanced study, 199; as editor, 203; and Vanderbilt group, 205

Warton, Thomas, and *History of English Poetry*, 94

Whitehead, A. N., mentioned, 180

Wilde, Oscar, mentioned, 182

Wilson, Dover, and bibliographical method in literary history, 93

Wilson, Woodrow, on scholars, 192; as teacher, 202

Winckelmann, Johann Joachim, and *Geschichte der Kunst im Altertum*, 118

Windelband, Wilhelm, mentioned, 110

Winesburg, Ohio, mentioned, 179

Winters, Yvor, and *Primitivism and Decadence*, 164; on poetry, 164–165

Witchcraft in Old and New England. See Kittredge

Wolf, F. A., and new Hellenism, 9

Wolfe, Thomas, and graduate work, 197–198, 200

Wood, Grant, and *Dinner for Threshers*, 184

Woodberry, George Edward, as teacher, 196

Word, borrowing, 65 ff.

Wordsworth, William, mentioned, 188, 211; poems of, 141

Yeats, William Butler, 195

(The index was made by a member of the staff of the University of North Carolina Press.)